The Destruction and Recovery of Monte Cassino,
529–1964

Italy in Late Antiquity and the Early Middle Ages

The Destruction and Recovery of Monte Cassino, 529–1964

Kriston R. Rennie

Amsterdam University Press

Cover illustration: *Succisa Virescit* [*Montecassino Triptych*], 1946. By Jan Henryk de Rosen (1891–1982). Wax tempera and gold leaf on panel, 64 × 120 1/4 inches (open), 64 × 60 inches (closed). Saint Vincent Archabbey Collection, Latrobe: Pennsylvania. Photo: Richard Stoner.

Cover design: Coördesign, Leiden
Lay-out: Crius Group, Hulshout

ISBN	978 94 6372 913 0
e-ISBN	978 90 4855 212 2
DOI	10.5117/9789463729130
NUR	684

© K.R. Rennie / Amsterdam University Press B.V., Amsterdam 2021

All rights reserved. Without limiting the rights under copyright reserved above, no part of this book may be reproduced, stored in or introduced into a retrieval system, or transmitted, in any form or by any means (electronic, mechanical, photocopying, recording or otherwise) without the written permission of both the copyright owner and the author of the book.

Every effort has been made to obtain permission to use all copyrighted illustrations reproduced in this book. Nonetheless, whosoever believes to have rights to this material is advised to contact the publisher.

Printed and bound by CPI Group (UK) Ltd, Croydon CR0 4YY

And there, uplifted, like a passing cloud
That pauses on a mountain summit high,
Monte Cassino's convent rears its proud
And venerable walls against the sky.
– *Henry Wadsworth Longfellow*[1]

---

1   Longfellow, 'Terra di Lavoro'.

Table of Contents

Acknowledgements	9
Abbreviations	11
Prologue: The Oak Tree	13

Part I *Animus* and Anchor

1. An Enigma: The Legend of Saint Benedict	29
2. The 'Citadel of Campania': Growth and Prosperity	55

Part II Rise and Fall

3. A Destiny Repeated: Episodes of Destruction	87
4. *Floreat Semper:* Rebuilding, Stone by Stone	127

Part III Preservation and Valorisation

5. The People's Patrimony: Defining Historical Value	159
6. A New Europe: Erasing the Destruction	187
Epilogue: Lighthouse	213
References	219
Index	241

Acknowledgements

This book began as a conversation about my own shortcomings. Over time, it blossomed into a fully fledged research project. For their help in its intellectual formation, I want to thank Yaniv Fox, with whom I shared my ill-formed ideas before fully understanding the scale of what I was proposing to undertake. I would also like to thank the Cassinese archivist and historian Dom Mariano Dell'Omo for his kindness, ease of communication, and overall willingness to help a fellow scholar. Professor Dr Gert Melville once again provided his support throughout the life of this project, encouraging me to pursue the subject after spending some time at his research centre (FOVOG) in Dresden. A Faculty Fellowship at the University of Queensland's Institute for Advanced Study in the Humanities (IASH) in 2019 provided the first burst of uninterrupted writing, during which time the general framework of this book came to life. A sabbatical soon followed in Toronto, where – as Visiting Fellow at the Pontifical Institute of Mediaeval Studies – I managed to find some closure.

This book has benefitted from a fantastic selection of images – medieval to modern. For their permissions, I'd especially like to thank the abbey of Monte Cassino (Archivio and Biblioteca Statale del Monumento Nazionale di Montecassino), PIMS Library in Toronto, and Saint-Vincent Archabbey in La Trobe, Pennsylvania.

And finally, I owe a debt of gratitude to my editor, Erin Dailey, for entertaining my initial proposal and challenging me to think more broadly about the bigger questions framing this book. The two reviewers of my manuscript likewise provided incisive comments and encouragement, which has ultimately led to the final product.

Abbreviations

Chron. Cas.   *Chronica monasterii Casinensis*
Gregory the Great,
   Dialogues   *Grégoire le Grand: Dialogues*, ed. Adalbert de Vogüé
JE   Jaffé-Ewald, *Regesta pontificum Romanorum* (590–882)
JL   Jaffé-Loewenfeld, *Regesta pontificum Romanorum* (882–1198)
MGH   *Monumenta Germaniae Historica*
    Conc.   *Concilia*
    DD O III.   *Ottonis III. Diplomata*
    SS   *Scriptores* (in Folio)
    SS rer. Lang.   *Scriptores rerum Longobardicarum et Italicarum*
    SRM   *Scriptores rerum Merovingicarum*
PL   *Patrologiae cursus completus, series Latina*
Rule of Saint Benedict   *La règle de saint Benoit*, ed. Adalbert de Vogüé

Prologue: The Oak Tree

Abstract

This prologue introduces the book's main themes and arguments. It poses and contextualises the central questions underpinning this historical investigation into Monte Cassino's 'destruction tradition' over 1,400 years. To this end, it proposes a conceptual model through which to examine the abbey's long historical tradition and representation of death and resurrection, destruction and recovery.

Keywords: destruction; recovery; tradition; identity; representation; reconstruction

Some shepherds chanced upon him. They discovered his secret hiding place, concealed in a narrow cave (grotto) in the Apennine Mountains near Subiaco, in the lonely wilderness 35 miles from Rome. There, through the thickets, they caught sight of a strange man. At first glance, because he was 'clothed in rough skins, they mistook him for some wild animal'.[1] A closer inspection identified him more clearly as a servant of God. The passing shepherds didn't know his name, or that he'd been living in this remote location for three years. They didn't know that he was 'born in the district of Norcia of distinguished parents',[2] or that he'd willingly abandoned his home, his inheritance, and his Roman liberal studies to 'go into solitude'.[3] Yet their encounter occurred just as this man's reputation for holiness was becoming known in the surrounding region.

A great following soon developed around this mysterious hermit. News quickly spread of his influence, signs, and wonders: 'Like a shining lamp his example was to be set on a lamp stand to give light to everyone in God's house.'[4] Great numbers visited his cave, trading food for spiritual

---

1 Vogüé, *Grégoire le Grand: Dialogues*, II. 1, p. 136.
2 Ibid., II (Prologue), p. 126.
3 Ibid., II. 1, p. 128.
4 Ibid., p. 134.

Rennie, K.R., *The Destruction and Recovery of Monte Cassino, 529–1964*. Amsterdam: Amsterdam University Press, 2021
DOI 10.5117/9789463729130_PRO

nourishment. Not everyone had the temperament, opportunity, or desire to follow his ascetic lifestyle, though many were inspired to live like him: in God's service. Some came to him seeking only advice, having heard of the miracles he performed. But increasingly, as 'the people of that whole region for miles around had grown fervent in their love of Christ', many 'forsook the world to place themselves under his guidance'.[5]

Wishing to please his visitors, this saintly figure agreed to many requests. Approached by an entire monastic community who had recently lost their abbot, he consented to become their superior. Showing great reluctance, he nevertheless agreed to instruct them in the practice of virtue, and to watch over their religious spirit. Before long, he had established twelve monasteries in the surrounding area, each populated with an abbot and twelve monks. He played a hand in their organisational structure, spiritual discipline, and overall direction. His wisdom and knowledge provided a constant source of encouragement. His personal role was key to their growth, prosperity, and success.

Yet this experience and fame came at a personal cost. As his popularity grew, he moved farther away from his initial goals. The life of austere spiritual solitude, which brought him to the mountains in the first place, was replaced by a duty-bound role of advisor and administrator. Although the progress of his work could not be stopped, the time for his departure from this region was imminent. His next move would prove decisive for the history of Western monasticism, a critical moment in the early institutional history of Western Christianity and the Roman Church.

The hand of God guided him in his decision to leave.[6] Three ravens, whom he was accustomed to feed, showed him the way. Circling above him, they offered solace and guidance. Still, he hesitated at every crossway, unsure of his journey's path and purpose. At a critical moment of self-doubt, however, two angels suddenly appeared to ease the man's confusion. Taking the form of young men, they showed him 'which way he ought to take'.[7] And with their help, this ascetic figure of growing repute eventually arrived and settled 'in the stronghold of Cassinum'.[8]

There, perched on a mountain top overlooking the rich, fertile Liri Valley and the ancient town known today as Cassino,[9] he established a spiritual

5   Ibid., II. 2, p. 138.
6   A source written more than four centuries after Benedict's lifetime suggests that he withdrew from Subiaco 'by reason of the persecution of the presbyter Florentinus' (*Chron. Cas.*, I. 1, p. 17).
7   Paul the Deacon, *Historia Langobardorum*, I. 26, p. 68.
8   Ibid.
9   Formerly known as Eulogimenopolis, San Germano, and, from 1862, Cassino. See *Chron. s. Ben.*, c. 15 (p. 476) and c. 20 (p. 479).

PROLOGUE: THE OAK TREE   15

community of 'many monks'.¹⁰ He wrote some basic instructions for the religious life that inspired a Western religious tradition and monastic order. 'Gradually,' as the earliest account of his life relates, 'the people of the countryside were won over to the faith by his zealous preaching'.¹¹

*

So begins the life of Saint Benedict of Nursia (480–547), a figure 'renowned for his great life and his apostolic virtues'.¹² A man who, after arriving on the mountain of Cassino in the early sixth century, 'restrained himself in great abstinence'¹³ and inspired a whole monastic tradition. An historic figure recognised today as the 'father', 'patron and protector of Europe', and 'gem of Italy'¹⁴: an architect of unity and a universal symbol of Christian perseverance, resilience, peace, faith, and goodwill.

And so begins also the history of Monte Cassino abbey – Benedict's 'house'¹⁵ – jointly founded in 529 with his twin sister, Saint Scholastica. Sitting 519 m above sea level (1,702 feet), approximately 125 km south-east of Rome along the ancient Via Casilina, this Benedictine abbey grew into one of the most important religious, political, cultural, and intellectual centres in Western Europe. Heralded in the modern era as a 'lighthouse of Western civilisation', European heritage, learning, and culture, it continues to house the name, spirit, memory, and tradition of its original founder, with whom the abbey is synonymous. 'Few places in the West,' noted one of the abbey's most eminent modern historians, 'represent the continuity of tradition between the ancient and the modern world as well as does Monte Cassino, the foundation of St. Benedict.'¹⁶

What sits atop the mountain today, however, is a distant relative of its original foundation. The so-called 'Citadel of Campania'¹⁷ stands there still, though much altered in appearance. Its imposing physical stature disguises fourteen centuries of adversity, material and cultural destruction, exile, loss, and death at the hands of Lombard, Saracen, Norman, Angevin, French, Spanish, Italian, German, and Allied advances and aggressions. As this

10   Paul the Deacon, *Historia Langobardorum*, I. 26, p. 68.
11   Vogüé, *Grégoire le Grand: Dialogues*, II. 8, p. 168.
12   Ibid.
13   Ibid.
14   'Segni di nuova vita', p. 2. See also Rea, in *Pacis Nuntius*, p. 27.
15   'Casa di san Benedetto', in *Ildefonso Schuster – Ildefonso Rea*, no. 119, p. 183.
16   Bloch, *Monte Cassino*, I, p. 3.
17   Vogüé, *Grégoire le Grand: Dialogues*, II (in the full title).

book argues, the abbey's intimate experience with suffering epitomises a 'destruction tradition'[18] (*Zerstörungstradition*), whose individual episodes have been incorporated into a monastic (Benedictine) narrative of progress, sovereignty, and triumph. Their enduring role has shaped and defined the abbey's core identity, historical representation, sense of community, spirit, and self-consciousness over the course of more than fourteen centuries.

This 'tradition' is historically and culturally constructed. It is not an antithetical concept but rather a 'central organizing principle'[19] conditioned by violent breaks with the past. This narrativised conception of reality reveals Monte Cassino's underlying structure: its relationship with the past and 'social form of knowledge'.[20] The abbey's experiences, therefore, ultimately define its meaning and value.[21] For this reason, the interplay between 'destruction' and 'recovery' is important to interpreting Monte Cassino's historical representation and consciousness; its perspective(s) and perceived coherence help explain what the community of monks sought to preserve, to rebuild, to remember, and to forget.

Monte Cassino's destruction was never so total as to render it obsolete. Its symbolism was ostensibly difficult to erase. After every episode of destruction, the abbey's authenticity was reconstituted, its meaning and value reanimated into a cohesive and arguably stronger whole. With every episode, it became what Gert Melville called a 'symbol of the destroyed symbol'.[22] As this book demonstrates, the physical acts of destruction unified rather than divided the religious community; historicizing this continuous existence across fourteen centuries reveals a conscious identity, whose narrative representation evolved with time and experience.

Destruction made visible the abbey's unifying power. Its character was 'transfigured by imagination'[23] with every subsequent recovery effort, its identity (re)conceptualised in relation to these significant historical moments and processes. Whereas the abbey's destruction is critical to its self-representation and story of perseverance, understanding the periods of its recovery is equally important to its characterisation as a prestigious religious house and symbol of universal human experience. For while the abbey suffered destruction at the hands of others, the process of rebuilding

18 Melville, 'Montecassino', p. 322.
19 White, 'The Value of Narrativity', p. 19.
20 Samuel, *Theatres of Memory*, p. 30.
21 White, 'Fictions of Factual Representation', p. 122. See also Rosenzweig and Thelen, *The Presence of the Past*, pp. 37–38.
22 Melville, 'Montecassino', p. 324.
23 Durkheim, *Elementary Forms*, p. 283.

was more deliberate and controlled by the community of monks; recording and interpreting their experience played a prominent role in shaping the abbey's long-standing tradition. Significant choices were made in this creative process, generating in turn the abbey's discursive representation and shared reality.

Monte Cassino's history cannot be told apart from war and its aftermath, death and resurrection, destruction and recovery; these experiences are among the abbey's most visible, intimate, and essential features. They validate it as an important 'memorial site',[24] one whose 'continuous memory [...] also generates its existence'[25] – a place whose 'inherent sanctity [...] is made not only explicit but also timeless'.[26]

But how exactly did this past emerge and develop? The story traditionally begins in the early Middle Ages, shortly after foundation, when Monte Cassino succumbed to a Lombard attack; the abbey was sacked c. 577 and the community of monks was exiled at Rome for over a century. Against all odds, however, they eventually returned to the mountain under a Brescian figure named Petronax, re-establishing a monastic community which grew in number, reputation, territory, and wealth until a second attack on the abbey in 883. On this fateful occasion, Saracens from the mouth of the Garigliano River sacked the abbey, killing the abbot (Bertharius) at the altar of Saint Martin – violent actions that initiated a period of prolonged exile at Teano until 915, followed by a further 25 years at Capua, in southern Italy.

The abbey's first 500 years were disruptive but formative nonetheless. Recovering from these disastrous experiences, Monte Cassino underwent a so-called 'golden age' under Abbot Desiderius (1058–1087) in the second half of the eleventh century. The competing political powers of Capua and Benevento, and the advent of the Normans through southern Italy in the same century, did not weaken the abbey's spiritual resolve and material purchase in the region. But unfortunately, as many histories of the abbey remind us, the impressive building programme initiated by this abbot (and future pope) was completely destroyed by a powerful earthquake in 1349, leaving very few historical traces beyond the abbey's famed bronze doors and remnants of mosaic floors; fragments of the latter material populate the abbey's contemporary museum, serving to reintegrate them into the long historical narrative.

---

24 Melville, 'Montecassino', p. 331.
25 Ibid., p. 322.
26 Remensnyder, *Remembering*, p. 44.

Another cycle of recovery, rebuilding, and resettlement in the late Middle Ages followed this natural disaster. Pope Urban V (1362–1370) initiated and oversaw a programme that took many decades to complete. By the fifteenth century, Monte Cassino had regained some of its former glory. But the political climate in Europe saw French and Spanish troops vying for the Kingdom of Naples, with the abbey of Monte Cassino occupying a strategic location at the crossroads of southern Italy. This historical and geopolitical landscape meant that the abbey suffered various depredations at the hands of opportunistic rulers, soldiers, and even local peasants. It was this setting which barely escaped the advancing French Revolutionary army in 1799, whose escapades in the nearby town of Cassino are well-documented but little known. Yet the abbey survived unscathed in a physical sense, only to experience the effects of feudal restructuring under royal orders in 1807 that threatened the administrative, organisational, fiscal, and jurisdictional independence it has enjoyed since the early centuries of its existence.

The impact of Italian unification in the second half of the nineteenth century weighed heavily on Monte Cassino. Yet the suppression of monasteries and religious institutions during this transformative political era did not extinguish the famed abbey; in fact, the emergent nationalism and internationalism of this time thrust it into the spotlight as a symbol of Western unity, faith, civilisation, learning, and culture. The articulation and expression of this historical significance and religious value has prevailed until today, a spirit that survived the abbey's most devastating experience with modern warfare and all its fury: the dreadful Allied bombardment of Monte Cassino on 15 February 1944, which reduced the abbey to a pile of rubble.

This précis of the abbey's 'destruction tradition' represents a familiar historical narrative. 'If there is a place where the great events of our history seem to crowd together,' wrote one of the abbey's former archivists, 'that place is Monte Cassino.'[27] It is the dichotomous representation of this past that informs this book's main argument: the relationship between harmony and discord, mourning and resurrection, 'tribulations and joys'.[28]

On several occasions between the sixth and twentieth centuries, peace was extinguished at Monte Cassino. Each attack on the abbey represented a sharp break in the continuum of time, threatening the community's identity and relationship to its original foundation under Saint Benedict – a rupture of the past. For the survivors, their spatial and temporal grounding was thrown askew, leading to periods of emigration – temporary but often long-term. Plans

27 Leccisotti, *Monte Cassino*, p. 312.
28 Ibid., p. 311.

1. The ruined monastery at Cassino, Italy, 19 May 1944.

and building programmes for reconstruction may have taken different forms over the centuries, but every time the historical memory of Monte Cassino triumphed over the tragedy of loss, displacement, and death. The abbey was always rebuilt and repopulated, the connection to its foundation re-established, and its fabric, identity, and history resuscitated: 'after whirlwinds of war had blown out the holy and benevolent flame',[29] peace was returned to the abbey. Yet what remains in the collective historical memory is a pastiche or bricolage – the appropriation of specific events into a cultural design and framework of knowledge, which conveys an unbroken or deliberate chain of progress.

To make sense of this historical and synthetic phenomenon is this book's main objective. It pursues the *idea* of Monte Cassino over time, asking how – from the Middle Ages to the present day – the abbey viewed itself and was viewed by others. The construction and politicisation of Monte Cassino's past presents the significant historical problem. Exactly how it is remembered in relation to destruction is distinctive and diagnostic. As an early monastic foundation in Western (Latin) Christendom, Monte Cassino generates many assumptions on monastic ideals, identity, sovereignty, socio-political and religious order in a longer European heritage. Remembering this history is a conscious and paradigmatic activity. Its cultural legacy has been crafted over many subsequent centuries, making it of great interest and relevance

---

29   Pope Paul VI, 'Discorso', in *Pacis Nuntius*, p. 9.

2. 'Succisa virescit'. Drawing by the painter, Pietro Annigoni.

to historians of all specialisms and time periods. As we'll see in the first two chapters, Monte Cassino quickly came to enjoy enormous prestige as Saint Benedict's monastery and the home of his monastic *Rule*; outside valuations of this esteem, and internal self-perceptions of its importance, created a spiritual community whose history was produced and fostered through its written records.

The resulting portrait is a truly global cultural site, born from the ashes of a small medieval religious community. The abbey's modern coat of arms embraces this generated identity. Its motto, *Succisa virescit* – which loosely means, 'the cut-off shoot grows verdant again' – invokes the 'age-old oak planted by St Benedict',[30] whose robust trunk took root 'at the dawn of the formation of the new Europe'.[31] '"Stripped of its leaves"' by the violence of the war,' as this book explores, the tree springs up 'even more vigorously than before'.[32] This powerful symbol of peace, regrowth, heritage, and continuity acknowledges the abbey's turbulent past. It embraces these defining

30 Pope Benedict XVI, 'Celebration of Vespers'.
31 Rea, 'Pro Montecassino', p. 2.
32 Pope Benedict XVI, 'Celebration of Vespers'.

historical experiences from which it recovered and flourished, time and again, from the sixth to the twentieth centuries. It also captures an internal (Benedictine) belief that 'the life of the abbey was not in the buildings and the possessions, but in the spirit that animated the community'.[33] As one of Monte Cassino's former archivists wrote, the monks of this mountain summit have, over the centuries, witnessed the rise and fall of dynasties, empires, and kingdoms. 'Sometimes they were caught in the storm and swept away,' he continued, 'but the [oak] tree planted here by St. Benedict always gave forth new shoots.'[34]

These 'shoots' are historical fragments of the abbey's past. Their number is many. They represent an idea 'kept alive through the vicissitudes'[35] of time, enduring more than fourteen centuries. Their reconstruction and configuration – that is to say, their description, representation, and narrative – presents Monte Cassino's 'semantic horizon'.[36] Nietzsche might have called it the 'fabric of existence'[37]: how segments of the past are ordered, for some purpose or implicit intention. Their inner coherence, articulation, acceptance, and relation over a long (diachronic) continuum of time generates our historical perspective; it also provides our principal source of coherence for understanding its meaning, value, and significance. The end result is an understanding of history that traverses multiple historical periods, national and international interests, and political boundaries. It is this vision of the past that effectively binds the abbey together into a cohesive and synthetic whole.

Interpreting this historical reconstruction is anything but straightforward. In many respects, its true characterisation is complicated by the countless scholarship on Monte Cassino. The abbey is both a subject and object of historical veneration most familiar to historians and general readers of twentieth-century warfare, nationalism, sovereignty, and politics on the one hand, and historians of early medieval religious life, orders, and institutions on the other. But as I argue, the key to realising the abbey's historical identity lies with harmonising these eras and synthesising them into a large-scale 'destruction tradition'.

Applying this 'conceptual apparatus'[38] considers the totality of Monte Cassino's experience: the material nature of its existence, its violent

---

33 Leccisotti, *Monte Cassino*, p. 100.
34 Ibid., p. 312.
35 Ibid., p. 311.
36 Koselleck, *The Practice of Conceptual History*, p. 124.
37 Nietzsche, *Use and Abuse of History*, p. 54.
38 White, 'Fictions of Factual Representation', p. 126.

breaks with the past, the imaginative reconstructions of its legacy, and the conceptualisation(s) and reconceptualisation(s) of its meaning, value, and coherence. These 'sub-plots' comprise the abbey's essential components, whose organisation into chronological sequence defines its narrative structure.[39]

By focusing on the singular abbey of Monte Cassino over 1,400 years, this book raises important questions that originate in the medieval world, but which culminate in the emergent nationalism and internationalism of the nineteenth and twentieth centuries. Interrogating the politics and culture of identity from medieval to modern times reveals the processes of historical writing and representation that have consistently shaped the abbey over centuries.

What emerges from this critical interpretation is an encomiastic narrative. Our sources are overwhelmingly Benedictine and almost exclusively Cassinese. This emic construction evokes a partisan view of the abbey and its legacy, one written primarily by monks inside the cloister walls. As we'll examine, this teleological version of the past seemingly ignores or overlooks the abbey's fragmentation, cultivating in its place a social memory of historical events far more cohesive than might first appear to the outside observer.[40]

Such a triumphalist narrative is problematic for the modern historian, who – advocating caution in this representation of progress – must operate above it. Interrogating this process of historical construction poses the ultimate interpretive challenge. Taking care not to rehearse or affirm the abbey's representation in any celebratory or deterministic fashion, this book ultimately asks how Monte Cassino saw itself, how the abbey interpreted and understood its own trajectory, experiences, and place in the historical record.

The making and contours of this tradition will become clearer with each subsequent chapter. But it bears mention at the outset just how the balanced concepts of 'destruction' and 'recovery' informed the abbey's own history from the Middle Ages onwards. Erchempert's *History of the Lombards of Benevento* (written c. 889)[41] and Leo Marsicanus's *Chronica monasterii Casinensis* (early twelfth century)[42] are essential starting points for evaluating this internal perspective. Both texts are significant 'histories'

---

39 Stone, 'Revival of Narrative', p. 3.
40 Pohl, 'History in Fragments', p. 362.
41 See Pohl, *Werkstätte der Erinnerung*, pp. 33–55.
42 Ibid., pp. 77–85.

of the abbey, whose authors provide 'information about the way in which the past had shaped the present'.[43] Both offer 'an inside history of the monastery's political culture and its perceptions of power'.[44] The former work, as Walter Pohl argued, was created as a strategy for dealing with the 'difficult time'[45] of the abbey's destruction in the late ninth century. But it is the latter work and its continuation by Peter the Deacon in the twelfth century that structures the abbey's narrative into defined temporal categories of 'pre-' and 'post-' destruction, introducing an early interpretative framework for Monte Cassino's identity.[46] This medieval textual community – what Pohl called a 'workshop of memory' – was central to the abbey's *Geschichtsbild*: the self-portrayal of its 'monastic, social, ethnic, and political identities',[47] which first came to light in the ninth and tenth centuries.

A 'golden chain'[48] of historiography connects the past and present through a linear process of identity construction.[49] And it reveals in its wake a long and uniform history, whose coherence and meaning were established by, and in relation to – *not in spite of* – its intimate experience with destruction and the much longer process of recovery. This link between the religious community and its lived experience was paramount to situating and explaining rather difficult historical conditions and circumstances in a much longer story of survival and perseverance. It is a modality of communication, an explanatory framework, a 'plot-structure of a historical narrative (*how* things turned out as they did) and the formal argument or explanation of '*why* things happened or turned out as they did'.[50]

Telling this story requires the evidence to speak for itself. This empiricist claim means interpreting how authors of that evidence fashioned 'fragments of the past into a whole whose integrity is – in its *re*presentation – a purely discursive one'.[51] There is a poetic and authoritative expression to this construction process, which is by no means unproblematic or uncritical. We might rightly ask whether the resulting portrait of Monte Cassino as symbolic of a universal human experience is consistent, accurate, or misleading. Are there contradictions or ambiguities in the way the abbey's past is

---

43 Pohl, 'History in Fragments', p. 361.
44 Ibid., p. 362.
45 Pohl, *Werkstätte der Erinnerung*, p. 36.
46 *Chron. Cas.*, p. 5 ('Epistola Leonis').
47 Pohl, *Werkstätte der Erinnerung*, p. 166.
48 The termed is used by Leccisotti, *Monte Cassino*, p. 196.
49 See Chapter 6.
50 White, 'Fictions of Factual Representation', p. 128.
51 Ibid., p. 125.

represented, organised, and rearranged across more than fourteen centuries of its existence?[52] How does its expression change over time, keeping in mind the role of communities and human agency in the process of identity creation and preservation. These questions are all the more poignant when considering – as this book does – the process by which Monte Cassino not only became legitimated as Saint Benedict's monastery, but how it 'saw itself in that light'.[53]

This *longue durée* or 'deep' historical approach offers a powerful lens through which to view Monte Cassino: how it developed its reputation as a centre of Western Christendom – a 'place of remembrance' (*Erinnerungsort*) or 'negative memory'[54] with a seemingly continuous past; how religious identity, cultivated and projected over so many centuries, is tied to the abbey's experience with war, destruction, and its aftermath; how the very idea of Monte Cassino is tied to a particular *locus* or *habitus*, environment, landscape, cultural heritage, and tradition; how the *animus* of Saint Benedict, and the venerable mountain on which he founded his abbey, have been harnessed into a universal symbol of hope, freedom, prosperity, Western culture and civilisation – historical agents of European identity, heritage, secularism, sovereignty, and unity in the modern world.

'Destruction' and 'recovery' present the main interpretive framework for pursuing such questions. These analytic categories provide a master key for understanding the abbey's true sense of its past. They offer a prism through which the categories of tradition, identity, and value can be interrogated. They also inform this book's main structure and argument. After establishing Monte Cassino's spiritual and historical esteem in Chapters 1–2, both as a product of human agency (the saint) and landscape-topography (the mountain), Chapters 3–4 look at each episode of destruction in detail, followed by the abbey's incredible (and successful) recovery efforts over the respective centuries. Before turning to this more detail-oriented, empirical side of the story in Part II: Rise and Fall, however, it is necessary to consider in Part I: *Animus* and Anchor: why Monte Cassino was a target of repeated aggression between the sixth and twentieth centuries; and why, in every case, it was deemed worth saving. Laying the foundation for this interrogation requires a look at the legend or 'invention' of Saint Benedict, whose persona plays a central role in attributions of holiness and historical significance for the venerable mountain on which he founded his abbey in the early sixth century.

---

52   For some discussion on these questions, see Pohl, 'History in Fragments', pp. 343–354.
53   Pohl, 'History in Fragments', p. 357.
54   Melville, 'Montecassino', p. 323.

This background is important. Indeed, without Benedict, Monte Cassino wouldn't exist. More precisely, the abbey's origins and prestige owe directly to the saint's role in foundation, and the memory generated from this pivotal event; the possibility of his corporeal absence from the abbey following the eighth century does little to diminish these identity claims (see Chapter 2), which suggests that the monks 'took the extraordinary prestige of being Saint Benedict's monastery for granted'.[55] This argument will be advanced on more than one occasion as a means to illustrate an important dual purpose, one whose meaning relies on reassessing the saint's integral role in defining the abbey's representation and reputation. Their interconnection over fourteen centuries evolves and produces a powerful religious, national, and eventually international symbol. Chapters 5 and 6 (Part III: Preservation and Valorisation) examine the origins and evolution of this vision, asking how it was interpreted in the nineteenth and twentieth centuries into the realm of preservation and heritage. This process of validation, what I refer to as the abbey's patrimonial expression, developed in a transformative world of nascent nation states, international law, and world war.

Such a deep historical analysis yields one preliminary conclusion: the Benedictine abbey of Monte Cassino is a cultural product; its historical meaning and value, and sense of its own unbroken and continuous past, have been constituted by centuries of antagonism and warfare. The historical representation of its long and turbulent past has been reinforced by the abbey's experiences with destruction and recovery, death and resurrection. The interpretation and use of these defining historical moments in both written sources and contemporary imaginings have strengthened the abbey's assigned (symbolic) value, historical agency, and overall significance. While its material existence and contiguous religious observance in the twenty-first century suggests a constant across the medieval, early modern, and modern eras, any semblance of continuity is man-made: the product of a constructed historical tradition and legacy. The meaning of its construction was informed by common experiences, which together forge the abbey's existence and core identity.

This book traces that story from foundation to the present day. It argues for the centrality of historical representation in building contemporary understandings of – and appreciations for – the medieval past and its religious heritage.

---

55 Pohl, 'History in Fragments', p. 364.

Part I

Animus and Anchor

1. An Enigma: The Legend of Saint Benedict

Abstract
This chapter introduces a few key features of Saint Benedict's life and death, considering the historical process by which he became known as Monte Cassino's *'animus'* and 'anchor' – the abbey's spirit and foundation. This line of enquiry means asking how his influence spread, shaped, and fostered the abbey's reputation as a centre of spiritual, religious, and intellectual culture. It also means considering the contested narratives surrounding his possible translation, in addition to the many discoveries of his relics and their contribution to the entrenched historiography.

Keywords: translation; relics; tomb; miracles; discovery; dispute; hagiography

> 'There was a man of saintly life; blessed Benedict was his name, and he was blessed also with God's grace.'[1]

With these words, Pope Gregory the Great (590–604) began his life of Saint Benedict of Nursia. His famous *Dialogues on the Life and the Miracles of the Italian Fathers* (written c. 593–594) – *Dialogues* for short – is our earliest witness to Benedict's character, actions, and influence. It is also our *only* witness. As Gert Melville has argued, 'what Gregory's contemporaries knew of Benedict, what many generations afterward knew, and indeed what we know of Benedict today we know from this one text alone'.[2] This includes even his very existence. For without this late-sixth-century account, 'no

---

1 Vogüé, *Grégoire le Grand: Dialogues*, II (Prologue), p. 126.
2 Melville, *The World of Medieval Monasticism*, p. 27.

Rennie, K.R., *The Destruction and Recovery of Monte Cassino, 529–1964*. Amsterdam: Amsterdam University Press, 2021
DOI 10.5117/9789463729130_CH01

"Benedictine" monasticism could ever have been established'.³ And, it follows, the abbey of Monte Cassino would never have been founded.

This opening chapter introduces a few key features of Benedict's life and death. It does not attempt a full summary of his actions or defence of his spiritual credentials; it rather considers the historical process by which Benedict became known as Monte Cassino's *'animus'* and 'anchor' – the abbey's spirit and foundation. This line of enquiry means asking how his influence spread, shaped, and fostered the abbey's reputation as a centre of spiritual, religious, and intellectual culture.⁴ Understanding this historical representation (or imprint) is key to our larger historiographical operation. Because to comprehend the abbey's spiritual and historical esteem – in the Middle Ages and the modern world alike – requires first a look at the man behind its foundation and rise to prominence. It becomes immediately clear that one cannot exist without the other.

Vita and *Regula*

There is no shortage of research into Benedict's life. So much ink has been spilled on this historic figure, about whom we know so little. He remains an enigma, precisely because of his minimal representation in early medieval sources. For this reason alone, Benedict's life should be viewed through the lens of memory rather than pure history.⁵ Over the course of many centuries, he has become a larger-than-life historical stalwart. Labelling him a great Christian thinker, Pope Benedict XVI equated the saint's works to

> heralds of an authentic spiritual leaven which, in the course of the centuries, far beyond the boundaries of his country and time, changed the face of Europe following the fall of the political unity created by the Roman Empire, inspiring a new spiritual and cultural unity, that of the Christian faith shared by the peoples of the Continent.⁶

'This,' the former German pope and namesake concluded, 'is how the reality we call "Europe" came into being'.⁷ The 'illuminating power'⁸ of his

---

3   Ibid.
4   For this argument, see especially Prinz, 'Montecassino ed Europa monastica'.
5   See Fried, *Schleier der Erinnerung*, pp. 344–357.
6   Pope Benedict XVI, *Great Christian Thinkers*, p. 126.
7   Ibid.
8   Ibid., p. 128.

monastic *Rule*, he further contended, inspired the sixth-century monk's promotion to 'Patron of Europe' on 24 October 1964.

The mediation of Benedict's sanctity – his reputation as a holy man – begins with Gregory's *Dialogues*. Through this work and its gradual diffusion throughout Western Europe between the seventh and tenth centuries, Benedict attained iconic status.[9] The stylised life, which occupies the entire second book of the *Dialogues*, set the stage for Benedict's future veneration. It was the first real narrative, portraying him as: a 'visionary prophet of the last days'[10]; 'the paternal leader of a community'; 'a mediator between the narrowly bound earthly matters of this world and God's boundlessness in heaven'.[11]

This solitary early medieval text has shaped our modern understanding of Benedict. It is not a biography in the modern sense, although Paul the Deacon described it as such in the late eighth century; its intention was rather 'to convey an ideal image of an ascetic and a charismatic leader of a monastic community'.[12] Through rich symbolism and description, it serves to highlight Benedict's sanctity, his power to perform miracles, and his divine gifts. By focusing on origins, it shaped the growth of monastic life in the medieval West. Because it was written by an influential bishop of Rome, it established a bond between Saint Peter and Saint Benedict – between Rome and Monte Cassino – that would be idealised by later medieval writers.[13]

The *Dialogues* effectively generated and transmitted Benedict's life, contributing to his historical and spiritual fame. It made him a household name. The wider its diffusion beyond Italy and Rome, the more famous this legend became. We know that Gregory's work was first mentioned in the early seventh century (613/614) in northern Francia. It became more widespread in Southern and Western Europe over the course of the seventh century. But it wasn't until the early eighth century that the saint's name was even mentioned outside of the *Dialogues*.[14] Given later claims for his sanctity, Benedict's absence from contemporary liturgical sources, such as seventh-century sacramentaries, the 'Hieronymian Martyrology', as well as

---

9   Hallinger, 'Benedikt von Monte Cassino', pp. 81–82. See also Clark, *The 'Gregorian' Dialogues*, chapter 16.
10 Leyser, *Authority and* Asceticism, p. 182. See also Leyser, 'St Benedict and Gregory the Great'.
11 Melville, *The World of Medieval Monasticism*, p. 27.
12 Ibid., p. 26.
13 On this argument, see Wollasch, 'Benedictus abbas Romensis'; also, Engelbert, 'Regeltext und Romverehrung', pp. 153–156.
14 *Vita Willibaldi*, c. 6, p. 105; Engelbert, 'Regeltext und Romverehrung', pp. 154–155.

calendars, lectionaries, church dedications, and anniversaries/feast days, is extremely curious (see below).[15]

For over two centuries, therefore, Benedict was known only through Gregory's eyes. Even though the material informing this hagiography was second-hand. Following the Lombard sack of Monte Cassino c. 577, the community of monks fled to Rome, allegedly taking up residence at a monastery near the Lateran Palace (see Chapter 3). This is how, when, and where Gregory first came into contact with them. He befriended their refugee leader, Valentianus, who was at Monte Cassino during Benedict's lifetime, before himself becoming abbot of the Lateran monastery.

Valentianus was a valuable source of information. So, too, were the other characters credited in the preface of Gregory's second book: Constantine, who succeeded Benedict as abbot of Monte Cassino; Simplicius, Benedict's second successor; and Honoratus, 'who is still abbot of the monastery where the man of God first lived' – that is, in the last decade of the sixth century.

Gregory's account was informed by a fifteen-year-long dialogue with Benedict's disciples. The pope didn't know Benedict personally. Separated in life by only a few decades, and in distance by just over a 100 km, they nevertheless lived worlds apart. Yet there is a genuine historical and spiritual connection between the two figures, a 'dialogue' built on more than just the testimony of Benedict's immediate disciples.[16] As the historian Peter Brown poetically wrote, 'the story of Benedict's life came to Gregory, like the ghostly bells of a sunken city, from a world before the furious impact of the Lombards'.[17] This story, written as an intimate conversation with his deacon, Peter, catapulted Benedict's fame. Further credit for his growing reputation is attributed also to his set of guidelines on the observance of the monastic life; together with his *vita*, this feature of Benedict's legacy adds a deeper layer to his historical relationship with the abbey of Monte Cassino.

The *Rule of Saint Benedict* laid out the norms of ascetic life. Working models for monastic observance already existed in the fifth and sixth centuries, but none quite as detailed and balanced as the regulations provided during Benedict's lifetime. Historians have long believed that this set of principles 'prepared the way for the growth of the reputation of Benedict and the power of Benedictine monasticism'.[18]

---

15 Clark, 'Authorship of the Gregorian Dialogues', p. 127; Clark, *The 'Gregorian' Dialogues*, chapters 14 and 18. See also Chapman, 'A propos des martyrologues', pp. 295–301.
16 On this connection, see Leyser, 'St Benedict and Gregory the Great'.
17 Brown, *Rise of Western Christendom*, p. 210.
18 Melville, *The World of Medieval Monasticism*, p. 29.

AN ENIGMA: THE LEGEND OF SAINT BENEDICT

3. The Rule of St Benedict copied into an eighth-century manuscript (MS Hatton 48, fol. 6ᵛ–7ʳ).

The *Rule of Saint Benedict* is undeniably linked to the expansion of Western monasticism. It was slowly diffused throughout a growing Christian world. A religious community at the Provençal monastery of Hauterive (Alta Ripa) was reportedly following its precepts in the early seventh century.[19] Widely known by the middle of that century in places like modern-day France, Germany, Switzerland, Italy, and England, the *Rule* became dominant in the Western European monastic tradition by the ninth.[20] In the tenth and eleventh centuries, it provided the organisational framework for a medieval monastic empire – more than a thousand religious houses, whose mother community was the Burgundian monastery of Cluny (est. 910).

The founding and support of monasteries assured the *Rule*'s adoption. The increasing desire for standardised liturgical practice under the Carolingians (eighth–ninth centuries) eventually led to its use as a normative guide for monastic life in many new communities across Western Europe. This relationship between Benedict's *Rule* and the religious life maintained a hold on the monastic way of life until the Cistercians established their first

---

19 For a look at the evidence and its arguments, see Engelbert, 'Regeltext und Romverehrung'; see also Dell'Omo, 'A proposito dell'esilio romano', and Wollasch, 'Benedictus abbas Romensis'.
20 Clark, *The 'Gregorian' Dialogues*, chapter 15; Hallinger, 'Benedikt von Monte Cassino', p. 78. See also Prinz, *Frühes Mönchtum im Frankenreich*, pp. 263–292.

community at Cîteaux in the late eleventh century. From this point onward, Benedictine monasticism lost its monopoly status, but not its deep-seated connection to the saint and his founding monastery at Monte Cassino.

The *Rule*'s legacy is really twofold. First and foremost, its 73 chapters offered preparation for hearts and bodies 'to do battle under the holy obedience of His commands'.[21] It was both spiritual and organisational in its purpose. Humility, obedience, charity, and manual labour define its commands. Its remit concerned spiritual practice, daily life, governance, and the monastery's existence in the surrounding world. In summary, it characterised four types of monks; described what kind of man the abbot ought to be; outlined disciplinary measures; detailed the instruments of good works; elaborated on the central rituals and variation of Divine Office and the observance of key celebrations like Lent; explained the procedures for entry and exit into the monastery; outlined behavioural, organisational, and administrative routines and expectations; as well as detailing many other features of day-to-day existence in the monastery such as sleep, personal possessions, sickness, food, drink, and clothes.[22]

Second, the *Rule* became synonymous with Benedict himself. To read it is 'to seize the essence of the man'.[23] It's what he left behind, what defined his everyday life, and what established his memory firmly in the Western monastic tradition. To borrow Gregory's near contemporaneous description in the *Dialogues*, it was 'outstanding in its discernment and radiant in its language. Anyone who wants to know more about the holy man and how he lived, should look at the *Rule*, because the holy man could not have taught other than he lived.'[24] It is part legacy, part heritage.

For these very reasons, the autograph manuscript of the *Rule* is particularly important to forging a relationship with the abbey of Monte Cassino. Its history has taken on a life of its own, rescued at the time of the Lombard attack and returned after the abbey's restoration in the mid-eighth century. Pope Zacharias is credited with returning the original manuscript to the newly formed community, which suggests that it was guarded in Rome during the Cassinese monks' long period of exile (c. 577–c. 718). The autograph copy was once again saved from obliteration following the Saracen attack of Monte Cassino in 883, transported – it is believed – by the monks fleeing

---

21 *Rule of Saint Benedict*, Prologue (verse 1), pp. 412–413.
22 For the most authoritative study, see Vogüé, *La règle de saint Benoît*. For a table of contents, see vol. 1, pp. 426–435.
23 Melville, *The World of Medieval Monasticism*, p. 29.
24 Vogüé, *Grégoire le Grand: Dialogues*, II. 36, p. 242.

to Teano, where it was accidentally destroyed by fire.[25] The twelfth-century chronicler of Monte Cassino, Leo Marsicanus, attributed this great loss to the 'unsearchable judgment of God'.[26]

Over the past fourteen centuries, the *Rule of Saint Benedict* has evolved into more than a daily rhythm of monastic life. In the second half of the twentieth century, it was heralded as a reminder of European identity, which had been 'deeply wounded by two world wars and the collapse of the great ideologies'.[27] As Europe emerged from these 'tragic utopias',[28] this early medieval monastic *Rule* came to represent a valuable resource and symbol for modern progress. Without it, Pope Benedict XVI declared, 'a new Europe cannot be built'.[29] Because its roots were so deeply ingrained on the European continent, it was the 'vital sap'[30] capable of awakening the ethical and spiritual renewal deemed necessary in the wake of twentieth-century tragedy (i.e., the Second World War).

These are lofty words founded on tenuous origins. Benedict's representation in the written sources is sparse. Yet the successful transmission of his *Rule* and Gregory's *Dialogues* fuelled his legacy. So, too, did the saint's continuous and uninterrupted connection to Monte Cassino, which, through a gradual process of validation, was reinforced continually over the medieval and modern centuries

Pope Gregory I was the first to mention Benedict's association with the abbey. His *Dialogues* describe the man's journey and settlement there. Melville has argued on numerous occasions for the story's fabrication. 'From the point of view of historical criticism,' he contends, 'the text itself becomes a problem.'[31] A series of core questions immediately follow: Is it even accurate? How do we know? What is the basis for our trust in its details? Melville argued that 'for those in search of historical facts, the panegyric of the text both clouds the subject matter and in equal measure idealises it in ways that move beyond history'.[32]

Paul the Deacon tells us that Monte Cassino was 'renowned' for Benedict's 'great life and his apostolic virtues'.[33] When he wrote his *History of the*

---

25 *Chron. Cas.*, I. 44, pp. 114–115; I. 48, pp. 126–127.
26 *Chron. Cas.*, I. 48, p. 126.
27 Pope Benedict XVI, *Great Christian Thinkers*, pp. 128–129.
28 Ibid.
29 Ibid., p. 129.
30 Ibid.
31 Melville, *The World of Medieval Monasticism*, p. 27.
32 Ibid.
33 Paul the Deacon, *Historia Langobardorum*, I. 26, p. 64.

Lombards in the 780s, this was accepted truth. Or at least, it was a common understanding. Yet the historical proof is little more than a textual trace – a brief or passing mention in a few early medieval sources. It is hardly representative or concrete in its evidence. Nor is it very persuasive.

Yet this brief historical account was ammunition enough. Since the Middle Ages, Monte Cassino has been recognised and admired as Benedict's abbey, precisely because of his association with its foundation. This was true despite the overwhelming paucity of early medieval sources, despite all the textual sparsity and historical doubt, despite its destruction by the Lombards in the late sixth century (which left no tangible link to its original founder), and despite the absence of any 'Benedictine' life at Monte Cassino throughout the seventh century, for a period of more than 110 years.

Against all odds, this tenuous historical connection developed into a permanent bond. It was likely a conscious and politicised move, which might be attributed to the early medieval papacy. This is a critical point that historians often underestimate. In the early eighth century, the abbey was firmly re-established c. 718 under Petronax through a process of rebuilding and repopulation (see Chapter 4). With the papacy's assistance, the religious community was restored and the connection to Benedict's tomb was re-established or resuscitated. The *Rule of Saint Benedict* became the community's guiding principles once again. The abbey even achieved a measure of autonomy from secular and ecclesiastical rule through the acquisition of exemption privileges, from local, imperial, and papal rulers.

The eighth century plays a big part in this institutional story, thrusting the abbey into the spotlight once again. As the greatest modern historian on Monte Cassino, Herbert Bloch, wrote:

> It was this paean to St. Benedict, together with the *Rule*, which assured the survival of Benedictine monasticism and the resurrection of the abbey of Monte Cassino on its ancient site early in the eighth century, in time for it to play an important part in the Carolingian Revival.[34]

This resurrection was surely no accident. In more ways than one, Monte Cassino became a model of Western monasticism in this era. When Charlemagne, the Frankish king and future emperor, visited the abbey in 787, he asked for a copy of the *Rule*, which ultimately helped him to establish a normative practice throughout his kingdom. (This copy, now housed at the

---

34 Bloch, 'Monte Cassino's Teachers and Library', p. 566.

Abbey Library of Saint Gall in Switzerland, is considered the most precious surviving manuscript version; the oldest copy (c. 750), however, remains at the Bodleian Library in Oxford.[35])

But the *Rule*'s popularity only partially explains Monte Cassino's resettled status in the Carolingian era. Benedict was still the main attraction. Monte Cassino is where he lived and died. It was 'his' abbey. The holiness and historical significance of this site derived from his presence, in life and in death. Yet this latter point in particular raises some serious questions for the historian. Following the Lombard sack of Monte Cassino c. 577, suspicions were introduced about the location of his bodily remains. It is a complex and emotional subject which remains unresolved today. It presents an historical 'thicket of thorns'[36] (*densum spinetum*) more than deserving of our attention here.

The reason for our interest is simple: the question of Benedict's remains speaks directly to the importance of Monte Cassino as a site of religious, cultural, and intellectual heritage. It poses what Francis Clark called a 'historical and devotional problem'.[37] The physical location of the saint's relics is related to claims of sanctity and historical relevance, which for the history of Monte Cassino return time and again to the man behind its original foundation. For without Benedict, Monte Cassino wouldn't exist. Without Benedict, there would have been little justification for rebuilding and reconsecrating the abbey after every episode of destruction over the last 1,400 years.

Thicket of Thorns

Benedict died on 21 March 547.[38] But his sister died before him. After witnessing Scholastica's soul 'entering the court of heaven in the form of a dove', Benedict informed his brethren at Monte Cassino of her death. He then sent 'some of them to bring her body to the monastery and bury it in the tomb he had prepared for himself. The bodies of these two were now to share a common resting place, just as in life their souls had always been one in God'.[39]

---

35 On the subject, see Meyvaert, 'Problems Concerning the 'Autograph' Manuscript'.
36 Baronius, *Annales ecclesiastici*, XI, c. 24.
37 Clark, *The 'Gregorian' Dialogues*, p. 305.
38 For the historical evidence surrounding this date, see Schmitz, *Histoire de l'Ordre de Saint Benoit*, vol. 1, pp. 357–362.
39 Vogüé, *Grégoire le Grand: Dialogues*, II. 34, p. 234.

As Gregory later explained in the *Dialogues*, when Benedict eventually died, 'his body was laid to rest in the Chapel of Saint John the Baptist, which he had built to replace the altar of Apollo'.[40] That Benedict was buried with his sister originates with this singular account. For the most part, it is an accepted historical event. How long the two saintly figures remained interred at Monte Cassino, however, is more controversial. Two competing traditions have developed around a body of narrative, liturgical, and hagiographical sources. The ensuing debate – or 'thicket of thorns' – concerns the rightful possession of holy relics.[41] The reasons for contention will become obvious as we attempt to navigate through the material and its varied interpretation over the centuries. The abbey's identity and significance as a spiritual, cultural, and intellectual centre are entangled in this historical representation.

The first question to ask is whether Saints Benedict and Scholastica ever left Monte Cassino. The answer cannot be taken for granted, because doubt on their whereabouts is introduced early on in the historical narrative. In his *History of the Lombards*, Paul the Deacon offers the following account of their translation from Italy. 'About these times,' he wrote,

> when a great solitude existed for a number of years past in the stronghold of Cassinum where the holy body of the most blessed Benedict reposes, there came Franks from the regions of the Celmanici [Le Mans] and of the Aurelianenses [Saint-Benoît-sur-Loire, Fleury, in the diocese or Orléans], and while they pretended to keep a vigil by the venerable body they bore away the bones of the reverend father and also of the revered Scholastica his sister, and carried them to their own country where two monasteries were built, one in honour of each, that is, of the blessed Benedict and of Saint Scholastica.[42]

A French tradition was born from this early medieval account.[43] The *Historia translationis sancti Benedicti* presents the earliest corroborative reference to Fleury as Benedict's resting place.[44] Its author, a monk named Adrevald of Fleury, also popularised the story in his late-ninth-century *De miraculis sancti Benedicti* (written c. 878/879).[45] His basic interpretation was repeated

---

40 Ibid., II. 37, p. 244.
41 For the most recent account, see Galdi, 'S. Benedetto tra Montecassino e Fleury'.
42 Paul the Deacon, *Historia Langobardorum*, VI. 2, p. 165.
43 For a brief summary of the evidence, see Mundò, 'Posthuma Sancti Benedicti', pp. 262–264.
44 (BHL 1116) PL 124:901–910; see also Mabillon, *Vetera Analecta*, IV, pp. 451–452.
45 Vidier, *L'Historiographie à Saint-Benoît-sur-Loire*, pp. 168–170. See also Berland, 'Présence du corps de saint Benoît à Fleury-sur-Loire'.

by Regino of Prüm in the tenth century, whose account dates the translation to 685–695.[46] Paul the Deacon provides a more likely timeline to the rule of the Lombard duke Gisulf I of Benevento, between 690 and 707. Historians, however, tend to support an earlier date.

Suffice it to say that the '*loculus*' of Benedict's bones was repeatedly confirmed.[47] Around two centuries after Adrevald, the monastery of Fleury produced another collection of miracle stories (*Miracula sancti Benedicti* (BHL 1135)) that drew attention to Benedict's glory on the feast day commemorating his death (21 March).[48] In the late thirteenth century, these claims were spread to an even wider audience through the use of vernacular, following a summary in French of the *Historia translationis sancti Benedicti* and another account known as *Illatio sancti Benedicti* (Ms. Paris franç. 13 496, f. 277–280).[49] By the early modern and contemporary era, a chain of historical analyses was published which bolster Fleury's claims. These include Jean Dubois's *Floriacensis vetus bibliotheca benedictina* (1605), Dom Simon-Germain Millet's treatise on the translation (1624), Jean Bollandus's account in the *Acta Sanctorum* (1658), Charles Le Cointe's *Annales Francorum* (1668),[50] and especially Dom François Chamard's *Les reliques de Saint Benoît* (1882). Writing from the French abbey of Maredsous in the first half of the twentieth century, Dom Philibert Schmitz – seeing no need for explanation or elaboration – unreservedly noted that 'the body of the saint was taken and brought to Fleury, around 672–674. It rests there still today.'[51] There is a plaque mounted at Saint-Benoît-sur-Loire at Fleury, which affirms the local reception of this belief; it reads simply: 'Here lies the body of Benedict.'

This view is informed by – and embedded in – the early medieval liturgical evidence.[52] The rise of Benedict's cult first came to prominence between 670 and 750.[53] The date of his birth (21 March)[54] was well recognised already by the late eighth century, especially in Italy. But the appearance of a second

46 Regino of Prüm, *Chronicon*, Book I, a. 612–613, p. 33.
47 Berland, 'Présence du corps de saint Benoît à Fleury-sur-Loire', p. 283.
48 *Les Miracles de Saint Benoît*, cc. 14–17, pp. 271–276.
49 See Vidier, *L'Historiographie à Saint-Benoît-sur-Loire*, pp. 221–226.
50 Leclercq, 'Fleury-sur-Loire,' cols 1718–1720. See also Berland, 'Présence du corps de saint Benoît à Fleury-sur-Loire', pp. 284–295.
51 Schmitz, *Histoire de l'Ordre de Saint Benoit*, vol. 1, p. 30.
52 For a summary of developing traditions, see especially Galli, *Saint Benoît en France*, chapter 7 (pp. 53–65).
53 See especially McCurrach, 'The Veneration of St. Benedict in Medieval Rome'; Clark, *The 'Gregorian' Dialogues*, chapter 18, pp. 279–304.
54 See Frank, 'Die älteren Zeugnisse'.

date (11 July) began to appear around the same time, marking his translation from Monte Cassino to Saint-Benoît-sur-Loire at Fleury.[55] Our earliest reference to this event appears in the Anglo-Saxon Calendar of St Willibrord, in the first half of the eighth century (possibly based on the martyrology of Bede). The early-eighth-century 'Hieronymian Martyrology' mentions 11 July as the feast day for Benedict's 'deposit' in the church of Sainte-Marie at Fleury (*Depositio sancti Benedicti abbatis*). A mid-eighth-century Frankish source, known as the Gelasian Sacramentary (extant in more than a dozen manuscripts), notes the July feast and the mass provided in honour of the saint.[56] And from the same period, the martyrology of Gellone (among others) shows both dates, adding a third (4 December) which commemorates 'in the monastery of Fleury, the arrival [*adventus*] of the body of Saint Benedict from the parts of Rome' (*monasterio Floriacensi a partibus Romae adventus corporis sancti Benedicti abbatis*).[57]

There is a long list of manuscript evidence from the Middle Ages – including sacramentaries, breviaries, missals, lectionaries, antiphonies, and martyrologies – which shows the celebration of more than one feast day for Saint Benedict.[58] The diffusion of this common liturgical practice and its associated dates soon reached Germany and Italy, effectively taking root more widely in the Carolingian Empire.[59] The fact that Adrevald of Fleury noted both the July and December dates in his *Historia translationis* (cc. 12 and 15), moreover, provides even greater impetus to the reception of Benedict's *transalpinus* residence.[60]

The monastery of Fleury certainly profited from its association with Benedict. 'Within a generation or two of its foundation,' it had 'gained enormously in prestige.'[61] By the late seventh century, Benedict was considered a patron of the abbey; there is no reason to doubt the monks' genuine belief in possessing the holy relics. Questions nevertheless remain on the manner in which they were acquired, and even more so on the duration of their stay in northern France. That the story is fabricated – a mere legend or fiction used to validate Fleury's prestige – also remains a possibility.[62]

---

55 For arguments concerning the latter date, see Quentin, 'Le Martyrologe Hiéronymien Benoît'.
56 Vogel, *Medieval* Liturgy, p. 73.
57 Chapman, 'A propos des martyrologues'; Wollasch, 'Benedictus abbas Romensis', pp. 132–133.
58 For the manuscript transmission, see Leclercq, 'Fleury-sur-Loire', cols 1735–1743. For Monte Cassino, see Morin, 'Les quatres plus anciens calendriers'.
59 For a complete account, see Deshusses and Hourlier, 'Saint Benoît dans les livres liturgiques'.
60 Adrevald of Fleury, *Historia translationis*, cols 906C and 908C.
61 Head, *Hagiography and the Cult of Saints*, p. 23.
62 For this argument, see especially Clark, *The 'Gregorian' Dialogues*, chapter 20.

In truth, there are few certainties beyond faith-based speculation. But the stakes over the question of ownership remain high. Representing a tradition of continuity, the Cassinese argue that neither Benedict nor Scholastica ever left Monte Cassino. Confusingly, the origins of this interpretation also stem from Paul the Deacon's *History of the Lombards*.[63] 'It is certain', he wrote,

> that the venerable mouth, sweeter than all nectar, and the eyes beholding ever heavenly things, and the other members too have remained to us, although decayed. For only the body of our Lord alone did not see corruption; but the bodies of all the saints have been subjected to corruption, to be restored afterwards to eternal glory, with the exception of those which by divine miracles are kept without blemish.[64]

The fragility of relics surely could not survive transportation. Or so this source seems to imply. This understanding was supported by Abbot Bertharius of Monte Cassino (857–883), who in a poem about Benedict mentioned a singular 'golden reliquary' or 'golden vessel' (*aurea arca*)[65] at Monte Cassino, which 'contains the relics of the holy saints'. After all, decaying body parts are impossible to remove. Besides, wasn't Petronax 'drawn to the holy remains of the blessed father Benedict',[66] as Paul the Deacon relates, which in turn led to the abbey's refoundation under his care c. 718?

But there is more to the story still. Abbot Theodomar of Monte Cassino (777/778–796) mentioned that the brethren of his community, prior to burial, were taken 'before the sacred body of the venerable father' (*ante sacrum patris venerabile corpus*).[67] Paul the Deacon, in a homily on Saint Benedict, also mentions a miracle that took place before his body (*ante eius hoc corpus sacratissimum*).[68] Both references invoke the corporeal presence of Saint Benedict, without which these liturgical practices (and their associated miracles) would never have taken place. In other words, these early medieval accounts were intended as further proof of the abbey's possession claims.

And they were clearly believed. Charlemagne journeyed to Monte Cassino in 787, 'in order to pray to the blessed father Benedict'.[69] In 866, to cite

---

63 On this subject, see especially Hourlier, 'Le témoignage de Paul Diacre'.
64 Paul the Deacon, *Historia Langobardorum*, VI. 2, p. 165.
65 *Versus domni Bertharii abbatis de miraculis almi patris Benedicti*, p. 397.
66 Paul the Deacon, *Historia Langobardorum*, VI. 40, p. 178.
67 See Winandy, 'Un témoignage oublié', p. 265 (c. 31).
68 Paul the Deacon, *Homiliae*, col. 1575.
69 *Chron. Cas.*, I, c. 12, p. 45. He may also have issued a privilege: see MGH DD Kar. 1, no. 158, pp. 213–216 (28 March 787); MGH DD Lo I, no. 24, pp. 96–98 (Pavia, 21 February 835) (for the

another example, Emperor Louis II made an official visit to the abbey. 'There with sacerdotal dignity,' it is recorded,

> he was honourably welcomed by the venerable abbot Bertharius, with lamps and with thuribles and with praise from the brothers. Ascending the mount where the holy *corpus* of the beloved father Benedict is buried, he was received with equal fanfare and there, having offered gifts to Saint Benedict and viewing with praise and marvelling at the whole monastery, he descended.[70]

A handful of papal bulls and imperial decrees from the ninth and tenth centuries can be added to this list, confirming a contemporary belief among German emperors (Otto I, II, and III) and medieval popes (John IX, Marinus I, John XII, Benedict VIII, John XV) that Benedict's body was safely buried and venerated at Monte Cassino.[71]

Yet such readings lack sufficient historical conviction. In the first instance, they rely too closely on the ambiguous meaning in Paul the Deacon's *History*. The first part of his account suggests the saints' whereabouts at Le Mans and Fleury, which in the second half of the same chapter is seemingly refuted. Scholars and ecclesiastics have seized upon Paul's contra-position and choice of Latin vocabulary, in order to advance their own arguments on both sides of the debate.[72] Secondly, the argument is based heavily on textual affirmations of the saints' corporeal presence over many centuries, which themselves do not count as veritable proof.[73] In this regard, the Cassinese tradition is fraught with uncertainty.

The 'opposite thesis'[74] is more historically grounded. Early medieval accounts tend to corroborate the relics' relocation to northern France.[75] The *Annals of Lorsch* refer in brief to a translation in 703 of Benedict alone: *translatio corporis sancti Benedicti abbatis de monte Cassino*.[76] (No mention is made of Scholastica. While some of the later witnesses do mention her

---

property in the latter grant, see Bloch, *Monte Cassino*, II, p. 831, no. 324). See also Falco, 'Lineamenti', pp. 509–510; Caspar, 'Echte und gefälschte'; and Bloch, *Monte Cassino*, I, p. 252.

70   *Chron. s. Ben.*, c. 4, p. 471. See also Erchempert, *Historia Langobardorum Beneventanorum*, c. 33, p. 247.
71   Leccisotti, 'La testimonianza storica', pp. 148–149 (see especially footnotes 97–104).
72   Meyvaert, 'Peter the Deacon', p. 8.
73   See especially Leccisotti, 'La testimonianza storica', pp. 131–185.
74   Ibid., p. 189.
75   See Hourlier, 'La translation après les sources narratives'.
76   *Annales Laureshamenses*, p. 22. See Galli, *Saint Benoît en France*, chapter 2 (pp. 11–17).

fate, the importance of Benedict's whereabouts quickly overshadows his sister.) An eighth-century manuscript from the monastery of Saint Emmeram at Regensburg, first discovered in 1685 by Jean Mabillon, describes the circumstances of Benedict's translation in great detail.[77] Its account fits the medieval literary conventions of *furta sacra* (theft of relics), complete with dream visions revealing the location of the tomb and rightful claims to the newly acquired relics.[78] A priest in France, we are told, inspired by the lessons of his pious abbot, set off to Italy in search of Benedict's bones. After an arduous search, and with God's help, a tomb was eventually discovered, wherein the priest and his search party uncovered the bones of Saint Benedict and his sister, Scholastica. The relics were then washed and prepared for travel to the monastery of Fleury, where they presently lay in peace awaiting their glorious resurrection.

It is easy to understand why such claims might be refuted. At stake is Monte Cassino's claim to unity from the sixth century to the present day, which is possible only with the continuous presence of Benedict's relics.[79] Consequently, there is more than an element of invention and intrigue to the story, whose details have been fashioned into a grand monastic narrative or legend. In an influential study on the subject, the Benedictine scholar and former Monte Cassino archivist Tommaso Leccisotti resuscitated a connection between a Brescian relic (possibly an arm – *lacertus* or *radius*) and Saint Benedict, believed to have been given to the monastery at Leno in 758/759, only to be returned in 1878. The brief chronicle for this abbey mentions that 'certain parts of the body of the most blessed and excellent confessor' (Saint Benedict) were brought to Leno.[80] Building on the work of his predecessors, Leccisotti harnessed this brief narrative account as proof for the existence of Benedict's bones at Monte Cassino[81] – a connection made possible after remains were discovered in the post-Second World War recovery efforts, which offered a more 'scientific' basis for comparison (see below).

But once again, Fleury's claims to the relics present a convincing historical counterpoint. Adrevald of Fleury's account of the translation (*Historia translationis*) gained significant traction throughout the Middle Ages. A

77 Mabillon, *Vetera Analecta*, IV, pp. 451–453. See also Weber, 'Un nouveau manuscrit', pp. 141–142, and Galli, *Saint Benoît en France*, pp. 2–5.
78 For the Latin and French translation, see Leclercq, 'Fleury-sur-Loire', cols 1720–1721.
79 Meyvaert, 'Peter the Deacon', p. 4.
80 *Chronicon Brixiense*, p. 239.
81 Leccisotti, 'La testimonianza storica', pp. 135–143, 238. For the presentation of these claims and a strong counterargument, see Morin, 'La Translation de S. Benoît'.

number of manuscript copies between the tenth and sixteenth centuries strongly supports the reception of this narrative in the French region.[82] His version of events dates the incident to the reign of Clovis II (d. 657/658), king of Neustria and Burgundy.[83] This timeline coincides nicely with the monastery's foundation in 651, which provides a good motive behind the translation – namely, the need and/or the desire for a patron saint.[84]

Adrevald also named the culprit: a monk called Aigulf. According to his account, after reading Gregory's *Dialogues*, Abbot Mummolus of Fleury dispatched this monk to Italy with the express purpose of acquiring the saint's body.[85] Upon discovering the relics (with some help from a local *senex*), which lay abandoned on the venerable mountain following the Lombard sack of Monte Cassino c. 577, the search party was emboldened to smuggle them out by nightfall. Locating the tomb, they broke it open and made off with the remains of both saints, with the pope and the Lombards in hot pursuit.[86]

The theft was clearly premeditated and politically motivated.[87] Simply put: it was known that Benedict's relics would bring fame to the abbey, in turn ensuring the support of wealthy patrons while guaranteeing its importance as a pilgrimage site. Fitting with the traditional narratives of the time, this account further serves as religious justification for the translation to France.[88] According to such contemporary views on theft, Fleury had every right to remove the relics of Saint Benedict and repurpose them in founding their own monastery. Incidentally, we are told, Aigulf was joined on his journey by a team of clerics and monks from Le Mans, themselves dispatched on a similar mission by their bishop, Berarius.[89] Once the relics of both saints arrived in France, and Benedict was safely enshrined at Fleury, the latter group transported the remains of Saint Scholastica to her final resting place at Le Mans.[90]

Further details on the theft of Benedict's relics took centuries to emerge. Problematically, this information is contained in the *Epitome Chronicorum*

82 Vidier, *L'Historiographie à Saint-Benoît-sur-Loire*, pp. 141–144.
83 Adrevald of Fleury, *Historia translationis*, col. 901B.
84 See Laporte, 'Vues sur l'histoire de l'abbaye de Fleury'.
85 Adrevald of Fleury, *Historia translationis*, cols 901–910. See Clark, *The 'Gregorian' Dialogues*, pp. 306–307.
86 Ibid., col. 905A–C. See Goffart, 'Le Mans, St. Scholastica'.
87 Wood, 'Between Rome and Jarrow', pp. 305–306.
88 See Geary, *Furta Sacra*, pp. 83–84.
89 *Vita s. Berarii*, cols 157–160 (BHL 1177).
90 Adrevald of Fleury, *Historia translationis*, cols 906C–907D. See Hourlier, 'La translation de sainte Scholastique au Mans'.

Casinensium, a forgery once attributed to Anastasius Bibliothecarius in the ninth century, but now believed to have been written in the twelfth century by Peter the Deacon – the continuator of the Monte Cassino *Chronicon*.[91] Notwithstanding problems of authenticity, however, the *Epitome* introduces a few important pieces of material to the debate. First, it corroborates the most likely timeline for the translation, attributing the relic theft to the post-Lombard era (i.e., after 577), when the monastery of Monte Cassino lay abandoned and desolate for over a century. Second, the collection contains a series of papal forgeries, which assert that Rome's concern for Benedict's whereabouts began as early as the seventh century.[92] Five letters attributed to Popes Vitalian (657–672), Leo II (682–683), and Constantine (708–715) are cited to this effect. The Vitalian letters in particular support Adrevald's account of the relic theft, confirming also his dating of the translation to sometime between 657 and 663.[93] Unsurprisingly, the transfer is condemned; from Monte Cassino's perspective, the removal was entirely unjustified and without permission from the saints or the displaced community of Cassinese monks.

It must be said, however, that such a view acknowledges the translation story on some level. The open criticism and denunciation of the theft reflects its occurrence. But the discussion quickly shifts to the saints' restitution at Monte Cassino. By including these seventh-century (forged) papal letters into the abbey's narrative, Peter the Deacon effectively enrolled the papacy's help in preserving Benedict's name and honour. Choosing Pope Vitalian as the foil was strategic and deliberate; historically speaking, he was the 'first known pope after Gregory demonstrating explicit concern for the memory of Benedict'.[94] This common knowledge made him an ideal agent or literary device for transmitting a Cassinese tradition, expressing grave concern for the surreptitious activities undertaken by the monks from Le Mans and Fleury.

The papacy did in fact play a genuine role in the dispute. The monks of Monte Cassino, at the insistence of their abbot, Optatus (749–759), and King Carloman of the Franks, had implored the papacy for Benedict's safe return. In the mid-eighth century, decades after the event, Pope Zacharias lamented and condemned the furtive theft. In an authentic letter

---

91 Muratori, *Epitome Chronicorum Casinensium*, pp. 345–370. See Caspar, *Petrus Diaconus und die Monte Cassineser Fälschungen*, pp. 111–121; Martin, 'L'*Epitome Chronicorum Casinensium*'.
92 JL 2099, 2100, 2101, 2117, and 2150.
93 Muratori, *Epitome Chronicorum Casinensium*, pp. 355–357.
94 Mews, 'Gregory the Great, the Rule of Benedict and Roman Liturgy', p. 132.

dated 750–751, and addressed to all the bishops and priests in France, he requested that the relics be repatriated to Italy.⁹⁵ This communication did not result in any immediate action, but mounting pressure from the pope and the Frankish king certainly put the monks at Fleury 'in an awkward position'.⁹⁶ What this papal source shows is that around this time 'the translation of St. Benedict's relics was recognised at Monte Cassino as an historical fact'.⁹⁷

Our next point of discussion then becomes one of duration. How long was Benedict absent from Monte Cassino? Or, put another way, when was his body returned? A forgery was later introduced to address this lingering question. Pope Stephen II – with the help King Carloman – is credited with securing the safe return of both saints. This account offers a rather lengthy description of the contiguous burial of Saint Benedict beside his sister, to the right of the altar.⁹⁸ Their bones, it is stated, which were brought back (*reduco*) from France, were 'put back again' (*recondo*) at Monte Cassino.⁹⁹ This repatriation allegedly took place in the mid-eighth century, which anchors the abbey's possession tradition from this date onward.

We might reasonably expect the dispute to end here, with Benedict's return. Yet this is far from being the case. Curiously, the memory of Benedict's translation to Fleury – however brief – appears to lapse. Up to this point in the narrative, there is a general recognition in the Cassinese tradition of the saints' theft; anger and political efforts for their return; and their subsequent repatriation. 'Gradually,' however, as Paul Meyvaert noted, 'Monte Cassino refused to believe that any relics had ever been taken away.'¹⁰⁰

This change in the abbey's representation is noticeable by the late ninth century, suggesting an active medieval dimension to eradicating the past. Abbot Bertharius's poem on Benedict (mentioned above), and a sermon on Scholastica, are frequently cited as evidence for extinguishing all traces of the translation story; their accounts suggest a rupture in historical attitude about what actually happened.¹⁰¹ Whether denial or a genuine forgetting

95 Pope Zacharias, MGH Epp. 3, no. 18, p. 467 (JE 2290). See Hourlier, 'La lettre de Zacharie'. See also Galli, *Saint Benoît en France*, pp. 31–35.
96 Meyvaert, 'Peter the Deacon', p. 10.
97 Ibid.
98 Muratori, *Epitome Chronicorum Casinensium*, p. 362.
99 Ibid.
100 Meyvaert, 'Peter the Deacon', p. 12.
101 Lentini, 'Il sermone di S. Bertario su S. Scolastica', p. 230 (c. 131): 'Ecce in paradyso ab angelis collocatur; ecce in terris monachorum manibus aptatur in tumulo fratris, ut munus quod una mater contulit, nec caeli ianua nec terrae sepultura separaret; et quibus una fuit semper mens in Christo, una esset corporum arca.' See Davril, 'La tradition cassinienne', pp. 384–386.

of past events, the Cassinese narrative from the ninth century returns to stringent claims of unity, advancing the argument for Monte Cassino's uninterrupted possession of the holy relics since the sixth century.

Miracles and serendipitous discoveries helped strengthen this position; together, these two features widened Monte Cassino's claims for a continuous history of the saints' corporeal presence. Abbot Desiderius of Monte Cassino (1058–1087) dedicated his *Dialogues* to the very subject.[102] His work, *Dialogi de miraculis sancti Benedicti*, shows a particular forethought into guarding the story of Monte Cassino's sanctity through its most treasured patron and founder, thereby transmitting the abbey's memory for future generations.[103] Desiderius's prologue notes precisely this authorial intention, fearing that without active conservation – and through the negligence of writers – Benedict's miracles would escape memory and be delivered into oblivion.[104] Similarly, Abbot Oderisius (either I or II) wrote a letter to the monks at Fleury, in which he acknowledged the existence of both claims to the relics of Saint Benedict.[105] Yet he then proceeded to boast about the many miracles, omens, and revelations which he had witnessed with his own eyes. The implication of possession is obvious.

The miraculous in this sense justified the saints' presence. This belief was reinforced with each subsequent experience. In his *History of the Normans*, for example, Amatus of Monte Cassino tells a story about Henry II, which counters the rumours of Benedict's translation to France with the claim of a miracle. The German emperor was suffering from a severe pain in his side, and so wished for the powers of Saint Benedict to restore his good health. 'As the Roman Empire which is subject to use was raised up among the other kingdoms of the world by the keys of the Apostle Peter and by the teachings of St Paul,' he said,

> so do we intend to increase it by means of the order of holy father Benedict and are resolved to have his body presently with us. For by the preaching of these two apostles the Faith was spread throughout the world, but because of the superior abilities of Father an order has been founded and all monks given a rule for monastic life.[106]

---

102 For example, see Desiderius, *Dialogi de miraculis*, II. 14–15 (pp. 1134–1135) and II. 17–18 (pp. 1135–1137).
103 Dell'Omo, *Montecassino*, p. 246.
104 Desiderius, *Dialogi de miraculis*, prologus, pp. 1116–1117.
105 *Recueil des chartes de l'abbaye de Saint-Benoît-sur-Loire*, vol. 1, no. XCIII, p. 245.
106 Amatus of Montecassino, *History of the Normans*, I. 30, p. 54.

The emperor proceeded to fall asleep; the saint appeared to him, touching and curing him.

Benedict then delivered a message to the emperor. 'O emperor,' he reportedly said, 'why do you want my corporeal presence? Do you think that I want to leave the place where I was brought by the angels, where I wrote the rule of monks and where the major part of my body was buried?"' Amatus explained that, with these words, Benedict 'showed that when the bones of a saint are translated from one place to another, the place where the flesh first became earth should always be revered by men'. He continued by saying to the emperor that '"You should know beyond any doubt that my body wishes to remain here. Of this I shall give you a sign with my pastoral staff which will be revealed to you and the sign will be clear."'[107]

This account is copied from Monte Cassino's *Chronicon*, with one notable distinction.[108] The continuator of the latter work, Peter the Deacon, mentions that the emperor had suspicions about the presence of Benedict's body at Monte Cassino.[109] Yet his vision of the saint during the night assuaged any lingering doubts or fears. Not only was Henry II able to pass the kidney stones through his urine without the use of medicine, but – the *Chronicon* relates – he was now, because of his cure, more than convinced that Benedict and his sister were at peace in this place.[110]

Hard 'proof' came in the form of a miraculous discovery. During an ambitious rebuilding programme in the second half of the eleventh century, Abbot Desiderius 'suddenly found the venerable tomb of St. Benedict'. Upon this discovery in 1068, he

> expressed the opinion to his brethren and to other men of good judgment that he should not venture to change the tomb in the least, and in order that no one could snatch away anything from so great a treasure, he recovered the tomb where it was with precious stones and above it, running north and south at right angles to the axis of the basilica, he built a sepulchre of Parian marble five cubits long – a wonderful work. By this device, the sanctuary remained in great eminence, so much so that one has to descend from its pavement to that of the basilica by eight steps under the large arch which is, of course, above the sanctuary.[111]

---

107 Ibid., pp. 54-55.
108 See *Chron. Cas.*, II. 43-44, pp. 247-452. See also Smidt, 'Die Historia Normannorum von Amatus', pp. 211-212.
109 *Chron. Cas.*, II. 43, p. 242.
110 *Chron. Cas.*, II. 43, p. 248.
111 *Chron. Cas.*, III. 26, p. 395.

There is an element of surprise noted in the discovery. In his *Historica Relatio*, Peter the Deacon once again mentions the abbot's sudden find (*subito, ignorantibus cunctis, sepulcrum invenitur*),[112] which suggests something unexpected but providential. Abbot Bertharius's earlier reference to a single 'golden vessel' in his dedicatory poem to Benedict was later modified to accommodate the new and more favourable circumstances. In particular, a change was made to reflect Desiderius's discovery of two *loculi*[113] instead of one. The revised manuscript text in Vat. lat. 1202 (written at Monte Cassino c. 1070–1071) thereby eliminated any uncertainty or contradiction about what lay buried at Monte Cassino. The new account read: 'Now a single vessel contains the relics of *both* saints, whom God has joined on earth and in heaven' (emphasis added).[114]

With his discovery, Desiderius reignited the abbey's claims for continuous possession. Its significance was swiftly reinforced among his contemporaries. Alexander II's consecration of the altar in 1071 suggests the papacy's blessing of the Cassinese tradition. Peter the Deacon's dedicatory statement to the abbot in 1072 immortalised the find, noting that 'after the passing away of the most holy and noble father Benedict, in this his venerable monastery at Cassino, where the most sacred bodies of the same Father our lawgiver and of his peerless sister Scholastica rest honourably buried'.[115] Furthermore, two forged bulls attributed to Popes Alexander II and Urban II were also meant to confirm the verity of the details.[116]

The case for Monte Cassino was ostensibly mounting. By the late eleventh century, the abbey

> was the better able to counter the monks of Saint-Benoît-sur-Loire, who claimed to possess St. Benedict's relics. Its new basilica was now equipped to be a centre of pilgrimage and devotion without peer among the churches of monastic saints in the western world.[117]

This confidence grew even more when, after almost four centuries, the saints' tombs were uncovered once again. On 18 November 1484, Cardinal John of Aragon, the commendatory abbot of Monte Cassino from 1471 to

---

112   Ibid. See also *Acta Sanctorum*, Mar. III, Dies 21, col 288C (BHL 1142).
113   Newton, *Scriptorium and Library*, p. 231.
114   See Meyvaert, 'Peter the Deacon', pp. 23–24; Davril, 'La tradition cassinienne', p. 386.
115   Newton, *Scriptorium and Library*, p. 276.
116   Tosti, *Storia della badia*, I, pp. 432–435; II, pp. 211–113. See Galdi, 'S. Benedetto tra Montecassino e Fleury', p. 568.
117   Cowdrey, *Age of Abbot Desiderius*, p. 14.

1485, removed the high altar as part of a larger renovation project. An official act written two years later by the abbey's notary, Cristoforo Perone, bolstered the abbey's claims with a detailed account the tomb's position and location.[118] One witness to the event was Raphael Maffeus (1451–1522), whose *Commentariorum Urbanorum Libri XXXVIII* (published in 1506) offers a succinct précis on the discovery.[119] In a chapter devoted to the saint, he refers to the calamitous translation of Benedict's bones to Fleury – the very same relics, however, that were returned from France and unearthed by the Aragonese cardinal.[120]

The monks of Monte Cassino were never in doubt, especially after Desiderius's discovery centuries earlier. On 18 November 1486, the military-governor or vice-regent of the king of Naples, John Antonio I Carafa (1446–1454), completed the abbey's restoration. He placed a marble slab over the tomb, which would serve future generations in identifying the remains of both saints. A plaque was attached to the tomb's lid, with the inscription: 'In this tomb lies the body of the most blessed father Saint Benedict and his sister, Scholastica, rebuilt on the order of John Antonio Carafa.'[121] When Abbot Girolamo II Sclocchetto of Piacenza (1541–1546) was renovating the abbey six decades later (12 March 1545), he found Carafa's inscription.[122] On this occasion, the tomb was opened, only to witness the bodies of Saints Benedict and Scholastica, which brought tears to the monks' eyes.[123] Further renovation works by Abbot Simplificius Caffarelli in 1637 uncovered the tomb's base, which was easily identified by its marble plaque. When Abbot Angelo VI della Noce (1665–1669) opened the tomb on 7 August 1659, he discovered the saints' bones inside before transferring them to a cypress box, which was placed inside an alabaster urn.[124] And when Pope Benedict

---

118 Leccisotti, 'Sul documento', p. 119. See also Leccisotti, 'La testimonianza storica', pp. 169–174 (BHL 1143). For the manuscript tradition, see Meyvaert, 'L'invention des reliques Cassiniennes', p. 288, no. 5; De Witte, 'Notes sur la découverte des ossements'. For the act itself, see Bartolini, *Di s. Zaccaria papa*, no. 26, pp. 68–72 (*documenti*).

119 For the Latin, see Meyvaert, 'L'invention des reliques Cassiniennes', p. 309.

120 Maffeus, *Commentariorum Urbanorum Octo et Tringinta Libri*, lib. 21, col. 753 (see also *Reg. Aven.* fol. 408r).

121 'In hac sepultura iacent corpora beatissimi patris sancti Benedicti et Scolasticae eius sororis recondita ex ordinatione Iohannis Antonii Caraffa militis, filii comitis Mataloni viceregis Casinensis ob suam spontaneam devotionem.'

122 Leccisotti, 'La testimonianza storica', p. 175. See also Davril, 'La tradition cassinienne', pp. 388–391.

123 Quote from Onorato dei Medici, *Annali Cassinesi* III, p. 452, as cited in Leccisotti, 'La testimonianza storica', p. 175.

124 Leccisotti, 'La testimonianza storica', p. 180.

XIII consecrated the basilica on 19 May 1727, the occasion represented yet another 'historic relation'[125] with Rome, signalling once again the papacy's acceptance of the Cassinese claims.

Mystery of the Grape

The controversy continues today. It 'has the wonderfully enduring quality of good wine', wrote one observer. 'One can savour its bouquet, argue its finer points, knowing that there is no provable solution to the mystery of the grape that gives so much pleasure.'[126] After the Allied bombing of Monte Cassino on 15 February 1944, human remains were discovered where the altar once stood. Upon closer inspection of the uncovered (and still intact) tomb, which had miraculously escaped damage from the destructive aerial raid, the skeletal remains were declared as belonging to two humans, possibly of the same genetic pool. 'Scientific' findings reinforced this uninterrupted and continuous Cassinese argument, providing the religious community a final link in the historical chain of memory.

The narrative is a familiar one. Similar to the discoveries in 1066, 1484, 1545, 1637, and 1659, the 1950 recovery programme for Monte Cassino miraculously unearthed the abbey's patron saints.[127] On this occasion (1 August 1950), the alabaster urn was opened. Under its lid was the inscription: *Ssmi P. Benedicti et Scholast. sacra ossa et cineres.*[128] Inside the urn was the cypress box fashioned for the saints' remains in the seventeenth century by Abbot Della Noce; it bore the further inscription: *SS.mus PP. Benedictus et Scholastica.*[129] Under the direction of Monte Cassino's abbot at the time, Ildefonso Rea (1945–1971), and the collaboration of two monks,[130] the human remains were examined. In the coming weeks of August 1950, medical experts and radiologists from Rome and Naples were invited to examine the remains further.[131] Significantly, despite the advancement in

---

125 In Leccisotti, "La consacrazione della basilica cassinese', p. 326 (c. 24, col. 170v).
126 Hall, *Eagle Argent*, p. 4.
127 For a contemporary report, see Leccisotti, 'A Montecassino'.
128 See Leccisotti, 'Il recente rinvenimento delle reliquie', p. 22; a picture can be found in *tavola* V.
129 See the detailed account in 'La ricognizione dei sacri corpi', pp. 3–9.
130 'Relazione dei periti', p. 10.
131 For a day-by-day outline of events and a brief composition of the team, see Leccisotti, 'Il recente rinvenimento delle reliquie'; for the official proceedings, see the 'Attie Ufficiali' in the second volume, pp. 11–92. See also Avagliano, 'Montecassino "com'era e dov'era"', p. 145 (citing the abbot's letter from 5 August 1950).

medical and technological processes, radiocarbon dating was not used as a scientific method.

Serious and swift efforts were made to authenticate the Cassinese tradition.[132] The positive results of these examinations were first published by Professor L. Olivieri, from the University of Naples's Faculty of Medicine, and Domenico Catalano from the Institute of Human Anatomy at the University of Naples.[133] After witnessing the bones first-hand, Ildefonso Schuster, the cardinal-bishop of Milan, argued for their authenticity in his testimony dated 5 November 1950.[134] Archaeological and historical accounts of the exhumation appeared alongside the scientific study, published at Monte Cassino in the first of two volumes entitled *Il sepolcro di S. Benedetto* (1951).[135] The significance of the discovery is advanced on the opening page of this volume: 'After so much destruction, after the losses and indigences, after the exiles and wanderings', the abbey's archivist/historian wrote, Monte Cassino could now boast its newest restoration in its long and uninterrupted past.[136] Abbot Rea issued a number of decrees and acts to communicate the news as widely as possible to all Benedictine monasteries, congregations, the Cassinese community, and Italian government officials.[137]

Meanwhile, on the 'study and research' side of things, the newly minted journal *Benedictina* provided a welcome outlet for publishing Monte Cassino's claims, inspiring a generation or more of scholarship on the abbey's long and continuous tradition. Indeed, many of the seminal articles on this subject from the 1950s to the 1960s were later published in the second volume of *Il sepolcro di S. Benedetto* (1982). Assembled in preparation for the fifteenth centenary of the saint's birth, this sophomore book also sought to engage with recent counterclaims (and criticism) published in the academic journal *Studia monastica* (1979).

Fleury's tradition is comprehensively represented in this special journal issue entitled 'Le culte et les reliques de saint Benoît et de sainte Scholastique'. Also prepared for Benedict's centenary, this series of journal articles

---

132 For a brief summary of events, see Scarafoni, 'Il sepolcro di S. Benedetto', pp. 167–171. See also the Atti Ufficiali in *Il sepolcro di S. Benedetto*, vol. 2, pp. 13–92.

133 Olivieri and Catalano, 'Studio anatomo-radiologico'. A brief account is reprinted in Davril, 'La tradition cassinienne', pp. 393–401. The examination also included Professors Mario Mazzeo, Gastone Lambertini, Pasquale Scrocca, and Girolamo Matronola (see 'Relazione dei periti', p. 15.)

134 Schuster, 'Una testimonianza', p. 23. See also the cardinal's correspondence with Abbot Rea in *Ildefonso Schuster – Ildefonso Rea*, no. 153, pp. 211–213.

135 Sections III and IV.

136 Leccisotti, 'Il recente rinvenimento delle reliquie', p. 13.

137 See *Ildefonso Schuster – Ildefonso Rea*, no. 158, pp. 223–224.

combined decades of analysis and scholarly discourse first begun in the early 1950s, after the bishop of Orléans, Monsignor Picard de la Vacquerie, initiated a formal enquiry into the historic matter (12 November 1952).[138] Competing anatomical studies on the bones of Saint Benedict at Fleury (and at various other French monasteries) were examined, which complement the objective archaeological and historical studies.[139] The whole enterprise, it is proclaimed, was conducted without any polemical spirit, as an exercise in intellectual honesty.[140] In that same year (1952), moreover, M.-H. Laurent published a lengthy and critical review of *Il sepolcro di S. Benedetto* in the French journal *Revue d'histoire ecclésiastique*, which prompted a strong rebuttal by Tommaso Leccisotti, Luigi Olivieri, Gian Alberto Blanc, and Cesarina Cortesi, who sought to counter lingering claims of authenticity with a thorough reappraisal of the scientific, anatomical, historical, and archaeological evidence.[141] A few years prior, Dom Déodat Galli had published a short book intended to 'present the historical arguments on which the Fleury tradition is based and to show how the relics of Saint Benedict have always been preserved since the seventh century to our days despite the invasions, wars and revolutions'.[142] He wanted to make the proof more accessible to the public, since it transpired that many Benedictines themselves were not aware of the saint's transfer from Monte Cassino to Fleury; or they considered it legend. As he concluded, the translation should not be a subject of contestation between the sons of Saint Benedict. Because it is historical fact, he suggested, amply proven by the evidence, French and Italian monks should 'love' in this event the 'designs of divine Providence'.[143]

These intentions notwithstanding, the findings are far from conclusive. To begin with, the links to Saints Benedict and/or Scholastica are themselves rather tenuous. There is no definitive source or putative evidence that connects the post-Second World War discovery with our earliest reference in the *Dialogues* of the saints' original burial site – what Gregory the Great described as a shared and 'common resting place' in the Chapel of St John the Baptist, which Benedict 'had built to replace the altar of Apollo'.[144] As one historian concluded, 'neither medicine, nor archaeology, nor history

---

138 See Davril, 'Historique des travaux'.
139 For example, Beau, 'Rapport anatomique'.
140 Davril, 'Conclusion générale', p. 423.
141 Laurent, 'Review of Il Sepolcro di S. Benedetto'; Leccisotti, 'Ancora del sepolcro di S. Benedetto'.
142 Galli, *Saint Benoît en France*, p. vi.
143 Ibid., p. 72.
144 See Vogüé, *Grégoire le Grand: Dialogues*, II. 34 (p. 234) and 37 (p. 244), respectively.

authorise us now to consider as authentic the bones exhumed at Cassino in 1950'.¹⁴⁵ A more recent account laments that

> we are left with the agnostic reflection that the truth about the grave and remains of St Benedict, author of the great rule that has inspired Western monasticism and patron of Europe, lies beyond our reach. It has been obscured by age-old literary falsifications and pious frauds, leading to age-long historical misapprehensions.¹⁴⁶

*

This conclusion does not alter localised belief, which comprises part history, part hagiography.¹⁴⁷ The second half of the twentieth century certainly breathed new life into the Cassinese tradition. But it also provoked historical criticism, particularly around the polemical nature of the studies – a reality that adds another historiographical layer to an already long debate.¹⁴⁸

For our present purposes, the sheer breadth of historical materials affirms a central argument in this book: Monte Cassino's identity was cultivated and forged through the figure, life, memory, and tradition(s) of its patron saint. The possibility of his corporeal absence from the abbey has scarcely diminished its symbolic value. While this conviction runs counter to much modern, critical scholarship, the Cassinese belief in the saint's whereabouts remains steadfast – a dominant tradition and self-portrayal that both justifies and affirms the abbey's legacy as a *locellus aureus*.¹⁴⁹

Over the last fourteen centuries, the conflation of Benedict's life and death has irrevocably shaped how the abbey is viewed historically and spiritually – in essence, how we measure its esteem and historical value. Through his monastic *Rule*, he determined the bonds of a religious community centred on obedience, humility, and manual labour. In the wider history of early monasticism, Benedict embodies the whole programme of Western religious life, discipline, and governance. He is the emblem of spiritual devotion and practice. And, as we'll see in the next chapter, the record of his achievements and historical importance lives on the venerable mountain which houses his foundation.

---

145 Laurent, 'Review of Il Sepolcro di S. Benedetto', p. 659.
146 Clark, *The 'Gregorian' Dialogues*, p. 318.
147 For the latter category, see especially Grégoire, *Storia e agriografia*, Part III.
148 On this subject, see Galli, *Saint Benoît en France*, chapter 3 (pp. 19–24).
149 Pohl, *Werkstätte der Erinnerung*, p. 175.

2. The 'Citadel of Campania': Growth and Prosperity

Abstract

This chapter examines Monte Cassino's long-standing reputation as a sacred mountain. It asks how the abbey conditioned, reinforced, and engendered its place in the history of the Western religious tradition. Its physical location and environment are critical to understanding its history of settlement and inhabitation, time and again, after repeated episodes of destruction and exile. But how exactly did the abbey achieve this sacralised status? And what historical conditions contributed to Monte Cassino's growth and prosperity beyond a localised influence? As argued throughout this chapter, the abbey's spiritual and historical allure are defining features of its past, demonstrating formative qualities for understanding the abbey's identity and sense of its own history, culture, and tradition.

Keywords: mountain; *locus sanctus*; library; scriptorium; reputation; visitors

> Eternal benedictions rest
> Upon thy name, Saint Benedict!
> Founder of convents in the West,
> Who built on Mount Cassino's crest
> In the Land of Labor, thine eagle's nest.[1]

Monte Cassino was broken ground well before the advent of Christianity. At the mountain's base stood the ancient town of Cassinum, a Volscian settlement transformed from the third century BC into a flourishing site

---

1 Longfellow, *Christus*, p. 158 (first interlude, The abbot Joachim).

under Roman rule. 'Antiquity reports that the well-known [Marcus Terentius] Varro, famed throughout so many generations and, as Cicero bears witness, the wisest of all the Romans, was the founder of this dwelling place.'[2] This 'consul of the Romans', the abbey's eleventh-century chronicler attests, 'chose this place for himself out of all the places of the Roman Empire, built it up, and made it notable with many monuments. After his death, Caesar turned over the aforesaid *Castrum Casinum* to Antony.'[3]

On the mountain's summit stood an ancient acropolis, which served more than a strategic military purpose.[4] On this site there existed also 'a very old temple [of Jupiter], in which the ignorant country people still worshipped Apollo as their pagan ancestors had done, and went on offering superstitious and idolatrous sacrifices in groves dedicated to various demons'.[5] This area of worship was surrounded by groves and a portico, enclosed within the ancient walls, which defensive structures the Romans rehabilitated and fortified.

This sacred landscape changed with Saint Benedict's arrival in the early sixth century.[6] When this 'man of God arrived at this spot', Gregory the Great wrote in his *Dialogues*, he

> destroyed the idol, overturned the altar and cut down the trees in the sacred groves. Then he turned the temple of Apollo into a chapel dedicated to Saint Martin [of Tours], and where Apollo's altar had stood, he built a chapel in honour of Saint John the Baptist.[7]

His actions foreshadowed Gregory's famed instructions to Abbot Melitus in 601: that pagan shrines should only be purified so that 'the people, seeing that their temples are not destroyed, may abandon their error and flocking more readily to the accustomed resorts, may come to know and adore the true god'.[8] Thus pioneering what eventually became widespread practice throughout the early medieval West, Benedict founded his so-called 'Citadel

---

2   *Chron. Cas.*, I. 1, p. 17.
3   *Chron. Cas.*, IV. 112, p. 581. See also Cicero, *Philippics*, II, 40, pp. 154–157; Dell'Omo, *Montecassino Medievale*, pp. 173–174; Ildefonso Schuster's account in D'Onorio, Spinelli, and Pirozzi. *L'Abbazia di Montecassino*, pp. 53–66.
4   On this subject, see especially Pantoni, *L'Acropoli di Montecassino*. See also his brief account in *Pacis Nuntius*, pp. 49–62.
5   Vogüé, *Grégoire le Grand: Dialogues*, II. 8, p. 168.
6   Peter the Deacon, *Ortus et vita*, XV, pp. 18, 20.
7   Vogüé, *Grégoire le Grand: Dialogues*, II. 8, p. 168. The chopping down of sacred trees is emulated by Saint Martin of Tours and Boniface in the West; John of Ephesus in the East.
8   Bede, *Ecclesiastical History*, I. 30.

4. Benedict of Nursia Orders the Destruction of the Temple of Apollo at Monte Cassino. By Jan Erasmus Quellinus (1634–1715). The Edward Pearce Casey Fund and Elisha Whittelsey Collection, 2012.

of Campania'.[9] As one modern French philosopher noted: 'At the time [when] the School of Athens, founded by Plato, was closed/the light of reason/was sublimated in faith.'[10]

By planting his Cross on the summit, Benedict transposed existing religious customs. He took shelter in a Roman tower, a two-storey headquarters connected by an internal staircase, which would later be incorporated into the abbey's designs. According to an encomium allegedly given at the First Lateran Council in 1123, the saint's arrival on this mountain represented a continuation of God's mission, which in turn 'rendered it famous throughout the world and made it the head of the whole monastic order'.[11] In this view, the original abbey was founded '"neither by men, nor through man"' (Galatians 1:1), the pope said, 'but through Jesus Christ, by whose command Saint Benedict came to that place, purged it of the filthiness of idolatry, and by writing the *Rule*, by the working of miracles, and by the burial of his body there'.[12]

The venerable mountain was a powerful metaphor for the monastic life: an isolated, elevated, and semi-inaccessible location where devoted religious men could aspire to encounter the divine through spiritual purification. On its summit stood an earthly house, Benedict's house, through which countless souls could ascend to heaven along 'the ladder once mounted to the sky'[13] – a 'magnificent road covered with rich carpeting and glittering with thousands of lights'. This was the path taken by Benedict himself, stretching 'eastward in a straight line until it reached up into heaven'.[14] Immutable and stable, the mountain in this sense symbolised a close proximity with God, the promise of transcendence between heaven and earth[15]; it represents a 'window of God'[16] (*fenestra Dei*), where he was 'present to all' who believed.[17] It held an almost cosmic significance as the *axis mundi* – the central meeting point, sanctuary, and 'revelatory landscape'[18] for contact between humans and the divine.

9   Vogüé, *Grégoire le Grand: Dialogues*, II (part of the full title). For a more modern usage, see the record of Archbishop Guido Maggiori, appendix III in Avagliano, 'Montecassino "com'era e dov'era"', p. 155.
10 Guitton, 'Ricordo'.
11 *Chron. Cas.*, IV. 78, p. 543.
12 Ibid.
13 Peter Damian, *Opusculum* 36, col. 621.
14 Vogüé, *Grégoire le Grand: Dialogues*, II. 37, p. 244.
15 Grégoire, *Storia e agriografia*, pp. 23–24.
16 Carmen 32, *Item eiusdem [S. Mauri] metrum*, vv. 190–194, p. 177 (cited in Grégoire, *Storia e agriografia*, p. 33.)
17 *Chron. Cas.*, III. 30, p. 402.
18 See Eck, 'Mountains'.

The abbey embraced this religious landscape and symbolism. From its lofty heights, situated nearly 2,000 feet above sea level, this 'eagle's nest' was a physical and spiritual landmark. Built on the mountain's crest, it overlooked the Liri Valley, the Land of Labour (Terra di Lavoro), at the confluence of the Rivers Liri, Rapido, and Garigliano. The mountain itself, positioned along the ancient Via Casilina (the modern Highway no. 6), 125 km south-east of Rome, became Benedict's 'chief dwelling place and the main theatre of the Holy Patriarch's virtue and sanctity'.[19] For this connection alone, it swiftly rose to prominence in the medieval world and imagination. 'That mount, upon whose slope Cassino lies,' as Dante wrote in the early fourteenth century, 'was erst thronged on its summit by people deceived and ill-disposed.' It was Benedict, as this famous canto in the *Paradiso* relates, who 'first brought up there the name of Him who brought to earth that truth which lifts us so high'; it was he 'who drew the places round about away from the impious cult which seduced the world'.[20] 'It may be rightly asserted', therefore, as Pope Pius XII reflected in his mid-twentieth-century encyclical praising Saint Benedict, 'that the holy monastery built there was a haven and shelter of highest learning and of all the virtues' – a 'pillar of the Church and a bulwark of the faith'".[21]

But how exactly did the abbey achieve this sacralised status? And what historical conditions contributed to Monte Cassino's growth and prosperity beyond a localised influence? If we explore these questions beyond the contours and confines of Benedict's *animus* and aura (see Chapter 1), the answers are not immediately transparent. At first glance, the abbey's precipitous and remote mountaintop location offered few advantages for a thriving religious community; it was isolated, exposed to the elements and natural hazards. Such realities made it an unlikely place for long-term settlement, growth, and prosperity. But as I argue in the following pages, Monte Cassino's reputation as a sacred mountain conditioned, reinforced, and engendered its place in the history of the Western religious tradition. Its physical location and environment are critical to understanding its history of settlement and inhabitation, time and again, after repeated episodes of destruction and exile. Its functional purpose as 'a laboratory for the life of the spirit',[22] moreover, was realised through its material existence. The abbey's sustained fame as the fountainhead of Western monasticism rendered it a perennial attraction

---

19 Pope Pius XII, *Fulgens Radiatur*.
20 Dante, *Paradiso*, XXII, in *The Divine Comedy*.
21 Pope Pius XII, *Fulgens Radiatur*.
22 Leccisotti, *Monte Cassino*, p. 258.

to pilgrims and tourists alike. Its spiritual and historical allure are defining features of its past, demonstrating formative qualities for understanding the abbey's identity and sense of its own history, culture, and tradition.

Locus sanctus

It didn't take long for Monte Cassino to gain recognition as a premier religious community. Its spiritual and political status was swiftly reinforced by contemporaries, both secular and ecclesiastical. When Jonas of Bobbio wrote his *Life of Columbanus* c. 642/643, the monastery was already recognised in the medieval West as a 'holy place' (*locus sanctus*).[23] On a practical level, it enjoyed freedom and protection from the administrative, fiscal, and legal/jurisdictional control of local bishops and secular rulers.[24] Its modest origins in the early sixth century provided exceptional spiritual credentials, which translated over the course of many centuries into privileges of immunity and exemption from Capuan and Salernan princes, Beneventan dukes, Carolingian and Ottonian emperors, and medieval popes.[25] Together, these special prerogatives enabled the abbey to operate independently, to manage its own finances and resources, and to elect its own abbots.[26] As a direct consequence, the abbey became by the eighth and ninth centuries a centre of political activities.

On a more spiritual plane, it was Benedict's fame that drew people to the mountain. His 'gift of prophecy'[27] was widely known even during his lifetime. When the Goths were still in power, King Totila paid a visit to Monte Cassino to meet in person with the saintly figure.[28] The future bishop of Eichstatt, Willibald, visited the recently repopulated abbey in 729.[29] The Frankish mayor of the palace, Carloman, came to Monte Cassino in 746/747, exchanging his worldly possessions for the life of a monk; after his death in 755, moreover, the abbey received his body (in 757) 'in a golden casket'.[30] The Lombard king, Ratchis, retired to the abbey as a

---

23   Diem, 'The Carolingians and the Regula Benedicti', p. 261.
24   Pohl, 'History in Fragments', p. 365; Whitten, '*Quasi ex uno ore*', p. 51.
25   *Radelgisi et Siginulf divisio ducatus Beneventani*, c. 3, p. 221. See also Cowdrey, *Age of Abbot Desiderius*, pp. xxxii–xxxiii; Tabacco, 'Montecassino e l'impero'.
26   For some administrative and juridical examples, see Guiraud, *Économie et société*, chapter 2.
27   Vogüé, *Grégoire le Grand: Dialogues*. II. 14, p. 180.
28   Ibid.
29   *Vita Willibaldi*, c. 5, p. 102.
30   *Chron. Cas.*, I. 7, p. 33. See also *Annales Einhardi*, p. 141; Paul the Deacon, *Continuatio Casinesis*, c. 4, p. 199; *Chron. s. Ben.*, p. 487; Peter the Deacon, *Ortus et Vita*, c. 22, pp. 29–30.

Cassinese monk in 749.[31] The famed abbot of Fulda, Sturmi, visited in 747.[32] The Lombard historian, grammarian, poet, and teacher, Paul the Deacon, was there sometime in the 780s–790s. Charlemagne journeyed there in 787, 'in order to pray to the blessed father Benedict'[33]; Louis II made an official visit in 866, in order to visit the saint's burial place (see Chapter 1).[34] When Emperor Henry II of Germany visited Monte Cassino in late June 1022, he lavished the abbey with a Gospel Book (now at the Vatican Library, Codex Vat. Ottoman. lat. 74), in addition to 'a cover from the altar of St. Benedict which had belonged to King Charles' and 'a very large chalice in Saxon silver, with its paten, which Theodericus, King of the Saxons, had once sent to St. Benedict'.[35] And in 1072, Empress Agnes (Henry III's wife) came to Monte Cassino 'from the farthest regions of Germany', residing for 'almost half a year'. During her prolonged visit,

> she offered to Blessed Benedict, as befitted her august dignity, splendid gifts, namely a chasuble of white silk completely interwoven on all sides with gold; an alb finely decorated with fringe at the shoulders, the head, and the hands, but edged at the feet with a fringed border measuring about a cubit in breadth, and at the same time an amice with embroidery; two purple copes adorned with precious gold borders; and a large *pallium* with elephants, which they call a dossal; a Gospel Book with a cover cast in silver, relief work most beautifully gilded; and two candelabra also cast in silver, weighing twelve pounds.[36]

The abbey's privileged, autonomous status owes directly to its saintly patronage. As we saw in the previous chapter, it is explained also by the wide-scale adoption of Benedict's monastic *Rule*, which became a standard across Western Europe under the Carolingians. A royal council convened in 742 mandated that all religious houses should strive to live 'according to the rule of Saint Benedict' (*iuxta regulam sancti Benedicti*).[37] The Carolingian reform of spiritual life during the late eighth and early ninth centuries regulated the monastic life by applying the *Rule* throughout its widening

---

31 Erchempert, *Historia Langobardorum Beneventanorum*, c. 9, 238.
32 Eigil, *Vita Sturmi*, c. 14, pp. 145–147; Rudolf of Fulda, *Vita Leobae*, c. 10, pp. 125–126.
33 *Chron. Cas.*, I. 12, p. 45.
34 *Chron. s. Ben.*, c. 4, p. 471; cf. Erchempert, *Historia Langobardorum Beneventanorum*, c. 33, p. 247.
35 *Chron. Cas.*, II. 43, p. 250. See Bloch, *Monte Cassino*, I, pp. 19ff.
36 *Chron. Cas.*, III. 31, pp. 402–403.
37 *Concilium Germanicum* (a.742), c. 7, p. 4.

empire. Serving to regulate the day-to-day activities within each Frankish monastery, it now framed a wider network of relations between religious houses, abbots, local bishops, and secular authorities, in addition to early medieval kings, emperors, and popes.

The holiness of Monte Cassino can thus be attributed first and foremost to Benedict's life and works – his legacy. The Roman and pagan heritage which sustained this mountain summit for centuries before was officially supplanted with his advent to the mountain in the early sixth century. Gregory the Great's *Dialogues* forged a strong connection between this saint (and his relics), his monastic *Rule*, and the abbey's physical location. Writing almost 1,500 years later, Pope Benedict XVI drew on this sixth-century source to explain Monte Cassino's unique spiritual and cultural inheritance. For this twenty-first-century pope, it was 'a heritage that bore fruit in the passing centuries and is still bearing fruit throughout the world'.[38]

Much of this sentiment originates from the abbey's material construction, which grew in size, stature, wealth, and fame between the eighth and eleventh centuries.[39] Following the community's resettlement and repopulation in the early eighth century, its building and decorating programme accelerated rapidly. This historical process of reconstruction and renovation, which in many ways has continued throughout the abbey's long history, was a main contributor to its representation as a premier holy place. Abbot Gisulf (796–817) is responsible for refurbishing the hilltop location (*sursum*) of Monte Cassino, in addition to constructing the church and monastery of San Salvatore, built at the base of the mount (*deorsum*).[40] The latter monastery, which was burned by the Saracens in the late ninth century – and eventually replaced by a Baroque version in 1694 – 'became the *praepositura maior*, the major priory of Monte Cassino, its administrative center, the place where the majority of the monks lived and the abbots usually dwelt'.[41]

Situated at the foot of the mountain, San Salvatore was a 'gateway to the shrine of the Founder'[42] above. Its diverse buildings and facilities permitted the community's self-sufficient lifestyle, in accordance with the Benedictine *Rule* of monastic life and governance. Whereas the hill of Saint Benedict housed his body, spirit, and memory, the more practical day-to-day

---

38 Pope Benedict XVI, *Great Christian Thinkers*, p. 127.
39 See Morin, 'Pour le Topographie ancienne'.
40 *Chron. Cas.*, I. 17, p. 57. See Pantoni, 'La basilica di Gisulfo'.
41 Citarella and Willard, *Ninth-Century Treasure*, p. 41.
42 Ibid., p. 44.

operations developed in its shadow (e.g., abbot's accommodation, visitors' quarters, refectory, kitchen, dormitory, wine cellar, etc.). In between was the Rocca Janula, a fortress-like complex (*castrum/castellum*) constructed on a rock above the inhabited area of San Germano. First built during the tenth-century abbacy of Aligernus (948/950–985), this 'piccola porta del Monastero'[43] was defended and restored over many centuries thereafter.[44] Originally conceived for the collective defence of the town below and the monastery above, its ruins now lie almost unnoticed to the many tourists who visit the mountain summit each day.

To complement the building works at the mountain's base, Abbot Gisulf set about replacing the main church of Saint Martin. He used the Oratory of Saint John – originally built over the shrine of Apollo, home to the tomb of Saints Benedict and Scholastica – as the basis for an ambitious westward expansion of a new basilica. Leo Marsicanus recorded the embellishments in the Monte Cassino *Chronicon*, noting how

> the same abbot acting no less energetically above, built there some decent housing; and the church in which the *corpus* of Saint Benedict was buried, because it was small, making it altogether larger and covering with lead the roof of cypress timbers, he embellished with *ornamenta* in gold as well as in silver. Furthermore, above the altar of Saint Benedict he placed a silver ciborium, adorning it in part with gold and likewise with enamels, while the remaining altars he covered with silver plates.[45]

Under Abbot Bertharius (856–883), the monastery was fortified 'in the manner of a castle'(*in modum castelli*).[46] A town (*civitatis*) was also built around the lower church of San Salvatore, which became known in the Greek language as Eulogimenopolis, or the 'city of Benedict' (*Benedicti civitatis*).[47] At some point between 866 and 875, however, the abbey acquired a relic of Saint Germanus (a finger) from Emperor Louis II of Italy, who had removed the entire *corpus* from its resting place at Capua.[48] For this reason,

---

43 Baldizzi, in Pistilli, *La Rocca Janula*, p. 55.
44 *Chron. Cas.*, II. 1, p. 167. For a good historical and architectonic study of this fortress, see Pistilli, *La Rocca Janula*.
45 *Chron. Cas.*, I. 18, p. 59 (translation in Citarella and Willard, *Ninth-Century Treasure*, pp. 44–45).
46 *Chron. Cas.*, I. 33, p. 90.
47 *Chron. Cas.*, I. 33, p. 90; *Chron. s. Ben.*, c. 15 (p. 476) and c. 20 (p. 479); Fabiani, *La Terra di S. Benedetto*, I, pp. 30–31.
48 See Citarella and Willard, *Ninth-Century Treasure*, p. 118, no. 198.

the surrounding city became known as San Germano by the early tenth century[49]; it wasn't until 1863 that the official name of Cassino was adopted.

Monte Cassino came to represent much more than a singular physical locale. Its influence not only stretched down the mountainside, but it also extended well into the surrounding countryside. The abbey's material wealth derived primarily from its landholdings in this region between Latium and the Campania, which it accumulated primarily by donation and expansion from the eighth century onward.[50] At its apogee in the High Middle Ages, the extent of this territory – known from c. 982 in contemporary sources as the *Terra sancti Benedicti* – measured approximately 800 km² (80,000 hectares).[51]

Considering the humble origins of Monte Cassino's foundation, this landed property represents centuries of growth and territorial-economic expansion.[52] Yet its core was established early on with a lump-sum donation, when in 744 Duke Gisulf II of Benevento granted lands to the abbey in the fertile valleys of the Rivers Liri and Rapido.[53] As we'll see in Chapter 4, this substantial acquisition of approximately 600 km² formed part of the abbey's restoration under Abbot Petronax in the early eighth century.[54] With this one endowment, the 'lands of Saint Benedict' grew exponentially, expanding over the next few centuries into central and southern Italy with the further acquisition of various dependent *cellae* and churches.[55]

Given the abbey's intimate experience with destruction (see Chapter 3), its growth is correspondingly linked to periods of its restoration. In the mid-ninth century, Abbot Aligernus (948/950–985) helped regain some of the possessions lost to Saracen raiders in 883.[56] Doing so hinged on his successful political negotiations with local lords like the *gastaldus* of Aquino and the count of Teano, in whose hands the abbey's former territories now lay. A charter from 952 provides a definitive statement on the boundaries of Saint Benedict's reconstituted lands in the post-Saracen era, whose continued expansion relied on the support and patronage of Princes Landulf II and Paldulf II of Capua.[57]

49 For a direct reference to this name change, see *Chron. Cas.*, II. 32, p. 229.
50 Hoffmann, 'Zur Geschichte Montecassinos', p. 4.
51 For the most extensive account, see Fabiani, *La Terra di S. Benedetto*. For the term's use in Otto III's diploma (15 October 999), see MGH DD O III., no. 333, p. 761.
52 Dell'Omo, *Montecassino Medievale*, pp. 61–72. See also Guiraud, *Économie et société*, esp. pp. 18–26.
53 Whitten, '*Quasi ex uno ore*', pp. 50–51.
54 *Chron. Cas.*, I. 5, pp. 25–28; *Chron. s. Ben.*, c. 21, pp. 479–480.
55 For the most extensive coverage, see Fabiani, *La Terra di S. Benedetto*.
56 *Chron. Cas.*, II. 1–3, pp. 166–173.
57 Gattola, *Ad historiam*, I, pp. 57–58. See also Zeller, 'Montecassino in Teano', pp. 126–130; Cowdrey, *Age of Abbot Desiderius*, p. 2. *Registrum Petri Diaconi*, nos 214A (pp. 658–659) and 312 (pp. 926–927).

THE 'CITADEL OF CAMPANIA': GROWTH AND PROSPERITY

Consolidation of the *Terra sancti Benedicti* was integral to the abbey's medieval building programme. Abbot John III (997–1010) continued Aligernus's work on the abbey, completing a circuit of fortifications[58]; Abbot Atenulfus (1011–1022) built a bell tower (campanile) and renovated the abbey church of San Salvatore.[59] Abbot Theobaldus (1022–1035) continued these works with even greater energy and vision than his predecessors. As the *Chronicon* notes, he

> acquired very many ornaments for the church here. He had made a silver procession cross for Sundays, and two bells of marvellous size and beauty. He adorned the altar of St Gregory with a silver front of very fair workmanship. He made also a silver vessel in which he reverently placed the fragment of the wood of the Lord's cross. [...] He also clothed in fair workmanship – also of silver – a pastoral staff with its *titulus*. He added to the church of Blessed Benedict, on the north side next to the abbot's chamber, a tiny church in honour of St Nicholas, and he built an equally tiny church in honour of St Severus Bishop of Casinum, in the place that was of old called 'at the St Severus turn'. He also constructed high walls, and the two towers on this side and that in front of the atrium of the church, in the manner of a cloister.[60]

The German abbot Richerius (1038–1052) extended this building work on the abbey's east side, though the majority of his efforts were limited to securing the lands and possessions belonging to the great abbey. 'By reason of countless oppressive actions of those who lived about him,' our chronicler recorded,

> he was not able to carry out work in the monastery itself, yet he was the beginning and entire material source from which the present works derive, since by his diligence and hard work, yet with God's help through the merits of St Benedict, he rescued this land from the hand of the Normans.[61]

This measure of independence, peace, security, and wealth benefited Monte Cassino's most famous medieval abbot, Desiderius (1058–1087).[62] Without question, his abbacy signals an era of great artistic, architectural, and

---

58 *Chron. Cas.*, II. 25, p. 210.
59 Ibid., II. 32, p. 229.
60 Ibid., II. 53, p. 265.
61 Ibid., II. 89, pp. 340–344. See also Wühr, 'Die Wiedergeburt Montecassinos'.
62 For a brief account of his character, see Amatus of Montecassino, *History of the Normans*, c. 52, pp. 105–108.

intellectual achievement – a so-called 'golden age' in the abbey's history. With unprecedented vigour, ambition, and speed, Desiderius immediately set about refurbishing the old basilica of Saint Benedict, first built under Abbot Gisulf. Desiderius saw

> that the necessary buildings of the entire monastery were both cramped in compass and misshapen in shape and towering by reason of their age and their poor construction, so that they all seemed to be covered over with roofing that touched, and the grass from one was entangled with the ingress to the next.

As a result, his 'heart was stirred to attach them and renew'.[63]

Desiderius's work was framed as a continuation of the abbey's original foundation. A close friend, Archbishop Alfanus of Salerno (1058–1085), commemorated the abbot's industry in a dedicatory poem. Recognising that 'blessed Benedict, coming to these regions, overthrew the statue and fashioned a house for the Lord,' the poem relates how

> The almighty Master said to him
> that by the merits of Benedict
> this place, sacred and venerable,
> was to be made more spacious.[64]

Desiderius's plans to enlarge the abbey soon evolved. In 1066, he completely demolished this mountaintop basilica and began an ambitious programme of building a new one (48.40m x 21.07m) dedicated to Saint Benedict, sourcing most of his materials (e.g., columns, marble) directly from Rome.[65] 'After having given orders to those who were to execute this work with the greatest dispatch,' we are told, 'he himself went to Rome, and approaching each of his best friends and generously and prudently distributing large sums of money, he bought huge quantities of columns, bases, epistyles, and marble of different colours.'[66] As the *Chronicon* further relates, the venerable abbot

> by merits of the most blessed father Benedict through divine will being established in all prosperity and peace and held in such honour by all

---

63 *Chron. Cas.*, III. 9, pp. 371–372.
64 Alfanus of Salerno, *I carmi*, 54 ('In laudem abbatis desiderii et montis Casini'), p. 217.
65 *Chron. Cas.*, III. 26, p. 394; Immonen, 'Building the Cassinese Monastic Identity', pp. 54–63.
66 *Chron. Cas.*, III. 26, p. 717.

those round about that not only those of moderate station, but also their very princes and dukes gladly strove to obey him and to follow his will in all matters just as they would that of their father and their lord, he directed his attention, not without divine inspiration, to the destruction of the old church and the building of new in a way fairer and more august.[67]

The third and fourth stanzas of Alfanus's poem captures the magnanimity of the whole enterprise:

When the world's heaven-given cycle
had unrolled many ages,
Desiderius, assuming the ruler of this Citadel,
greatly enlarged it.

He laid low all that was old in it;
straightaway he built it new,
this man sprung from the glittering line of the leaders of Benevento.[68]

The finer details of this new basilica are well-documented. 'In the larger apse on the eastern side,' Desiderius

set up an altar of Blessed John the Baptist, on that place in fact where once Father Benedict had established an oratory of the same saint, and on the south side an altar of the Blessed Mother of God Mary, with, on the north side, an altar of Blessed Pope Gregory.[69]

The abbey's elaborate decorations and ornamentation did not escape mention[70]; in fact, they inspired much admiration among contemporaries. Their splendour included mosaics and pavements from highly skilled craftsmen from Constantinople and Alexandria[71]; cloths from Greece, 'varied in colour'; and marbles contributed from Rome, 'with which this house is made lovely'.[72] An elaborate fresco programme was also undertaken, one whose pictorial representation of Saint Benedict's hagiographical cycle has been linked

---

67 Ibid., III. 26, pp. 393–394.
68 Alfanus of Salerno, *I carmi*, 54, p. 217.
69 *Chron. Cas.*, III. 26, p. 395.
70 Ibid., III. 32, pp. 403–405.
71 Ibid., III. 27, p. 396. See also Cigola, *L'Abbazia Benedettina*, pp. 27–50.
72 Alfanus of Salerno, *I carmi*, 54, p. 218.

to the abbey's identity construction in this significant era of medieval rebuilding and Roman renewal.[73]

Abbot Desiderius committed serious thought, energy, and financial capital to the abbey's artistic development. He sent envoys to Constantinople

> to hire artists who were experts in the art of laying mosaics and pavements. The mosaicists were to decorate the apse, the arch, and the vestibule of the main basilica; the others, to lay the pavement of the whole church with various kinds of stones. The degree of perfection which was attained in these arts by the masters whom Desiderius had hired can be seen in their works. One would believe that the figures in the mosaics were alive and that in the marble of the pavement flowers of every colour bloomed in wonderful variety. And since Roman mastery of these arts had lapsed for more than five hundred years and deserved to be revived in our time through his efforts, with the inspiration and help of God, the abbot in his wisdom decided that a great number of young monks should be thoroughly trained in these arts, lest this knowledge be lost again in Italy. Yet he provided for himself devoted artists selected from his monks eager to become skilled not only in these arts but in all works of art that can be fashioned from gold, silver, bronze, iron, glass, ivory, wood, alabaster, and stone.[74]

As the *Chronicon* further relates, Desiderius

> laid the pavements of the entire church, including the adjoining oratories of Sts Bartholomew and Nicholas, and his own house with a marvellous diversity of cut stones hitherto quite unknown in these parts (particularly the pavement near the altar and in the choir). The steps leading to the altar were inlaid with precious marbles of harmonious diversity. He enclosed the front of the choir, which he established in the centre of the basilica, with four large parapet slabs of marble, one of which was red porphyry, one green (porphyry), and the remaining two – like all the others surrounding the choir – white (marble).[75]

In a relatively short time, the new basilica was complete. This pinnacle achievement, which offered 'visible proof of the power and wealth'[76] of Monte

---

73   See especially Immonen, 'Building the Cassinese Monastic Identity', pp. 63–76.
74   *Chron. Cas.*, III. 27, p. 718.
75   Ibid., III. 28, p. 719.
76   Cowdrey, *Age of Abbot Desiderius*, p. 16.

Cassino, was celebrated among a great and illustrious crowd at the basilica's consecration on 1 October 1071. 'Of the great ones' in attendance were

> Richard prince of Capua with his sons Jordan and his brother Rainulf, Gisulf Prince of Salerno with his brothers, Landulf also, Prince of Benevento, and Sergius Duke of Naples and Sergius Duke of Sorrento, as well as a sizeable crowd of the counts of the Marsi and of Valva and of the sons of Borrellus. And as to the rest of the powerful or noble figures, both out own people and the Normans, of all the lands round about, there was absolutely no possibility or through of reckoning up their numberless number.[77]

Yet this momentous activity was only just the beginning. Desiderius also succeeded in rebuilding the abbot's house, constructing a range of accommodation (*palatium*), a new monastic cloister, dormitory, chapter house, infirmary, bakery, library, and vestry.[78] He also improved the abbey's walls and gates, and rebuilt the church of Saint Martin. For the choir (*schola cantorum*), moreover, he

> made little silver doors at the entrance […] weighing about 30 pounds. He also made wooden seats with their own backs all around the choir, which were adorned with sculpture and also painting. But he also set up a quite lovely set of steps, equally of wood and of the same workmanship, outside the choir, formed like an ambo, from which in fact both the lessons at night and the epistle and Gospel lessons from the masses of the principal feasts were to be read.[79]

The abbey's bronze doors were arguably his most lasting architectural and artistic contribution. Inspired by the cathedral doors in Amalfi, which he encountered on a visit in 1065, Desiderius

> soon afterwards sent off to Constantinople the measurements of the doors of the old church, along with the order to make those doors which still exist today. For he had not yet decided to rebuild the church; and that is the reason why the door turned out to be as short as they have remained up to the present time.[80]

---

77 *Chron. Cas.*, III. 29, p. 399.
78 See ibid., III. 33–34, pp. 405–410; Immonen, 'Building the Cassinese Monastic Identity', pp. 52–54.
79 *Chron. Cas.*, III. 18, pp. 384–385.
80 Ibid., III. 18, p. 711.

Dated to 1070, the doors' 54 panels contain dedicatory inscriptions, names of saints and apostles, in addition to a list of the abbey's possessions.

The abbey's library also benefited from Desiderius's industry. Formerly (and traditionally) a part of the scriptorium, the abbot built a separate wooden building to house Monte Cassino's growing collection.[81] 'Not only in buildings, but also in copying books', it was noted, the abbot 'strove to devote the very greatest effort. For he ordered a number of books to be copied in this place'.[82] The collection was likely substantial already by the third quarter of the eighth century, serving a crucial purpose in the *ars grammatica* as well as liturgical use.[83] The abbey's scriptorium, moreover, continued to be productive even following the exile caused by the Saracens in the late ninth century. Abbot Aligernus's first efforts were to re-establish and repopulate the monastery and the library. This programme was continued in earnest by his successor in the early tenth century, Abbot Theobald, who 'also ordered a number of books to be copied (there has been a very serious want of these down to this time)'.[84]

Desiderius's commitment to the scriptorium and its scribal activity fuelled the abbey's reputation as an intellectual centre.[85] As a consequence, modern scholars frequently refer to Monte Cassino in this era as the 'greatest centre of book production in South Italy in the High Middle Ages'.[86] 'Many as the leaves with which Boreas is wont to strew the steep hillsides', Alfanus wrote, 'so many the titles of various books from various regions he [Desiderius] has brought'.[87] The continuator of the Monte Cassino *Chronicon*, Peter the Deacon, provides a detailed inventory of the works copied during this abbacy, which include (among others): patristic works by Augustine, Ambrose, Jerome, Hilary, and Cassian; letters, sermons, papal registers, sacramentaries, and liturgical manuscripts for service; histories by Bede, Anastasius, Gregory of Tours, Paul the Deacon, Jordanes, and Erchempert; legal and grammatical works used for instructional/educational purposes, such as Justinian's *Institutes* and *Novellae*; and classical works by the likes of Cicero, Terence, Virgil, Ovid, Horace, and Seneca.[88]

---

81   Ibid., III. 10, p. 327; Immonen, 'Building the Cassinese Monastic Identity', p. 52.
82   *Chron. Cas.*, III. 63, p. 444.
83   Bloch, 'Monte Cassino's Teachers and Library', p. 569.
84   *Chron. Cas.*, II. 53, p. 265. See also Newton, *Scriptorium and Library*, chapter 2; Leccisotti, *I Regesti*, I, pp. x–xxii.
85   See Howe, *Church Reform*, p. 146.
86   Newton, *Scriptorium and Library*, p. 5.
87   Alfanus of Salerno, *I carmi*, 54, p. 218.
88   *Chron. Cas.*, III. 63, pp. 444–446. For a detailed discussion on this list, see Newton, *Scriptorium and Library*, pp. 21–26.

This furious copying activity helped to preserve numerous rare texts. The justification for such work surely related to the Benedictine emphasis on the use of books in teaching and learning, which the *Rule* itself explained as 'tools to fashion virtues' in pursuit of perfecting the 'true monastic life'.[89] Reading (*lectio divina* or *lectio*) played a critical part 'in the regimen of the life of a monk according to St. Benedict's Rule'.[90] And significantly, this work – much like the donations of churches, land, and villages that were made to Desiderius – was considered a gift to Saint Benedict himself. A 'very beautiful book' written at the abbot's order, and presented by a Cassinese monk named John, confirms this important connection. Composed at his 'own expense' for his 'own salvation and that of his family', the monk offered the book 'devoutly to Saint Benedict on his holy altar'.[91]

The abbey's scriptorium and library embodied its central character. The *Chronicon*'s inventory of book copying (mentioned above) associated Desiderius's industry 'with the erection of buildings',[92] treating the two achievements of his abbacy (intellectual and material) on equal footing. they were complementary explanations for the abbey's growing prestige in the second half of the eleventh century. The production during this era of an estimated 600 manuscripts demonstrates more than the outcome of human industry[93]; it shows a level of contemporary care and the influence of various teachers; its material remains, moreover, reveal an impressive diversity in ornamentation (e.g., precious stones, gems, and enamels; miniatures; gold, silver, and ivory bindings, etc.) and calligraphy (Beneventan 'hand and script'[94]), reflecting also in their content a variety of pedagogical practices.[95] Leccisotti noted, in particular, the copying of treatises on music, calculus, and astronomy, Vitruvius's work *De Architectura*, the works of Esculapius and Ippocrates, that of Pliny on the natural sciences, and that of Apuleius on quadrupeds.[96]

The glory of Desiderius's achievements at Monte Cassino became known throughout the Christian world.[97] We've already considered the poetic and

---

89 *Rule of St Benedict*, chapter 73, pp. 672–675.
90 Bloch, 'Monte Cassino's Teachers and Library', p. 564.
91 Translated in Bloch, *Monte Cassino*, I, pp. 78–79 (Cas. 99 = Bibl. Cas. II, p. 398).
92 Newton, 'The Desiderian Scriptorium at Monte Cassino', p. 42.
93 On the importance of this collection, see Newton's introduction in Adacher and Orofino, *Manoscritti Cassinesi*, pp. 7–13.
94 Newton, 'The Desiderian Scriptorium at Monte Cassino', p. 51. See especially Loew, *Beneventan Script*, pp. 49–51.
95 See Loew, *Beneventan Script*, pp. 124–126.
96 Leccisotti, *Monte Cassino*, p. 247
97 *Chron. Cas.*, III. 30, p. 402.

dedicatory praise for his work, which appeared in two works composed by his close friend, Alfanus of Salerno. Leo Marsicanus also wrote a book on the abbey's consecration and dedication (*Narratio de consecratione et dedicatione ecclesiae Casinensis*), as well as providing ample description in his *Chronicon*.[98] Still further testimony on Desiderius's achievements can be found in a chrysobull issued by Byzantine Emperor Michael VII Dukas (April 1076), which stated that

> The most celebrated and famous church built in the name of our most blessed father Benedict in Italy, because it is most venerable and cared for, is praised, propagated, and revered not only in the West but also in the East, not so much for its splendour and riches as rather for the virtues of its present Abbot Desiderius, our father, and his disciples.[99]

Desiderius's eulogy commemorated his building and decorating achievements, which 'combined to assure his fame until the world should end'.[100] In his wake, 'the venerable mountain, the house of God, another Zion, leader of the faith, the mountain where God bestowed on his people the Law written with his finger' was once again 'teeming with monks'.[101] A dedicatory verse, inscribed in the central apse of the main basilica of Saint Benedict, just below the figures of John the Baptist and John the Evangelist, likened the abbey to Mount Sinai; like this famous allusion to the Israelite tradition, 'which issues the sacred commandments, as the Law', the renovated abbey also 'leads minds from the lowest depths' and spreads 'light through the regions of the world'.[102] Alfanus even went so far as to suggest that the ancient church of Hagia Sophia in Constantinople, built by Emperor Justinian, 'would prefer to trade places'[103] with Monte Cassino. '[B]eautiful in appearance, material, furnishings, and art',[104] the medieval abbey had become a sight to behold.

---

98 *Cod. Cas.*, 47, fols 23r–24v. See also Leccisotti, 'Il racconto della dedicazione', especially his transcription of the manuscript text on pp. 219–225.
99 *Registrum Petri Diaconi*, no. 145 (fol. 67r), p. 450; cf. *Chron. Cas.*, III. 39, p. 731. See also von Falkenhausen, 'Montecassino e Bisanzio', pp. 92–98.
100 Cowdrey, *Age of Abbot Desiderius*, p. 19. *Chron. Cas.*, III. 74, pp. 456–457.
101 Alfanus of Salerno, *I carmi*, 32, p. 173; see also *I carmi*, 15, p. 139. For discussion, see Grégoire, *Storia e agriografia*, p. 32.
102 Alfanus of Salerno, *I carmi*, 15, p. 139; *Chron. Cas.*, III. 28, p. 718.
103 Ibid., 32, p. 177.
104 From a dedicatory inscription (distich). See Bloch, *Monte Cassino*, I, p. 58.

The Towering Mountain

The abbey's reputation is a product of human ingenuity and industry: it was cultivated over time. Based on the abbey's direct association with Saint Benedict – his foundation, *Rule*, and enduring legacy – Monte Cassino became regarded as the epicentre of the Western coenobitic tradition. Its material footprint on the mountain summit contributed significantly to the daily rhythms of religious life; so, too, did its burgeoning power and influence hold sway over the surrounding region. While its 'golden age' did not last forever, the achievements of the Desiderian era furnished a rich historical legacy, which has attracted innumerable visitors to the mountain summit ever since. Many came – and still come – to the home of Benedictine monasticism for spiritual reasons, to pray at the saint's tomb, to offer blessings, donations, and gifts, or to visit the military cemeteries. Others came – and still come – to the 'towering mountain'[105] for intellectual pursuits, to tap the abbey's rich library resources, which have been accumulating for centuries.

The Italian writer and poet Giovanni Boccaccio was one such notable visitor. Coming to Monte Cassino on several occasions in the second half of the fourteenth century,[106] he found the abbey 'quite deserted and desolate'.[107] According to his young pupil, Benvenuto de Imola (c. 1330–c. 1387), Boccaccio 'climbed up [the mountain] happily', presumably expecting to revel in the abbey's glory. But to his surprise, he

> found the place of such great treasure without door or key, and as he entered he saw weeds growing through the windows and all the books and tables thick with dust. Marvelling, he began to open and turn over one book after another, and he found there many different volumes of ancient and exotic works. From some of them several gatherings had been removed; from others the edges of the pages had been cut away; and thus they were mutilated in many ways. At last, he went away grieving and in tears, regretting that the toil and effort of so many famous intellects had come into the hands of such corrupt and wasteful men. Running into the cloister, he found a monk and asked him why those precious books had been so foully mutilated. He

---

105 Vogüé, *Grégoire le Grand: Dialogues*, II. 8, p. 166.
106 His sojourns to the venerable mountain are associated with stories of intrigue and theft. Since the early twentieth century, claims have circulated over his role in discovering and stealing manuscripts from the abbey's library, suggesting the dilapidated state of the abbey and its care.
107 De Imola, *Comentum*, 5. 301.

5. Woodcut from the Nuremberg Chronicle, f. 144ʳ (fourteenth century).

replied that some monks, hoping to make a few solidi, would scrape off a gathering and make cheap psalters to sell to boys, and that they made gospels and breviaries out of the margins to sell to women.[108]

These early impressions have been incorporated into the abbey's history. Eight centuries later, after himself paying a visit to the hallowed abbey, the famed American poet and Harvard professor Henry Wadsworth Longfellow asked:

> What thought Boccaccio, in his reckless way,
> Mocking the lazy brotherhood, deplores
> The illuminated manuscripts, that lay
> Torn and neglected on the dusty floors?[109]

Yet there is no reason to dispute the ailing condition of Monte Cassino's library during the late Middle Ages. Dante related the same impression of decay, lamenting the fortunes of time that had inflicted the abbey:

---

108 Ibid., 5. 302.
109 Longfellow, 'Terra di Lavoro', p. 162.

> To climb it now, however, none makes haste
> to lift his feet from earth. My rule lives on
> only to fill the parchments it lays waste.
>
> The walls that were retreats in their good hour
> are dens for beasts now; what were holy cowls
> are gunny sacks stuffed of evil flour.[110]

This languishing state was not enough to deter later scholars from visiting the abbey's archives. Monte Cassino's reputation in this respect continued unabated, so famous were its collections, scriptorium, and historical and spiritual influence. Boccaccio's dismay at the abbey's dilapidated order, for example, did not prevent him from discovering – and reportedly stealing – an eleventh-century manuscript of Tacitus and Apuleius, now housed in the Laurenziana Library in Florence (Laura. 68.2). In 1429, the Italian humanist scholar Gian Francesco Poggio Bracciolini discovered a copy of Julius Frontinus's *De aquaeductu urbis* and Julius Firmicus Maternus's eight-book treatise on mathematics. After seeking permission, he 'carried the volume away [...] to copy the work of Frontinus'.[111] And when the French scholar and Maurist monk Jean Mabillon visited Monte Cassino in November 1685, he marvelled especially at the abbey's impressive collection of Latin and Greek codices, saints' lives, privileges, and charters.[112]

Such encounters demonstrate the abbey's continued attraction. Operating at a reduced scale, religious life nevertheless continued more or less uninterrupted. Notwithstanding the abbey's experience with destruction,

> the monks always sought to carry on with their program of prayer and work. In every era one can see them busy in restoring the ruins that piled up around them, in embellishing the house, and in transcribing codices. And even if the rapid and destructive course of time has always managed to destroy and scatter the fruits of their sacrifices, the memory of their work, tenacious and full of hope, confirmed by the documents and the surviving remains, is enough to command our admiration.[113]

110 Dante, *Paradiso*, 22. 73–78, p. 790, in *The Divine Comedy*.
111 Letter no. 73 in Bracciolini, *Two Renaissance Book Hunters*.
112 Mabillon and Germain, *Museum Italicum*, I, pp. 123–126.
113 Leccisotti, *Monte Cassino*, p. 273.

This 'admiration', embodied by the abbey's material stature, is best appreciated in situ. Anyone wishing to explore the abbey's manuscript collection, to pray at the site of the holy tomb(s), to offer blessings, gifts, or donations, or simply to revel in Monte Cassino's spiritual, historical, artistic, and architectural majesty, is required to follow the same preparatory steps: a difficult journey to the top of a towering mountain, whose slope 'stretches upward over a distance of nearly three miles'.[114]

Access to the mountain summit was a perennial problem. The abbey's natural environment presents some obvious physical challenges. When Benedict settled on the mountain top, no mention was ever made of his journey's initial obstacle. The remaining 'founders' of Monte Cassino, between the eighth to the twentieth centuries, surely encountered even greater challenges in their quests to build, renovate, and expand the abbey's material footprint. When large marble columns were transported up the mountain slope for the basilica's renovation in the 1060s, some indication was given in the sources of the arduous labour involved. Commenting on the job's material resources and manpower, the Monte Cassino chronicler noted how Abbot Desiderius brought the columns and marble

> from Rome to the Portus Romanus, from the Portus by sea to the tower of the Garigliano, and from there with great confidence on hired boats to Suium. But from Suium to this place he had them transported with enormous effort on wagons. And to admire the more the fervour and zeal of the faithful, a large number of citizens by themselves assumed the burden of the first column on their necks and arms from the foot of the mountain to this place. The labour was even greater, for the ascent then was very steep, narrow, and difficult. Desiderius had not yet thought of making the path smoother and wider, as he did later.[115]

The physical sacrifice paid dividends. When Mabillon visited the abbey in the late seventeenth century, he marvelled at the size of the abbey church, the height of the mountain's flanks, noting also how its magnificent and stately palaces were unreachable by vehicles.[116] An artistic impression of the mountain's prospect (*veduta*) – an engraving commissioned by Erasmo

---

114 Vogüé, *Grégoire le Grand: Dialogues*, II. 8, p. 166.
115 *Chron. Cas.*, III. 26, p. 717.
116 Mabillon and Germain, *Museum Italicum*, I, pp. 120–121: 'Mons. Casinus, in quo situm est monasterium, tantum habet in crepidine spatii, quantum satis ad continendas regulares aedes. Ecclesia, ut in loco angusto, magna et ampla; ut in ilia montis altitudine et asperitate, quo nulla possunt vehicula pertingere, magnifica et augusta.'

Gattola (from Neapolitan architect Arcangelo Guglielmelli) and sent to Mabillon for inclusion in his *Annales ordinis sancti Benedicti*[117] – shows just how winding and steep the journey must have been (see below); his own 'arduous ascent',[118] he recorded, took three hours to complete. But once the destination was reached, as his companion throughout Italy, Michel Germain, commented, the visitor could not help but be impressed by the 'illustrious monastery'; the performance of the divine office; the tranquillity and silence; the library collection (charters and manuscripts); even the condition and abstinence of the abbey's monks, whom he noted were of noble stock, most aged 60–70, and in great physical shape.[119]

The remote and impractical nature of Monte Cassino's location forms part of its legend. 'And there, uplifted, like a passing cloud/That pauses on a mountain summit high/Monte Cassino's convent rears its proud/And venerable walls against the sky.'[120] The abbey has repeatedly captured the imagination of its visitors, suggesting a natural environment that is just as important to its historical representation as the institutional and religious framework sustaining its daily operations.

The journey to the mountain summit was undeniably arduous. The zigzag paths through bare and rocky surrounds made the way impassable for carriages in the early nineteenth century; as the Allied Forces discovered a century later (in 1943–1944), tanks and trucks carrying military supplies were even more difficult to manoeuvre up the mountain without significant engineering feats to make the route passable. Today, the journey is made easier by road transport and a local bus, though the path remains precarious for the more adventurous travellers on foot or bicycle.

The weather is another impeding factor: unpredictable and potentially dangerous. Roadside-vaulted buildings greeted the wayfarer en route, providing necessary shelter against the inhospitable atmosphere and 'sudden impetuous tempests'.[121] The seasons could change in an instant, sending the weary traveller ducking for cover in one of these welcome asylums. 'At a distance,' one nineteenth-century traveller wrote,

> It only appears like a huge fabric surmounted by a line of machiculations, forming a kind of cornice under the roof; but a nearer investigation

---

117 Russo, 'Medieval Art Studies', p. 16.
118 Mabillon and Germain, *Museum Italicum*, I, p. 120.
119 Dantier, *Les monastères Benidictins d'Italie*, I, p. 411.
120 Longfellow, 'Terra di Lavoro', p. 161.
121 Craven, *Excursions in the Abruzzi*, vol. 1, p. 47.

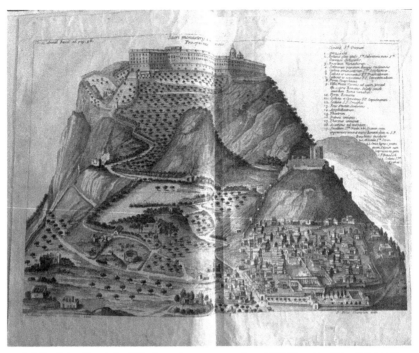

6. A. Guglielmelli, veduta of Montecassino, engraving from J. Mabillon, *Annales ordinis sancti Benedicti*, vol. 2 (Paris, 1704), between pp. 56 and 57. Biblioteca Statale del Monumento Nazionale di Montecassino.

7. Jean Mabillon and Michel Germain, *Museum Italicum*, vol. 1 (Lucca, 1687), p. 122.

shows some projections and recesses broken by arches and buttresses, which relieve the interminable succession of windows that occupy every front. The building covers the whole upper platform of the detached mountain on which it stands: the ground slopes from the walls on all sides; some of the adjoining borders being converted into enclosed gardens and furnished with fruit-trees and timber of larger growth, among which are some very fine pines. [...] The construction is of small stones covered with a reddish-grey stucco of a sober yet not dull hue.[122]

The architecture, as it stood in the early nineteenth century, 'offers no claim to regularity, nor can it be said to be impressed with any characteristic suitable to a monastic establishment. But the magnitude and simplicity of its mass stamp it with an aspect of dignity, which is nevertheless very imposing'.[123] The wanderer entered from the road through an archway in the corner, ascending under stone arches to a second gate, which opens onto a large court. Steps led to a quadrangle, surrounded by a cloister, whose arches 'are sustained by fine granite columns brought from the ruins of Casinum'.[124] Marble statues of the abbey's illustrious benefactors – including pontiffs and sovereigns – were carved into the wall's niches. Coming to the door of the church, the traveller used to see an inscription of the abbey's architectural history from 529 to its most recent restoration in 1649. The inside of the church was filled with fine works of art, chapels dedicated to saints, popes, abbots, and other distinguished guests. The bronze doors, manufactured at Constantinople in the eleventh century and installed during the 'golden age' of Desiderius's abbacy, were a main attraction. So, too, was the organ, considered by some as the finest in Italy. The archives contained invaluable 'manuscripts, diplomas, chronicles, and records, which justly constitute the proudest boast of the establishment'.[125]

These were just some of the reasons justifying Monte Cassino's fame. 'There is something extremely striking in the duration of these monastic establishments,' another nineteenth-century traveller noted. '[K]ingdoms and empires rise and fall around them – governments change – dynasties flourish and fade – manners and dresses alter, and even languages corrupt

---

122 Ibid., pp. 48–49.
123 Ibid., p. 48.
124 Ibid., p. 50.
125 Ibid., p. 54.

and evaporate."[126] Yet when you enter the gates of Monte Cassino, this author marvelled,

> the torrent of time stands still – you are transported back to the sixth or the tenth century – you see manners and habits, and hear the languages of those distant periods – you converse with another race of beings, unalterable in themselves though placed among mortals, as it appointed to observe and to record the vicissitudes from which they are exempt. Hitherto these monuments of ancient times and of past generations have been placed above the reach of that mortality, to which all the other works and institutions of man are subject.[127]

There is a performative, liturgical, almost spiritual aspect to this experience: one must arrive, approach, ascend, and discover. In the journey's first stage, the abbey remains obscured by the meandering direction of the road. When the road straightens and the valley widens, however, Monte Cassino's 'stately mass, crowing the highest pinnacle of the hill which terminates this plain, breaks on the eye with a very imposing effect'.[128] Celebrated still, in the nineteenth century, for its 'learning as well as piety', the abbey struck wonder into the hearts of its visitors: 'under whatever point of view it is regarded, it holds the primary rank among all religious institutions'.[129]

This admiration was shared by many of the abbey's visitors, in turn inspiring their writings. When the British author Charles Dickens visited Monte Cassino, 'perched on the steep and lofty hill above the little town of San Germano',[130] the experience left a vivid impression. He and his party wound their way up towards the summit on mules, 'moving solemnly and slowly, like a funeral procession'.[131] They did so until they saw through the grey mist 'at length the shadowy pile of buildings close before us: its grey walls and towers dimly seen, though so near and so vast: and the raw vapour rolling through its cloisters heavily'.[132] Dickens marvelled:

> How was this extraordinary structure ever built in such a situation, where the labour of conveying the stone, and iron, and marble, so great a height

---

126 Eustace, *A Classical Tour*, p. 219.
127 Ibid.
128 Craven, *Excursions in the Abruzzi*, vol. 1, p. 40.
129 Ibid., p. 46.
130 Dickens, *American Notes*, p. 427.
131 Ibid.
132 Ibid.

Le mont Cassin.

8. M. l'abbé C. Chevalier, *Naples, le Vésuve et Pompéi: croquis de voyage*, illustrated by Anastasi (Tours: Alfred Mame et fils éditeurs, 1871).

must have been prodigious? [...] How, being despoiled by plunder, fire and earthquake, has it risen from its ruins, and been again made what we now see it, with its church so sumptuous and magnificent?'[133]

These questions were not unlike those encountered in the mid-twentieth century. To French General and Commander-in-Chief of the French Expeditionary Corps in Italy Alphonse Juin, the mountain of Cassino was 'another Gibraltar'.[134] Although he never climbed the slopes himself, he admitted that 'for months the sight of this formidable obstacle, so long opposed to the progress of the allied forces, made me literally obsessed'.[135] According to an American war correspondent who climbed the towering mountain in May 1944, just after its capture, the route was almost inaccessible. 'I climbed it on hands and knees', he reported; 'it had taken three hours of strenuous climbing to reach our objective'.[136] The journey to the summit was anything but gentle, because 'on the Cassino side the hill rises abruptly, barren and forbidding. In places its gradients must be one in three or four'.[137] 'Rising out of the billowing artificial cloud,' he wrote elsewhere, 'and given

---

133 Ibid., pp. 427–428.
134 Juin, 'Pèlerinage au Mont Cassin', p. 580.
135 Ibid., p. 577.
136 Gander, 'Return to the Battlefields', p. 38.
137 Ibid.

majesty by them like a Himalayan peak poking through cumulus, was Monastery Hill. It was only 1,750 feet high, but it looked like Kinchinjunga to my excited imagination.'[138] Commenting on the abbey's reconstruction progress after the war, he concluded that 'few visitors can fail to be moved by the demonstration of faith and perseverance in the rising walls of the new Monte Cassino Abbey'.[139]

This mystique has been noted by many visitors, though few observations rival Longfellow's poetic licence, recounting his own personal journey:

Well I remember how on foot I climbed
The stony pathway leading to its gate;
Above, the convent bells for vespers chimed,
Below, the darkening town grew desolate.

Well I remember the low arch and dark,
The courtyard with its well, the terrace wide,
From which, far down, the valley like a park,
Veiled in the evening mists, was dim descried.

The day was dying, and with feeble hands
Caressed the mountain-tops; the vales between
Darkened; the river in the meadow-lands
Sheathed itself as a sword, and was not seen.

The silence of the place was like a sleep,
So full of rest it seemed; each passing tread
Was a reverberation from the deep
Recesses of the ages that are dead.[140]

*

The 'towering mountain' remains a constant feature in Monte Cassino's past. It has profoundly shaped human relationships with the abbey, awing and transforming through its physical character, majesty, and symbolism. Its summit, which once housed the Roman consul and Apollo's temple, assumed a new identity after Benedict's arrival in the early sixth century.

---

138 Gander, *After These Many Quests*, p. 179.
139 Gander, 'Return to the Battlefields', p. 41.
140 Longfellow, 'Terra di Lavoro'.

The mountain's intimate relationship with the saint provides an important connection to the narrative of this abbey's long historical representation; its spiritual and cultural inheritance are indissoluble historical features which transcend material loss and time. Their meaning is firmly rooted in the early Middle Ages, in the formation of an early monastic community.

Yet, as we'll see in the following two chapters, the abbey's historical tradition and memory owe considerably to its experience with death and resurrection, settlement and resettlement in the *longue durée*. Remaining a popular destination for popes, intellectuals, worshippers, and tourists alike, Monte Cassino through the ages became a repeated target of various aggressors, governments, and foreign militaries. Its remote location offered little solace from the ravages of war, political turmoil, and destruction.

Part II

Rise and Fall

3. A Destiny Repeated: Episodes of Destruction

Abstract
This chapter introduces numerous historical witnesses to the abbey's past, whose perspectives are preserved from the Middle Ages to the present day. Telling their stories is fundamental to understanding the abbey's representation over time. This historical exercise is critical also to framing Monte Cassino's resilience and rationalisation in the face of great adversity, which is a necessary step towards explaining its full-scale resurrection in the aftermath of destruction. Treating each case in tandem provides a wider view of the abbey's 'destruction tradition' over fourteen centuries; its focus also explains and positions these episodes in the construction of Monte Cassino's true identity during the process of recovery, which inevitably followed.

Keywords: Lombards; Saracens; earthquake; French Revolution; Kingdom of Naples; Risorgimento; Second World War

> I had seen the famous old Abbey, with its priceless and irreplaceable works of art, only from a distance, but with the thundering salvos that tore apart the hillside that morning, I knew there was no possibility that I ever would see it at any closer range. I remained at my command post all day and tried to work.[1]

The bombardment of Monte Cassino began promptly at 9:25 a.m. on the morning of 15 February 1944.[2] According to British General Henry Maitland Wilson, '142 flying fortresses dropped 287 tons of demolition bombs of 500

---

1   Clark, *Calculated Risk*, p. 319.
2   This precise time comes from the records of Major Bradford Evans, who led the aerial bombardment. He noted also the timestamp for the first impact of the bombs, which was automatically printed on each photograph taken from his plane. See Rosa, *Montecassino*, p. 115.

Rennie, K.R., *The Destruction and Recovery of Monte Cassino, 529–1964*. Amsterdam: Amsterdam University Press, 2021
DOI 10.5117/9789463729130_CH03

pounds and 66 and a half tons of incendiary bombs of 100 pounds, they were flooded by 47 B-25 and 40 B-26 which launched 100 tons of high explosive bombs.'[3] American General Mark W. Clark, tallied an even greater number of 255 Allied bombers (including B-17 'fortresses'), which dropped 576 tons of explosives.[4] Taking shelter in various parts of the abbey, many perished or were injured during the waves of attack. The following day, while the bombing continued from 150 aircraft, a group of approximately 40 souls (children, sick and wounded) surfaced from beneath the rubble. Despite repeated artillery fire, they slowly made their way down the venerable mountain along a mule path to a Red Cross station. Led by their abbot bearing a seventeenth-century crucifix, the procession of survivors 'took the way of the hills towards Monte Cairo and descended into the valley somewhere near Piedimonte'.[5] Fearing for the abbot's safety, the Germans sent an ambulance to escort him first to their headquarters at Castel Massimo, before eventually transporting him to Sant'Anselmo in Rome the following day.[6]

The famed battle of Monte Cassino continued for another three months. Considered 'the most gruelling, the most harrowing, and in one respect perhaps the most tragic, of any phase of the war in Italy',[7] it claimed the lives of over 75,000 German, American, British, French, Indian, New Zealand, Canadian, South African, Italian, and Polish soldiers. This tragic death toll in the Allied march towards Rome, and the abbey's near annihilation in the process, represents by far the most dramatic and destructive episode in Monte Cassino's 1,400-year history. But it was not the religious community's first such experience.

Monte Cassino has suffered a long history of destruction. It is a 'strange destiny', wrote one participant in the war, that the abbey was 'built on one of the paths where barbarism and war have frequented the most'.[8] 'Fate has destined the Abbey,' wrote another, 'perched on its 2,000 ft. peak, to symbolize, through the centuries, the mysterious balance of destructive and creative forces in the world'.[9] Its experience with both forces, and

3 General Sir Henry Maitland Wilson in Report to the Combined Chiefs of Staff, 8 January–10 May 1944, cited in Böhmler, *Monte Cassino*, p. 168.
4 Clark, *Calculated Risk*, p. 319.
5 Senger und Etterlin, 'Monte Cassino', p. 252. See also Senger und Etterlin, *Neither Fear nor Hope*, p. 203.
6 *Il Bombardamento di Montecassino*, p. 105
7 Clark, *Calculated Risk*, p. 311.
8 Juin, 'Pèlerinage au Mont Cassin', p. 585.
9 Gander, 'Return to the Battlefields', p. 36.

9. Flying Fortress of Monte Cassino.

the representation of these encounters, underpins the abbey's traditional historical narrative. These episodes of destruction are separated in time but closely related in interpretive purpose: considered together, they represent essential components in Monte Cassino's claims for a continuous, unbroken, and uninterrupted heritage. They are defining features of its identity, culture, and tradition, giving purchase to Monte Cassino's self-conceptualisation as a site of spiritual and historical importance and authenticity.

Advancing the basis for this claim requires a closer look at the historical records for each episode of destruction between the sixth and twentieth centuries. The objective here is simple: to restore these fragmented histories to their respective historical contexts and time periods, in order to appreciate their ordering and accumulated meaning to the contemporaries who experienced them. That is not to suggest that our records should be interpreted uncritically, but rather to acknowledge their distinct authorial voices and intentions.

This chapter introduces numerous historical witnesses to the abbey's past, whose perspectives are preserved from the Middle Ages to the present day. Telling their stories is fundamental to understanding the abbey's representation over time. This historical exercise is critical also to framing Monte Cassino's resilience and rationalisation in the face of great adversity, which is a necessary step towards explaining its full-scale resurrection in the aftermath of destruction – the focus of our next chapter. Treating each case in tandem not only provides a wider view of the abbey's 'destruction tradition' over fourteen centuries; its focus also explains and positions these episodes in the construction of Monte Cassino's true identity during the process of recovery, which inevitably followed.

Fulfilling a Promise

In the late sixth century, 'the Lombards were besieging Rome and causing much devastation in Italy'.[10] Their presence in this region was quickly established and, according to numerous medieval accounts, their invasion followed an invitation by the commander (and eunuch) of the Byzantine army, Narses. It was this influential figure who initially encouraged the Lombards to 'abandon the barren fields of Pannonia [modern-day Hungary] and come and take possession of Italy, teeming with every sort of riches'.[11]

From the late 560s, these 'barbarians' from north of the Danube – so-named for their 'long beards' (*Langobardi* in Latin)[12] – began occupying the Po Valley (east and south of Rome), the duchies of Spoleto and Benevento, and the Apennine Mountains. Their south-western expansion into Italy from the lands of Pannonia began under their king, Alboin (560–572). The political and military domination continued under Kings Grimoald (662–710) and Liutprand (712–744), who expanded and consolidated the Lombard power base in northern Italy and Tuscany until their eventual expulsion by Charlemagne and his Frankish army at the Battle of Pavia in June 744.

Early medieval historians have devoted considerable attention to the Lombard settlement of pre-Norman Italy. At the time of their expansion, more than a century had elapsed since the western half of the Roman Empire collapsed. During this era of dramatic political and economic decline, Rome and her surrounding region were rapidly destabilised. The ancient world, once renowned for its culture and society, was in the late sixth century a shell of its former self. Like the Ostrogoths before them, the Lombards entered Italy and capitalised on the absence of direct (or decentralised) local authority; most of Italy, from Ravenna down the eastern coastline, was being ruled at a great distance from the imperial city of Constantinople. Before the arrival of the Franks in the mid-eighth century, therefore, the Lombard kingdom 'was politically pre-eminent over both the Lombard duchies of the southern Apennines, Spoleto and Benevento, and the Roman-Byzantine

---

10   *Le Liber Pontificalis*, I, LXV (Pelagius), p. 309.
11   Paul the Deacon, *Historia Langobardorum*, II. 5, p. 75.
12   Ibid., I. 9, p. 52.

outposts, centring on Ravenna, Rome, Naples, and the southern extremities of the Italian mainland'.[13]

It was in this transformative world that the abbey of Monte Cassino was first established under Saint Benedict and his sister; it was also when it fell for the first time, succumbing to the aggression of Lombard military advances in central-southern Italy.

The exact date of the Lombard attack is a trivial matter. Historians have presented detailed manuscript evidence to suggest the most likely year of 577.[14] It certainly happened before the pontificate of Gregory the Great (590–604), whom we recognise – among other achievements – for his life of Saint Benedict in the second book of his *Dialogues*. For the abbey's established history, the Lombard attack signals the beginning of a long persecution. It provides a natural starting point, the first real episode in our wider discussion of Monte Cassino's destruction and recovery over 1,400 years.

Unfortunately, the surviving historical evidence for this event is scarce. Paul the Deacon informs us that, around the time that Teudelapius was crowned duke of Spoleto, the 'stronghold of Casinum' was attacked at night by the Lombards. They plundered everything, though miraculously, the monks of Monte Cassino managed to escape without harm. Not one of them was injured. As Paul's *History of the Lombards* relates: '[T]his was in fulfilment of a prophecy of the venerable father Benedict, which he made long before, in which he said: "I have been able with difficulty to obtain from God that the souls from this place should be yielded to me."'[15]

Gregory's *Dialogues* provide further context, suggesting that the lives of Benedict's community were narrowly spared. God, we are told, 'had decreed that this entire monastery and everything I [Benedict] have provided for the community shall fall into the hands of the barbarians'.[16] This prophecy was soon realised, as the Lombards 'came at night while the community was asleep and plundered the entire monastery, without capturing a single monk'.[17] According to this account, 'God fulfilled His promise to Benedict': he 'allowed the barbarians to destroy the monastery, but safeguarded the lives of the religious'.[18] In other words, there was a greater purpose to this place and its religious community. The buildings might (and did) crumble,

---

13   Wickham, *Early Medieval Italy*, p. 28.
14   See Brechter, 'Monte Cassinos erste Zerstörung'.
15   Paul the Deacon, *Historia Langobardorum*, IV. 17, p. 122.
16   Vogüé, *Grégoire le Grand: Dialogues*, II. 17, p. 192.
17   Ibid.
18   Ibid.

but the founding spirit would flourish once again. Symbolically, this historical event stands for the uninterrupted religious community and continuity of Benedict's life and monastic *Rule*.

Many subsequent interpretations stem from this solitary early medieval account. At this point of the narrative, the details of the story become contestable. Writing his *History* in the late eighth century, Paul the Deacon tells us that the monks fled from Monte Cassino to Rome, 'carrying with them the manuscript of the Holy Rule (of the order) which the aforesaid father had composed, and certain other writings'. The early medieval chronicler also deemed it worth noting that the monks secured a 'pound of bread and a measure of wine, and whatever of their household goods they had been able to snatch away'.[19]

Whether Rome was their final destination, and what happened to the monks on arrival, is not entirely clear. Some scholars suggest that the religious community was immediately dispersed, scattered across various Roman monasteries. Others argue that the entire community took refuge at the 'Lateran monastery' – a community first mentioned in Gregory's *Dialogues*, and later known as the monastery of Saint John the Evangelist, Saint John the Baptist, and Saint Pancratius.[20]

The most plausible version of historical events matters for a few reasons. First, it relates to the account of Monte Cassino's resettlement in the early eighth century under Abbot Petronax (see Chapter 4). Second, it plays an important role in our understanding of (and trust in) the early medieval evidence. Third, it is responsible for forging the earliest historical and religious connection between the abbey of Monte Cassino and the growing authority of the Western Church and its apostolic see in Rome.

We can trace the story's development over a number of centuries. Our earliest written account, Gregory the Great's *Dialogues* (written c. 593–594), doesn't mention the monks' exact destination after the Lombard sack of Monte Cassino. It states only that they fled. The lack of specifics is curious. If, in fact, they did take up residence at the Lateran monastery, we might expect an explicit reference to this effect in Gregory's writings. All that exists is some mention in the opening prologue to the source of Benedict's 'miraculous deeds': namely, the 'lips of four of his own disciples', one of whom (Valentianus) was 'for many years superior of the monastery at the Lateran'.[21]

---

19 Paul the Deacon, *Historia Langobardorum*, IV. 17, p. 122.
20 *Le Liber Pontificalis*, I, XCII (Gregory III), p. 419. See especially Dell'Omo, 'A proposito dell'esilio romano'.
21 Vogüé, *Grégoire le Grand: Dialogues*, II (Prologue).

Almost two centuries later, the general narrative gained some description. Writing c. 787, Paul the Deacon introduced the idea of the monks fleeing to Rome, bringing with them the autograph manuscript of Saint Benedict's *Rule*.[22] But it is the twelfth-century author Leo Marsicanus (d. 1115) whose chronicle of Monte Cassino provides the most elaborate account of the Lombard destruction and its aftermath. This narrative source relates how the monks of Monte Cassino came to Rome, where they established themselves near the Lateran Palace. There they remained for the next 110 years.[23] It is this account, which offers some of the finer details on the impact of destruction and displacement in the wake of the Lombard sack.

This account, in its entirety, is what the medieval evidence tells us. Admittedly, it's not as much as we'd like for such a monumental historical event. According to Suso Brechter, who has studied this historical problem extensively, the representation of Monte Cassino's first destruction is simply incorrect. Its transmission, he argues, is little more than a portrayal of various events by the twelfth-century monk and chronicler.[24] Yet this later representation has made the most lasting impression. Its account embellishes a connection between Monte Cassino and Rome that was not apparent at the time, in a deliberate attempt to establish historical continuity between Saint Benedict's foundation at Monte Cassino on the one hand, and the abbey's refounding under Petronax in the eighth century.[25] Brechter concludes that Leo's entire work has this tendency, which reveals a purposeful historiographical motive in the early twelfth century.[26] The chronicler interprets the sparse descriptions and elaborates with literary intent. The outcome is an embellished version of historical events, whose significance will become clearer in the following chapter.

For the moment, we can observe that the Lombard destruction of Monte Cassino did not erase the abbey's heritage. Quite the contrary: it strengthened the association between Saint Benedict and the location where he founded his monastery. We might reasonably expect the destruction of Monte Cassino and subsequent dispersal of its monks to terminate the abbey's history. After all, the Lombards laid waste to the abbey and its surrounding countryside, effectively severing all physical connections to this venerable mountain. But,

---

22 Paul the Deacon, *Historia Langobardorum*, IV. 17, p. 122.
23 *Chron. Cas.*, I. 2, pp. 20–21.
24 Brechter, 'Monte Cassinos erste Zerstörung', p. 149. See also Brechter, 'Die Frühgeschichte von Montecassino', p. 284.
25 Ferrari, *Early Roman Monasteries*, p. 249.
26 Brechter, 'Die Frühgeschichte von Montecassino', p. 285.

in fact, the story of this abbey and its inheritance was only just beginning, thanks in large part to how the event was memorialised by later writers.[27]

The principal historical referent in Monte Cassino's past became the *idea* of Benedict. His spiritual significance never waned amidst the chaos of Lombard destruction. A story of resilience is born through the retelling of its events: one that shapes future interpretations of the Lombard sack, but also of Monte Cassino's response, which would become a defining characteristic in the historical representation of the abbey's deep past.

A Swarm of Bees

The Arabs of ninth-century Europe were mobile marauders, who covered great distances and established bases throughout the Mediterranean. From Spain and North Africa, they launched many successful campaigns along the sea's basin. Following the expansion of the Islamic realm in the late seventh and early eighth centuries, the Muslims – variously called Arabs, Berbers, Moors, Africans, Agareni, Ismaelites, or Saracens in the Latin (Western) chronicles, annals, and *gestae* of the period – had established themselves as Europe's neighbours. In a lesser-known piece of early European history, they even settled for almost 90 years in the southern region of Provence (in the Camargue), before Christian forced expelled them and re-established political authority.

Saracen attacks in Italy are well-recorded in contemporary sources; they have also received ample attention among modern scholars. There are numerous incidents reported in medieval chronicles and annals. For southern Italy, these accounts concern Rome and her surrounding duchies – the heartland of Christian Europe. The first Arab attack likely occurred in 667. The islands of Sardinia, Sicily, and Corsica were paid frequent visits in the eighth century. Sicily, in particular, was the site of fierce and protracted battles with the indigenous and Byzantine forces, a struggle lasting almost 75 years. Appearing in these regions like a 'swarm of bees,' they are said to have devastated 'everything around'.[28]

Their presence in Italy introduces a much longer and complicated past. The Italian port cities of Naples, Gaeta, and Amalfi had long benefited from the economic advantages of Arab trade. But a more permanent threat

---

27 On the politics of memory, see especially Pohl, 'History in Fragments', and Pohl, *Werkstätte der Erinnerung*.
28 Erchempert, *Historia Langobardorum Beneventanorum*, c. 11, p. 239. See also *Chronicon Salernitanum*, c. 60, pp. 59–60.

had existed for some 40 years by the Lombard influence over Italy and the various attempts by competing polities to assert influence over the region. In the eighth and ninth centuries, the papacy, the Byzantines, the Franks, and the local authorities of Capua, Benevento, Salerno, and Naples vied for control of southern Italy. The Arabs were introduced into the conflict as hired mercenaries and quickly became a powerful force. Many scholars have recognised the majority of Muslim forays as maritime raiding expeditions. The ninth-century Cassinese chronicler Erchempert describes their military support and entrenchment in cities like Bari (on the Adriatic Sea), referring to their careful cultivation by Christian rulers as 'friends and familiars' who could be trusted in times of crisis.[29]

With the exception of Erchempert's *History of the Lombards of Benevento* (written c. 889), contemporary sources tend to present a different, more cynical account.[30] In the early 840s, according to our principal papal source, the *Liber Pontificalis*, a 'wicked and God-hated race of the Agareni were rising up from their own territory and compassing nearly every island and mainland district, and atrociously causing [...] the looting of men and the devastation of places'.[31] 'God sent the avenging pagans', the source further explains. The *Chronicon Vulturnense* plainly notes how around this time the Saracens from Africa and Babylon came and occupied Sicily.[32]

Owing to its historic and religious significance, an attack on Rome in 846 is richly documented.[33] The wealth and fame of the former imperial city was widely known. On 26 or 27 August of that year, 'the churches of the blessed princes Peter and Paul were thoroughly plundered by the Saracens'[34]; the sacred altar 'violated and reduced to such dishonour and vileness'.[35] The papal chronicle recounts the Saracen advances from the Roman shoreline near Ostia to Porto, culminating in this 'surprise attack'.[36] The contemporaneous Frankish *Annals of Fulda* and *Annals of Saint-Bertin* both corroborate the tale of destruction and looting.[37]

Writing centuries later, Leo Marsicanus expanded on a few important details. His interest in the attack on Rome looks beyond the apostolic city

---

29   Ibid., c. 16.
30   See Heath, 'Third/Ninth-Century Violence', pp. 28–35.
31   *Le Liber Pontificalis*, II, CIII (Gregory IV), p. 11.
32   *Chronicon Vulturnense*, I, p. 305.
33   Kreutz, *Before the Normans*, p. 26.
34   *Le Liber Pontificalis*, II, CV (Leo IV), p. 106.
35   Ibid., p. 113.
36   Ibid., CIIII (Sergius II), p. 101.
37   *Annales Fuldenses*, a. 846, p. 36; *Annales Bertiniani*, a. 846, pp. 33–34.

to the Saracens' movement immediately afterwards. To be more precise, the twelfth-century chronicler is more concerned with the events in Monte Cassino's own geographical vicinity. From the narrative account of this *Chronicon* we can trace the Saracens' southern advance, which led to a preliminary attack on the abbey in 846 that was waylaid only by divine intervention.[38]

On this first encounter, the abbey's peace was threatened but not extinguished. In its hour of greatest need, Saint Benedict came to his monastery's rescue.[39] Fearful of being killed, the monks went 'barefoot, in sackcloth and ashes' to the saint's tomb, seeking his intercession through prayer.[40] Summoning a violent storm, we are told, the saint proceeded to flood the banks of the River Liri, making it impassable for the assailants. The account of divine intervention ends with a moral lesson from a certain cleric and a monk, who appeared to the Saracens at sea, punishing them for their actions. The entire fleet was completely destroyed and there were no survivors to tell the tale.[41]

While the apostolic city of Rome suffered, Monte Cassino – thanks to the intervention of its founder, Saint Benedict – was spared. At least, this is the version of events later related by Abbot Desiderius in his *Dialogi de miraculis sancti Benedicti*.[42] It is this eleventh-century abbot who replaces the above-mentioned cleric and monk with Saint Peter and Saint Benedict, attributing their first-hand intervention in staving off the Saracen destruction of Monte Cassino. Desiderius explains that deliverance took the form of two miraculous changes in the weather: one that prevented the *barbari* from crossing the Garigliano River and completing their assault on the monastery, and another that later wrecked their ships as they returned to Sicily. Leo provides some additional information to supplement Desiderius's account, including information derived from Desiderius's main source: *Chronica sancti Benedicti Casinensis*. Heightening the effect of the central

38 See *Chron. s. Ben.*, c. 6, pp. 472–473.
39 For a good account, see Berto, 'Oblivion, Memory, and Irony', pp. 54ff.
40 *Chron. s. Ben.*, c. 6, p. 472.
41 Ibid.
42 Desiderius, *Dialogi de miraculis*, I. 2, p. 1119: '"Nos," inquiunt, "unus Petrus, alter Benedictus vocamur, quorum domos vos invasisse iactatis. Sed cuius virtute cuiusve potentiae simus, quam citissime experiemini." Et his dictis ab oculis eorum ablati sunt. Mox igitur undique furentibus ventis fluctibusque tumescentibus tanta subito tempesta exorta est, ut naves omnes vel collisae inter se vel impulsae scopulis confractae sint, ita ut ex omni illa paganorum copia vix pauci superfuerint, qui suis haec, a quibus missi fuerant, civibus nuntiare potuissent. Et quidem permisit omnipotens Deus ad tempus suas ab eis ecclesias divastari, sed non est passus eos super tanto facinore diutius gratulari.' See also *Chron. Cas.*, I. 27, pp. 76–81.

miracle, Desiderius tells us that, before the sudden downpour that made the river impassable, the sky was clear and the river low enough to have been easily crossed on foot.

Notwithstanding this account of divine intervention, which saved the abbey of Monte Cassino in 846, the Saracen threat in central and southern Italy still remained.[43] Commenting on the situation around Naples, Erchempert wrote that the Ismaelites 'devoured and exhausted everything'.[44] The whole region of Benevento c. 860, he further noted, was devastated by fire, sword, and cruel captivity, 'so that no means of sustenance remained there'[45]; Capua was depopulated at the hands of Sawdān, the emir of Bari, whose presence and activity in the region caused great social and political instability: '[H]e destroyed Benevento and its territories, so that no place except the principal cities could escape his savagery.'[46] According to a later account, this 'most wretched and wicked king of the Ismaelites' devastated the whole region by fire, sword, and cruel captivity so that no living breath remained.[47] The situation was so dire, the contemporary *Annals of Saint Bertin* report, that in the Spring of 866 Emperor Louis II of Italy and his wife, Engelberga, 'advanced to Benevento against the Saracens'.[48]

It is safe to assume that the monks of Monte Cassino anticipated a Saracen threat. In May 882, Abbot Bertharius 'fought them openly, reinforced with walls and towers the defences of the monastery on the mountain and began to build a city, Eulogimenopolis, enclosed in a defensive wall, around San Salvatore, the Cassinese establishment at the foot of the mountain'.[49] That same year, Pope John VIII issued protection to the monastery in the form of an exemption privilege.[50] Indeed, the abbey profited from a series of immunities, which benefited its jurisdictional horizon and claims.[51] Around 849, when Princes Radelchis and Siconulf were dividing the territory of Benevento, Monte Cassino – along with its neighbour, San Vincenzo al Volturno – was placed 'under the protection and immunity of Lord Emperors

---

43 Whitten, 'Franks, Greeks, and Saracens'.
44 Erchempert, *Historia Langobardorum Beneventanorum*, c. 75, p. 262; *Chronicon Salernitanum*, c. 141, pp. 148–149; *Chron. Cas*, I. 43; *Chron. s. Ben.*, c. 16, p. 476.
45 Ibid., c. 29, p. 245.
46 Ibid. See also Whitten, 'Franks, Greeks, and Saracens', pp. 264–266, and Heath, 'Third/Ninth-Century Violence', pp. 35–38.
47 *Chronicon Vulturnense*, I, p. 356.
48 *Annales Bertiniani*, a. 866. See also *Chronicon Vulturnense*, I, pp. 357–362, which relies heavily on Erchempert; Metcalfe, *Muslims of Medieval Italy*, p. 18.
49 Citarella, 'The Political Chaos in Southern Italy', p. 171. *Chron. Cas.*, I. 33, p. 90
50 *Chron. Cas.*, I. 32, p. 89. For the exemption privilege, see PL 126:950 (JE 3381).
51 Fabiani, *La Terra di S. Benedetto*, II.

Lothar and Louis'.⁵² In fact, the abbey and its growing territory of *cellae* profited from various arrangements with the Lombards, the Franks, the Ottonians, and the papacy in Rome.

There was good reason for such defensive actions. When the monks of Monte Cassino were visiting their brethren at San Vincenzo al Volturno in 881, this neighbouring Benedictine house was sacked by the Saracens.⁵³ While a ransom of 3,000 gold pieces was paid in 860 to prevent Arab raiders from pillaging and burning the monastery, it fell into their hands in October 881.⁵⁴ Many of the monks, including Abbot Maio, fled to Capua; they did not return for 33 years. With the assistance of some of the monastery's servants, the concealed treasure was eventually found⁵⁵; the monastery was subsequently pillaged and set alight.⁵⁶ Celebrating and triumphant, the 'nefarious Sawdān' dared to drink from the sacred chalice and burn incense in the golden vessel.⁵⁷

The twelfth-century *Chronicon Vulturnense* offers further description of the attack, noting how the Saracens

> suddenly attacked the monastery in a frontal assault, and surrounding it on all sides they set it on fire, and they also put to the sword the holy elders they found there [...] and so the blood of the holy monks which was shed for Christ is still there, providing clear evidence even today, as the rocks and stones of the church there were smeared or spattered with it.⁵⁸

The following planctus, still sung at the church of San Vincenzo, commemorates the fateful day (10 October):

> Let the pipe now proclaim, my heart sunk in grief,
> What is sudden cause for pity, and
> what brings so much destruction;
> And sounding from on high may it

---

52   *Chron. Cas.*, I. 29, p. 84: 'sub tutela et immunitate dominorum imperatorum Lotharii ac Ludovici constituta sunt'. Whitten, 'Franks, Greeks, and Saracens', pp. 258, 268.
53   *Chron. s. Ben.*, c. 18, p. 477; *Chron. Cas.*, I. 35, p. 96. See also Hodges, *Light in the Dark Ages*, pp. 144–153.
54   Erchempert, *Historia Langobardorum Beneventanorum*, c. 29, p. 245; Metcalfe, *Muslims of Medieval Italy*, p. 19.
55   *Chronicon Vulturnense*, I, p. 365.
56   Ibid., II, p. 8.
57   Ibid., I, p. 365.
58   Ibid., I, p. 364.

A DESTINY REPEATED: EPISODES OF DESTRUCTION

resound diverse laments to the people,
Who it allows to echo back their own
sad fates.
Thus far, Muse, the pipe mourns and
they utter their response in equal measure,
A destruction which is said to be too sweet.
They join such lamentation with their own songs,
So that the stars cry out, and given vent
to sad cantations.
When the very buildings fell,
They brought an end to many people
in this destruction,
Now the heathens come, the clamorous band rages.
They bring war down on the monks,
Then turning act as a scourge,
And with a rain of weapons make faith effeminate.
The impious rustic servants of the monks make a gift to this host.
They strike down their own masters in the slaughter.
They assail the strong fortresses, the opponents swiftly rush together,
The high buildings fall, the walls all collapse.
Neither age nor time, boyhood, youth, or old age,
None to whom life is a delight, can escape this.
Here blood is poured out, bodies are laid out over the fields,
And now they duly give up their spirits to God in heaven.
An end is put to things, not by wards,
And with men drenched in blood,
arms serve as standards of God.
And far away the flowers bloom in Macedonian fields,
The ground retains the purple glory.[59]

Monte Cassino soon followed a similar fate. According to Cassinese tradition, the decisive blow came on two separate days. On 4 September 883, the hilltop abbey of Monte Cassino (*sursum*) – the very place where Saint Benedict's body was buried – was sacked by the Saracens.[60] A second attack on the monastery of San Salvatore, at the base of the hill, followed more than one month later (22 October). On this occasion, according to Leo Marsicanus, the Saracens seized, devastated, and burned the abbey,

---

59 Ibid., I, pp. 366–368 (translation by Hodges, 'The Sack of San Vincenzo', pp. 19–20).
60 *Chron. Cas.*, I. 44, p. 114.

killing many who had taken refuge there. Notably, they also killed Abbot Bertharius (by sword) at the altar of Saint Martin in the church of San Salvatore.[61] And while the entire monastery was burning, they rejoiced in their spoils before returning triumphant to the mouth of the Garigliano River.[62] There they remained until the colony of Arab raiders was driven out at the Battle of Garigliano in 915.[63] (The significance of this victory was later commemorated by a tower, built by Prince Pandulf of Capua between 961 and 981).[64]

The record of the abbey's second destruction bears brief discussion. Our most contemporaneous author, the Cassinese monk Erchempert, offers a summary of the event. He mentions how the Saracens

> destroyed all of Benevento's territory and likewise Rome, and also part of Spoleto; they plundered all of the monasteries and all of the churches, cities and towns, villages, mountains and hills and islands; they burned the noble communities of the most blessed Benedict, honoured by all the world, and the monastery of the holy martyr Vincent, and numberless others.[65]

But the chronicler does not mention the brutal murder of Monte Cassino's abbot, Bertharius. This is an extremely curious omission. Armand Citarella rightly noted that 'from among all the contemporary chronicles, the history of Erchempert should be the most extensive and detailed source on the topic of the destruction of Monte Cassino'.[66] It is entirely plausible that one existed; the continuator of Leo Marsicanus's *Chronicon* of Monte Cassino, Peter the Deacon, explicitly mentions Erchempert's history on the abbey's destruction and reconstruction, which reinforces this suggestion.[67] But this remains the only surviving reference.

---

61 See also Peter the Deacon, *Ortus et vita*, c. 28, p. 51: 'Bertharius abbas nobilis carne, nobilis spiritu, in monasterio Domini Salvatoris iusta altarium sancti Martiri pro fide Christi a Sarracenis capita trancatus est. Sepultus vero est sursum in monasterio Casinensi. Passi sunt autem cum eo et alii multi, undecimo calendas Novembris.'
62 *Chron. Cas.*, I. 44, pp. 114–115.
63 Ibid., I. 52, pp. 133–135; Fabiani, *La Terra di S. Benedetto*, I, pp. 38–40.
64 See *Chron. Cas.*, II. 37, pp. 238–239. The epigraph reads: 'Hanc quondam Terram vastavit gens Agarena/Scandens hunc fluvium fieri ne postea possit/Princeps hanc Turrim Pandulfus condidit Heros/Ut sit structori decus et memorabile nomen.'
65 Erchempert, *Historia Langobardorum Beneventanorum*, c. 44, p. 253; *Chronicon Salernitanum*, c. 126, pp. 139–140.
66 Citarella, 'The Political Chaos in Southern Italy', p. 173.
67 Peter the Deacon, *De viris illustribus*, c. 15, col. 1023A ('De Erchemperto').

Once again, we are completely reliant on Leo Marsicanus, whose twelfth-century account 'kept alive the memory of the tragedy and of the glorious martyrdom of Bertharius'.[68] (The significance of this connection will be made clearer in the next chapter.) Suffice it to say that a cult quickly developed around the abbot, a devotion only reinvigorated with the rediscovery and cataloguing of his bones in the fourteenth century. (Another list dates from the late nineteenth century (1884), when the Latin and Italian ceremony was written.[69]) As Tommaso Leccisotti, a twentieth-century Cassinese monk and archivist, noted,

> his relics were always honoured through public worships until the time when the splendid chapel built by the pious don Ippolito Santarelli (1650) was completely restored and when on October 20, 1938, the abbot don Gregorio Diamare most solemnly consecrated his altar.[70]

The *Chronicon Vulturnense* situates the attack in familiar context. First destroyed by the Lombards, the chronicler notes, and re-established with Petronax's help, the abbey of Monte Cassino was once again destroyed. Following Leo Marsicanus's account, he briefly recounts the sequence of events: Abbot Bertharius's murder at the altar of Saint Martin; the subsequent fleeing of the monks to Teano, with their home-grown monastic *Rule* in tow[71]; the 30-year exile resulting from the abbey's desolation; and its eventual resettlement under Abbot Angelarius. Accentuating the extent of devastation, the author stressed the mental and visceral anguish, the increase of both suffering and pain, and the inconsolable grief caused by the attack.[72]

Like the Lombard attack in the late sixth century, the Saracen devastation of Monte Cassino was not total. To be sure, the abbot was murdered, the monks were displaced, and the abbey was razed to the ground. Yet as Leo Marsicanus noted, the abbey did not lose all of its treasure at this time. Anticipating the events, Abbot Bertharius had earlier sent some monks to Teano in Campania, taking with them whatever they could managed in the form of papal bulls, diplomas, bread, wine, sacks of flour. It was there, not at Monte Cassino, that some of the abbey's most precious items were ultimately

---

68 Citarella, 'The Political Chaos in Southern Italy', p. 179. See also Avagliano, 'Il culto di San Bertario'.
69 Avagliano, 'Il culto di San Bertario', p. 403.
70 Leccisotti, *Monte Cassino*, p. 40.
71 *Chronicon Vulturnense*, I, p. 370.
72 Ibid., I, p. 371.

destroyed after a great fire in 896.[73] Following this tragic event, the exiled monks sought refuge at the new city of Capua, under the protection of the dukes of Capua.[74] When the monks at last returned to Monte Cassino in the mid-tenth century, they discovered their region 'neglected and destitute, as if desolate'.[75] But as we'll see in the next chapter, this condition was no deterrent to its rebuilding programme, which more than succeeded in restoring the abbey to its former glory.

The Big One

On 9 September 1349, a great earthquake devastated the religious community at Monte Cassino, destroying the abbey completely and killing those gathered inside. An anonymous account from the period noted how 'the entire monastery totally collapsed and no building in it remained standing'.[76] The damage was all the more devastating because the earthquake happened during the hours of Mass (*hora missae*)[77]; many men, women, priests, and other religious figures were trapped inside the ecclesiastical buildings.

The 'great earthquake' (*magnus terramotus*) affected the whole Kingdom of Naples, but especially the diocese of Cassinum.[78] Structural geologists attribute the seismicity of this fourteenth-century event to the Latium-Abruzzi-Molise-Campani border area, a large 'damage distribution' region spread out over the southern-central Apennines.[79] In addition to the abbey, most of the homes, *castra*, and villages in the region were also destroyed.

The effects were felt as far afield as Rome and Naples, with the greatest damage affecting villages across the Latium-Molise border.[80] The contemporary Italian writer Petrarch was horrified by the violence of the unusual tremor, an unprecedented calamity that he attributed to divine wrath, a portend of things to come in Italy. About Rome in particular, he wrote that the earthquake was 'so strong that nothing similar had occurred since the

---

73   *Chron. Cas.*, I. 48, pp. 126–127; Zeller, 'Montecassino in Teano', p. 123; Pohl, *Werkstätte der Erinnerung*, pp. 154–155.
74   Fabiani, *La Terra di S. Benedetto*, I, pp. 36ff.
75   *Chron. Cas.*, II. 1, p. 166: 'neglectus ac destitutus et quasi desolatus'.
76   *Anonymorum monachorum Casinensium breve chronicon*, II, p. 836; *Annales Casinenses*, p. 320.
77   *Cronicon siculum*, p. 14.
78   Ibid.
79   Galli and Naso, 'Unmasking the 1349 Earthquake'.
80   Ibid., p. 131.

city's founding over two thousand years ago'.[81] 'Massive ancient buildings [...] fell', he continued, towers cracked and 'tumbled to the ground', and 'the beauty of many churches was destroyed'.[82]

At the base of the venerable mountain, half of the city of San Germano (modern-day Cassino) was destroyed, especially the part which was in the alluvial planes (i.e., the marshes), where a 'vast multitude of men, women, children, and religious died'.[83] If there is a silver lining here, it was surely the discovery of Abbot Bertharius's bones amidst the rubble; unearthing the ninth-century abbot, martyred during the ninth-century Saracen attack, initiated a cult following that eventually led to his official canonisation in 1884.[84]

There was little time or cause for celebration. This natural disaster struck an already weakened abbey. In the twelfth century, Monte Cassino's pre-eminence in southern Italy made it a target of ongoing political mischief. The arrival of the Normans did not have a direct impact on the abbey's fortunes, though their presence certainly unsettled the surrounding region and in turn threatened the stability of religious life and administration on the venerable mountain.[85] In 1139, Pope Innocent II was taken prisoner by Roger II of Sicily, who had broken through the defences of Rocca Janula – a Cassinese stronghold/fortress built in the tenth century, and whose remains stand on the mountainside today. Just under a century later, a modicum of peace was restored to the region with the signing of a treaty (at the same stronghold) between Pope Gregory IX and Emperor Frederick II.

The Norman presence in Italy did not presage the abbey's destruction. But it certainly disrupted the *Terra sancti Benedicti* around the middle of the eleventh century. According to Amatus of Monte Cassino, the *castello* of Saint Benedict (near the monastery) was 'at that time [1045] inhabited by the Normans, who had lordship over it, and from it they did much harm to the poor'. Abbot Richerius was plotting their exodus when the Normans arrived at the city of San Germano. 'There they dismounted and ungirded their swords and entered the church to make their prayers to God.' While inside, 'some guards appeared at the door and closed it', leaving them trapped, without weapons, and defenceless. Many were captured and others killed.

---

81   Petrarch, *Letters on Familiar Matters*, XI. 7, p. 99.
82   Ibid., XI. 7, pp. 99–100.
83   *Anonymorum monachorum Casinensium breve chronicon*, II, p. 836; *Annales Casinenses*, p. 320. See also Bloch, *Monte Cassino*, I, p. 483, no. 2.
84   Avagliano, 'Il culto di san Bertario'.
85   See Houben, 'Malfattori e benefattori'.

As the chronicler concludes: 'In a day all the *castelli* of St Benedict were recovered.'[86]

To prevent retribution, and to maintain the regained territory, Richerius divided the abbey's golden and silver vessels among his knights, 'whom he had called together to resist the Norman troops'. Both sides prepared for and engaged in battle, when Saint Benedict appeared as standard bearer. The Normans were then 'bound with strips of rope', and 'from this hour on they [the monks] knew no enemy in their land'.[87] As the Monte Cassino *Chronicon* relates: 'So through the power and merits of the Blessed Benedict his lands were all restored to his jurisdiction, and from now on through the mercy of God were free from attack by the Normans.'[88] Just to be safe, however, the abbot fortified the *castelli* on the lands of Saint Benedict for the peasants' protection.[89] The ongoing protection of Prince Richard of Capua, moreover, secured the abbey's autonomous and privileged place in the region. He punished 'those who persecuted and looted our church'; destroyed those 'who harmed the monastery's possessions'; wrested 'the monastery's *castelli* from the hands of the tyrants who occupied them', leaving many more to the monastery's care and direction. In all, 'because of the kind actions of this man, the entire monastery became resplendent'.[90]

Continued political pressures in the following century upset this harmonious relationship. As the modern abbey relates, this relationship languished following the death of Abbot Oderisius in 1105. The papacy's policy of cooperation with the Normans ended with Honorius II (1124–1130), who 'took on a rather different political strategy: one of ruthlessness and armed intervention'. As a consequence, Monte Cassino

> suddenly found itself being coerced into answering to papal rule. [...] The reversal of these previously cooperative policies in favor [of] anti-Norman policy, interference with abbot elections, dismissals and excommunications of Montecassino supporters and members (such as the young and influential Peter the Deacon, author of the *Chronicle of Montecassino*) all contributed to this era of instability.[91]

---

86 Amatus of Montecassino, *History of the Normans*, II. 42, p. 83.
87 Ibid., II. 43, p. 83.
88 *Chron. Cas.*, II. 71, p. 312.
89 Ibid., II. 73, p. 315.
90 Amatus of Montecassino, *History of the Normans*, VIII. 36, p. 205.
91 'XI-XII Centuries: Post Desiderius' "Golden Age"'.

The consolidation of Norman power in southern Italy directly influenced Monte Cassino's independence. The 'peace of her cloister' in the twelfth and thirteenth centuries 'was beset by the tragic necessities of sieges and the horrors of war'.[92] 'Many times,' Leccisotti wrote,

> the land of St Benedict was subjected to fire and sword; more than once those who survived the slaughter, with the vision of horrible cruelties still in their eyes, wandered in search of safer shelters. The horrors kept increasing with the mounting hostilities and the alternating fortunes of war.[93]

The Cassinese archivist is referring here to a period of 'Swabian oppression': a long and bitter struggle between imperial and papal forces, which resulted in 'total desolation on the sacred mountain'.[94] In 1229, the Monte Cassino was occupied by Emperor Frederick II, when it was attacked by cardinal legate Pelagius. Over a hundred armed men occupied the monastery, driving out the monks, treating them poorly, and pillaging their treasury. Ten years later (1239), the roles were reversed as the German emperor prepared to wage battle against the abbey's military occupants. In short order, the remaining monks were forced to abandon the monastery for 26 years, thereby reducing it to 'a den of thieves'.[95]

The rhetoric is strong in this statement; the reality was probably less dire, though others have remarked on the abbey's declining moral and material standards.[96] In the midst of much political instability, efforts were sometimes made to protect the abbey. Angevin rule introduced a measure of security found wanting under imperial rule. Pope John XXII made the abbey a direct dependent of the Roman church in 1322 (2 May), ruling that it become an episcopate with the responsibility to elects its abbot.

Unfortunately, despite these few positive measures, the fourteenth century 'turned out to be one of the most tragic in the history of the abbey'.[97] Both papal and imperial rule was weakening. The papacy began its lengthy 'Babylonian captivity' at Avignon (1305–1377), which effectively removed to a greater distance one of the abbey's most trusted custodians and allies. The Hungarians attacked the abbey in an act of vengeance for their deceased

---

92   Leccisotti, *Monte Cassino*, p. 65.
93   Ibid.
94   Ibid., p. 67.
95   Ibid.
96   Picozzi, 'Gli abati commendatari', p. 117.
97   Leccisotti, *Monte Cassino*, p. 68.

king, Andrea. Yet the greatest disaster of this period – the earthquake – was yet to come; and its destructive, earth-shattering force could not be blamed on any direct human action or interference.

The earthquake of 1349 ruptured the abbey's existence once again. Its immediate consequences on the religious life are poorly documented. More than a decade passed without much mention of the abbey's fortunes. Based on the few surviving accounts, however, the prevailing assumption is grim. A bull issued from the papacy at Avignon under Innocent VI (dated 22 April 1353) captures the first phase of a comeback, offering indulgences to anyone who might contribute financially to the abbey's reconstruction.[98] These were nominal but critical steps in yet another rebuilding programme, actions signalling the first phase in what became a decades-long recovery process.

Theatre of Bloody Encounters

Peace and prosperity did eventually return to Monte Cassino. But things were never quite the same. Reaching its thousandth year, the abbey 'was now losing its autonomy to become part, albeit a very important one, of a larger organism'.[99] In the late Middle Ages, as the administration of religious houses was being transferred to individual trustees – a system known as *commenda* – Monte Cassino struggled to maintain its traditional level of independence. Material and political realities of the temporal world began infiltrating the *vita religiosa*, which in turn led to a decline in Cassinese autonomy. The administrative and fiscal freedom exercised since the abbey's foundation was limited in the second half of the fourteenth century; it lasted until the time of Abbot Giovanni dei Medici (1486–1505), later Pope Leo X, when the abbey was placed directly under his care.[100] Unbeknownst to the monks at the time, this relationship brought Monte Cassino into a turbulent political struggle between the French and Spanish over the Kingdom of Naples. It placed them firmly in the former camp.

The abbey, it has been said, 'never had tranquillity due to the continuous wars that ruined the whole Neapolitan kingdom'.[101] King Louis XII of France was in Naples, when a territorial war broke out that directly

---

98 *Documenti Vaticani*, p. 14, no. 4. See Reg. Aven. 125, fol. 408r–v.
99 Leccisotti, *Monte Cassino*, p. 79.
100 On this figure, see Picozzi, 'Gli abati commendatari', pp. 168–176.
101 Picozzi, 'Gli abati commendatari', p. 175.

affected the mountain and her surrounding region. The commander-in-chief of the Spanish forces, Consalvo di Cordova, engaged the French forces along the Garigliano River. The nearby abbey of Monte Cassino provided a good defensive position for the French army, which – it is alleged – 'saw its cloister stained with blood in numerous acts of violence'.[102] However, it is not entirely clear whether the Spanish attacked the abbey in 1503 and defeated the French troops stationed inside. According to a contemporary Spanish chronicle, Consalvo did not want to attack Monte Cassino out of reverence for Saint Benedict's body, which he believed was buried there.[103] A more strategic manoeuvre has been suggested as the outcome, which saw the French abandon the abbey (without warfare or destruction) by the end of June, in order to concentrate their forces around Gaeta.[104] Whatever the case, the famed 'Battle of Garigliano' (1503) drove the French away from the region, surrendering the Kingdom of Naples into Spanish hands for centuries to come.[105]

While the abbey and its community of monks suffered during this turbulent era, the damage was not irreparable. What followed in subsequent centuries has been summarised as 'the vigorous recovery' of the sixteenth century, the 'magnificence' of the seventeenth, and the 'splendid and peaceful work' of the eighteenth.[106] Yet before Monte Cassino could enjoy its resurrected status, the repercussions of war and political-religious transformation in Western Europe continued to impact the abbey. After four commendatory abbots over a 50-year period (1454–1504), Monte Cassino joined the Congregation of Santa Giustina of Padua (est. 1408) in 1504/1505. While the abbey's power and influence had been weakened by the *commenda* system, the reforming statutes of this Congregation – which became known as the Cassinese Congregation – returned some peace and prosperity to this religious house.

That tranquillity, however, was upset with the arrival in Italy of the French Republican Army. 'The eighteenth century,' Leccisotti opined, 'would not end in peace.'[107] From 1796, the abbey of Monte Cassino found itself once again in a conflict zone, forced to contribute financially and materially to the region's military defences. Initial preparations for war saw the arrival of the Neapolitan Army under General Carl Mack von

102 Leccisotti, *Monte Cassino*, p. 73.
103 *Crónicas del Gran Capitán*, VII, c. 15, p. 383.
104 Pieri, 'La guerra franco-spagnola', p. 66.
105 For a thorough account, see Pieri, *La battaglia del Garigliano*.
106 See Leccisotti, *Monte Cassino*, chapter 6.
107 Leccisotti, *Monte Cassino*, p. 93.

Leiberich, an Austrian who stationed his troops along the banks of the River Liri. King Ferdinand IV, Queen Maria Carolina, their court, military advisors and guards set up their quarters in the defensive structure of Monte Cassino itself, whose ancient 'citadel' was once again put to good use over the next few years.[108]

The French encountered little resistance. Their army, led by General Maurice Matthieu, arrived at San Germano on 30 December 1798. Their objective was the Kingdom of Naples, which would eventually fall. In the new year (1799), 2,000 French soldiers arrived with General Jean-Antoine Étienne Championnet, whose army placed some immediate material demands on the abbey and its treasury. Their withdrawal was soon substituted by the occupation of General Olivier and 1,500 soldiers (1st Division), which transpired over the course of one day to the abbey's invasion and pillaging, first by the soldiers and then by opportunistic peasants.[109] Leccisotti relates that 'all the doors were broken down, and the store room, the cellars, and the bakery were emptied; what could not be carried – furniture, bedding, linens and other objects – were left strewn in the garden. Even the library and the archives were invaded.'[110] The monks were 'so threatened and insulted'[111] that they barely made it out alive, though they remained steadfast in their daily routines. The devastation inflicted on the church 'was even worse': vestments were cut and burned, relics and consecrated hosts were scattered on the floor, and the soldiers 'wearing sacred robes and driving donkeys, milled through the marble isles singing obscene songs'.[112] Because of the desolation and ruin suffered by this abbey, through which 'three thousand and more devastators' had passed, many religious could not return to their homes to live.[113]

The encounter was reminiscent of previous attacks on the abbey. A contemporary Cassinese monk, Giovanni Lamberti, likened the French soldiers to devils and monsters/dragons; their barbarous, violent, tragic, and dolorous actions were compared to the Saracen invasion of the ninth century.[114] His journal entry from 10 May 1799 offers a first-hand account of abbey's transition from religious house to temporary soldiers' quarters,

108 Jallonghi, 'Borbonici e Francesi', IV, pp. 11–12.
109 Ibid., pp. 235–236.
110 Leccisotti, *Monte Cassino*, p. 94.
111 Jallonghi, 'Borbonici e Francesi', p. 236.
112 Leccisotti, *Monte Cassino*, p. 95.
113 Jallonghi, 'Borbonici e Francesi', p. 249. See also Leccisotti, *Monte Cassino*, p. 95.
114 For this account, see Lena, 'Le vicende di San Germano', pp. 171–174.

detailing in particular the material goods and valued treasures that were seized by the soldiers over the course of their stay.[115]

The abbey's archivist at the time, Giovanni Battista Frederici, recorded the diabolical terror oppressing the religious at Monte Cassino and her surrounds, particularly the abbey palace and the town of San Germano, both at the base of the mountain. Recorded for posterity's sake, his journal account also notes the bloodshed, looting, profanities, and fires which led to the abbey's 'quasi destruction'[116] – an episode described as one of the most 'terrible shocks' to rock the abbey's foundation.

Writing from Rome in 1801, Pope Pius VII, a former Benedictine monk, expressed his deep sadness for the abbey, which 'has suffered so many calamities through the recent vicissitudes'. 'It is our desire,' he declared,

> that the monastery be restored to its old splendour and discipline as it stood for such a long course of centuries for the edification and glory of the Church. In this we promise our help through our resources and the use of our apostolic authority, in such a way that it will never be necessary again to implore our favour in behalf of your community.[117]

The situation for Monte Cassino did not improve with the army's departure. The French occupation of the Kingdom of Naples in 1806 led to a permanent reorganisation of the abbey's administration and long history of jurisdictional independence. A royal decree issued by Joseph Bonaparte (then king of Naples), dated 13 February 1807, noted that 'because of the great respect that we have, those celebrated places that during the barbarian age preserved the sacred fire of religion and saved for the ages the learning of past generations of men, are those sanctuaries deserving so much respect'.[118] This innocuous statement of respect and goodwill diminishes the realities of its enforced articles, which led to the closing of convents and abbeys, whose assets were turned over to the tax authorities. Article 1 explicitly declared that the religious orders of Saint Benedict and Saint Bernard, and their diverse affiliations, would henceforth be suppressed. Article 2 declared that all their properties would be joined to the crown, with the sales' profits going directly towards the state. Article 5 declared that the library, archives, and all manuscript deposits would be preserved, but with particular provisions

---

115 See also Dell'Omo, *Montecassino*, pp. 86–87.
116 Tosti, *Storia della badia*, IV, p. 77.
117 Ibid., IV, p. 38.
118 Ibid., IV, p. 41.

once again reserved to the state. Entrenching this right/power/influence more firmly, Article 6 further declared that custody of these deposits, and the religious constitution of the abbey, will be chosen – according to need – by the Ministry of Culture.[119]

These were profound changes to Monte Cassino's organisational life. For the next decade, until the period of Bourbon restoration (1815–1830), the abbey's spiritual and civil jurisdiction was 'suspended and the parishes of the Diocese of Cassino were entrusted to the victorious bishops who – in agreement with Rome – had appointed vicars general who acted in agreement with the abbot of Montecassino'.[120] As one contemporaneous (British) witness explained, 'the grants of land and feudal prerogatives, which rendered it a kind of little sovereignty, were suppressed by the French, who nevertheless respected the religious order'.[121] Some of its possessions were successfully restored with the return from Sicily in 1815 of King Ferdinand IV, who managed to place the abbey 'on a more respectable footing'. 'But still', wrote our observer, 'the revenue is diminished from more than one hundred thousand to twenty-four thousand ducats a year, and the number of monks from fifty to fifteen, with every other reduction in the same proportion'.[122]

After thirteen centuries of existence, Monte Cassino's autonomous power was greatly weakened. On this occasion, however, the reasons for its demise were notably different than before: 'not by ferocity of barbarians, nor by fury of war',[123] but rather through the introduction of new legislation. While political interference was nothing new to the abbey, the restrictions introduced in the nineteenth century were far less forgiving and more detrimental to everyday religious life. The new conditions at Monte Cassino 'allowed life to continue on new bases and with different horizons'. The 'hope of survival' helped to restore the abbey's normal activity, to repair the damaged buildings, and to resume 'the observance of the old Benedictine traditions'.[124]

This resilient spirit animated the abbey throughout the nineteenth century. Yet even though it supported the idea of Italian unification, the movement known as the Risorgimento weakened the abbey's position further. The limitation of ecclesiastical rights and freedoms in the previous decades (1840s–1850s) provided some indication of what was to come. Adding

119 Ibid., IV, pp. 41–42.
120 Avagliano, 'Montecassino nel primo Ottocento', p. 530.
121 Craven, *Excursions in the Abruzzi*, vol. 1, p. 56.
122 Ibid.
123 Tosti, *Storia della badia*, IV, p. 40.
124 Ibid., IV, p. 45. See also Leccisotti, *Monte Cassino*, p. 97.

to the laws of 1848,[125] a suppression law of religious corporations was issued on 29 May 1855, whose first article declared that 'religious communities established within the state by religious orders that are not dedicated to preaching, educating, or assisting the sick must cease to exist as moral bodies recognised by civil law'.[126]

More forceful measures arrived in the following decade. Similar to Bonaparte's 1807 royal decree, the Italian Parliament issued an abolition law (no. 3066) on 7 July 1866, whose 38 articles held direct ramifications for the Church in Italy and its religious orders.[127] To summarise: the 1866 law suppressed wealthy convents and abolished their feudal rights by seizing their property. Relating this suppression act to our present case, the monks of Monte Cassino were not driven from their abbey per se, but their activities were nonetheless restricted. Permission was granted for a few monks to remain, as caretakers of the archives and libraries of the institutions. Another law introduced on 18 August 1867 only complicated matters, declaring in its first article that abbeys and their priories would no longer be recognised as moral entities.[128]

The 'iniquitous ordinance'[129] of 1868 changed the rules of play. Against all promises, it effectively deprived Monte Cassino of its juridical status, its possessions, its lands, as well as its cultural and intellectual products. With this official decree, everything became the property of the state. Only one consolation was made: to declare the abbey a 'national monument', thereby entrusting the monks as its custodians. In practice, this meant that the abbot continued 'to have the role of Ordinary for the Cassino Diocese. The Abbatial Church constituted the residence of the capital and the monks could remain in the Abbey as cathedral church canons and custodians of the abbatial building.'[130] With this special concession, the abbey's lands were returned to Italy; the 'spirit' of Monte Cassino, however, could never be confiscated.

The political reorientation in the midst of Italian unification did not force the community of monks into exile. Rather, they remained in charge of their own internal administration and those of their surrounding lands. The strictness of the law was relaxed slightly, resulting in Monte Cassino's preservation. In the aftermath of religious suppression, the relentless pursuit of discipline and Benedictine observance, in addition to the 'unrelenting

---

125 D'Amelio, *Stato e Chiesa*, pp. 97–98.
126 Ibid., p. 100.
127 Ibid., pp. 528–536.
128 Ibid., p. 598.
129 Leccisotti, *Monte Cassino*, p. 99.
130 'Suppression and the early 20th century'.

zeal' of the abbots, 'lifted the community up in numbers and quality'.[131] The great library and art reserve were spared any seizure by the state; scholarly work continued in the scriptorium. 'On the eve of the fourth destruction', which occurred in the middle of the twentieth century, 'Monte Cassino, in the last recovery of its millenary life, remained faithful to the better traditions of its long activity'.[132] In a manner of speaking – according to such renditions of the past – very little had changed. The abbey remained steadfast, with a small group of monks maintaining its intellectual and spiritual lifeblood. However, this modicum of peace, tranquillity, and sovereignty would encounter its greatest threat in the following century with the outbreak of the Second World War.

Monastery Hill

The bombing of 'Monastery Hill'[133] on 15 February 1944 was an unequivocal mistake.[134] It resulted in the abbey's total destruction, 'the last in the order of time, but certainly the first for the intensity and extent of its violence'.[135] Monte Cassino's near obliteration represented a critical military phase in a long and brutal siege lasting from November 1943 to May 1944, as Allied Forces advanced northward towards Rome. Military historians have written tirelessly about the strategic errors and loss of human life during this fierce section of the war's 'Italian campaign'. Art, architectural, and intellectual historians have lamented the cultural losses and appropriations, which arguably set back Western culture and art by centuries. According to a later report by the Italian Ministry of Public Works, 'two hours of methodical bombardment thus shattered a millenary tradition of meditation, of operative charity that through so many fortunate events had given inexhaustible food to the most shining and true glory of Italy'.[136]

The scale and tragedy of loss was widely lamented at the time. German soldier-cum-historian Rudolf Böhmler called it 'a tragedy of world-wide historical significance'.[137] Writing after the war, English Prime Minister

---

131 Leccisotti, *Monte Cassino*, p. 100.
132 Ibid., p. 108.
133 Clark, *Calculated Risk*, p. 314. See also Gander, 'Return to the Battlefields'.
134 See Blumenson, *Salerno to Cassino*, p. 417. See also Lentini, 'Montecassino tra rovina e risurrezione'.
135 Leccisotti, *Monte Cassino*, p. 145.
136 'Relazione della commissione', p. 165.
137 Böhmler, *Monte Cassino*, p. 297.

10. A low aerial view of the monastery of Monte Cassino showing its complete destruction, 11–18 May 1944.

Winston Churchill described the 'formidable, strongly defended obstacle' whose steep sides were 'crowned by the famous building, which several times in previous wars had been pillaged, destroyed, and rebuilt'. 'There is controversy,' he admitted, 'about whether it should have been destroyed once again.'[138] He was referring in particular to what US Army General Mark W. Clark described as an unnecessary measure. Nevertheless, his opposition lost out to intensifying military arguments for its necessity, a cause strongly championed by New Zealand General Bernard Freyberg – actions ultimately approved by the British Field Marshal, General Harold Alexander.[139]

What actually happened was pieced together only in the aftermath. The impending disaster gathered steam in September 1943, when British

---

138 Churchill, *Second World War*, vol. V, p. 442.
139 Clark, *Calculated Risk*, pp. 316–318. On the sequence of events (hour by hour) leading to the ordering of bombardment, see especially Blumenson, *Salerno to Cassino*, pp. 403–407. Similarly, see Blumenson, 'The Bombing'.

forces (Eighth Army) landed in the south of Italy. The American forces (Fifth Army) landed at Naples. Both armies began their push northward towards the strategic Gustav Line, that German-defensive barrier that ran west-east across central Italy, following the courses of the Garigliano, Gari, and Rapido Rivers. In November of that year, the Allied Forces approached the valley of the Liri River, where the Germans had established their key defensive position. With their sights set firmly on Rome, they settled in for a long and bitter-cold winter.

The theatre of war was Monte Cassino's heartland and historic landscape. The abbey itself, exposed as ever on the mountain top, was an ideal outpost and defensive position. But few at the time thought it possible that it would ever become a direct target of modern warfare. Its location and defensive structures offered a promising site for works of art from the abbey of Cava, which were deposited at Monte Cassino for safekeeping during the war. But once the Italians signed the armistice with the Allies in September 1943, the abbey's neutrality changed; its history was effectively co-opted into contemporary warfare. Monte Cassino was no longer a passive historical agent immune to the tides of war. Yet notwithstanding the military advances that had devastated the town of Cassino below, Abbot Gregorio Diamare (1909–1945) 'was almost immovable in his security'[140] – so profound was his belief in the peace of his abbey during wartime, despite the signs of impending disaster that were visible everywhere from the mountain summit.[141]

Swift and decisive measures were taken nonetheless to protect Monte Cassino's heritage. In October 1943, a Viennese officer, Lieutenant Colonel Julius Schlegel, commander of the Divisional Maintenance Section – together with Captain Maximilian Johannes Becker[142] – convinced Abbot Diamare to move the abbey's literary, artistic, and cultural treasures to safety.[143] Schlegel provided his own recollection of the events after the war, describing the 'order'[144] of his conscience in defending 'one of the jewels of the crown of Western culture'.[145] Becker's memory, while casting some doubt on the authenticity of Schlegel's motives and authorisation, offers a similar

---

140 The account of Julius Schlegel, in *Il Bombardamento di Montecassino*, p. 221.
141 See Blumenson, *Salerno to Cassino*, p. 399.
142 See the account of Becker (18 February 1964), in *Il Bombardamento di Montecassino*, pp. 241–286.
143 Schlegel's own account appeared after the war in a series of articles published in *Die Oesterreichische Furche* (nos 45–50, 3 November–1 December 1951). Reprinted (in Italian) in *Il Bombardamento di Montecassino*, pp. 216–240.
144 Schlegel, in *Il Bombardamento di Montecassino*, p. 220.
145 Ibid., p. 218.

11. The transfer of art treasures from Monte Cassino, January 1944. Julius Schlegel (right) with Abbot Diamare (left). Bundesarchiv Bild 101I-729-0005-25.

narration. Important to both accounts was the initial task of convincing Abbot Diamare of the abbey's imminent danger – an effort greatly assisted by Emmanuel Munding, a German monk, and Mauro Inguanez, a librarian.

The efforts of both military men contributed to a plan for evacuating Monte Cassino's archive and library collections (*Monumentale, Paolina*, and *privata*). According to Schlegel, the former consisted of some 80,000 documents while the latter contained around 70,000 volumes. The archive, he says, was a treasure belonging not just to the abbey but to all of Italy: codices, *incunabuli*, documents, and volumes in parchment, in addition to historical works from the likes of Gregory the Great and Thomas Aquinas.[146] Added to this list of literary treasures were artistic works by Titian, Raphael, Tintoretto, Ghirlandaio, Bruegel, Da Vinci, among others, as well as various ancient vases, sculptures, reliquaries, and crucifixes.[147] The entire collection, which had been growing in size and splendour since the ninth century (see Chapter 2), 'was without any doubt one of the oldest and most precious in the world'.[148]

An extensive transport and salvage operation was mobilised in a matter of days. After some initial hesitation, the entire religious community reluctantly consented to the proposal for German assistance and relocation. Over the

---

146 Ibid., p. 222.
147 Ibid., p. 235.
148 Leccisotti, *Monte Cassino*, p. 253.

course of three short weeks, the remaining monks, Italian refugees, and German soldiers 'scrambled to crate and haul away the priceless collection as quickly as possible. Every night trucks full of treasures and artefacts accompanied by two monks would make its way towards Rome, away from their sacred home yet towards somewhere safe.'[149] 'In this way,' Schlegel noted,

> something like 70,000 volumes were safely transported from the archives and the library. The original documents – some 1,200 in all – many of them hundreds of years old, of priceless historical value and bearing the seals of Robert Guiscard, Roger of Sicily and many distinguished Popes and rulers, were brought to a place of safety.[150]

Meanwhile, monk and archivist Tommaso Leccisotti left for the Benedictine college of Sant'Anselmo in Rome in order to 'announce and prepare'[151] the arrival of his fellow monks and their treasured goods.

The entire task required some 700 crates and 100 trucks, the last of which departed Monte Cassino on 3 November 1943. Most of the crates were transported to the neutral territory of the Vatican and its Library for safekeeping; yet because the abbey's archive belonged (since the late nineteenth century) to the Italian state and not the Church (see Chapter 5), some of the crates were transported to a German military storage depot (castle) in Spoleto[152]; these treasures eventually joined their counterparts in Rome.[153] In the presence of General Maelzer, the German commander in the city of Rome, and other Italian (civilian and ecclesiastical) dignitaries, trucks arrived at Castel Sant'Angelo from Spoleto on 8 December 1943[154] carrying the remaining crates belonging to the abbey.[155]

---

149 '1943: The Removal of Treasures'. See also *Il Bombardamento di Montecassino*, p. 20.
150 *Il Bombardamento di Montecassino*, 226 (translation in Böhmler, *Monte Cassino*, pp. 106–107).
151 Grossetti and Matronola, in *Il Bombardamento di Montecassino*, p. 20.
152 For the suggestion of safekeeping and the deposit in the Vatican Library, see especially the letters of Tommaso Leccisotti in the appendix to Dell'Omo, 'Tommaso Leccisotti e Montecassino', pp. 56–58. See also Senger und Etterlin, *Neither Fear nor Hope*, p. 202. A letter from d. Martino Matronola to Leccisotti provides a division of the abbey's materials along 'church-state' lines, a status likewise recognised by Abbot Diamare in his discussions about the move. See 'Lista del materiale inviato a Roma trasmessa da d. Martino Matronola a d. Tommaso Leccisotti', in *Il Bombardamento di Montecassino*, p. 182, and Becker, in *Il Bombardamento di Montecassino*, p. 266, respectively.
153 Schlegel, in *Il Bombardamento di Montecassino*, p. 240.
154 Ibid.
155 See also Leccisotti, *Monte Cassino*, p. 116.

12. The unloading of property from Monte Cassino in the Piazza Venezia, Rome. Bundesarchiv Bild 101I-729-0003-13.

There is some lingering suspicion around the reunion. In the aftermath of war, and particularly following *The Times* publication on 8 November 1951, 'the truth about Cassino and the behaviour of the German troops became known throughout the world'.[156] According to an Allied broadcasting station, some of the abbey's crates were taken directly to Hermann Göring, whose Panzer division – it was claimed – was 'busily engaged in looting the monastery of Monte Cassino'.[157] A chronicler of the Royal Air Force, Norman Macmillan, further claimed that 'one statue was stolen from the altar and handed over to Göring, and of the 187 cases taken from the monastery fifteen were later missing, and a number of other valuable articles were stolen'.[158]

Countering these claims in his memoirs, German Field-Marshal Albert Kesselring noted how 'the world-famous art treasures' of Monte Cassino were removed to Orvieto by Göring's Panzer division, and subsequently 'handed over to the Vatican on my orders for storage in Rome'.[159] According to its own records, the abbey of Monte Cassino

> held an important collection of some 800 papal documents, 100,000 prints, 200 fragile parchment manuscripts, over 80,000 volumes from the libraries, 500 incunabula (=a type of book which was printed and not handwritten before the 16th century), and pieces of priceless art and

---

156 Böhmler, *Monte Cassino*, p. 113.
157 Schlegel, in *Il Bombardamento di Montecassino*, p. 228 (translation in Böhmler, *Monte Cassino*, p. 107).
158 Cited in Böhmler, *Monte Cassino*, p. 114.
159 Kesselring, *Memoirs*, p. 308.

precious tapestries. Some of these books and documents had actually originally been transferred from the Keats-Shelley house in Rome to Montecassino for safe-keeping during WWII, only to then be sent back, but this time to the Vatican City and its fortified fortress Castel Sant'Angelo, nearly 80 miles away.[160]

There is even some photographic, filmic, and other documentary evidence of the transfer. Becker recorded the deliberate plans for publicising the salvage operation through all available media,[161] a move intended to counter any Allied claims of German theft or appropriation. It seems clear that some accusations of this nature were anticipated. Ceremonies were sometimes organised to accompany the occasion, in recognition of the treasure's importance and the care taken to protect the abbey's cultural patrimony.

More interesting still is what the treasure's safe-keeping represented to contemporaries. Writing on 31 December 1943, the Director General of the Fine Arts – in the name of the Minister of National Education – expressed his profound thanks to German military and political authorities for their collaborative efforts in safeguarding the 'national artistic patrimony'.[162] He emphasised the significance of such physical and juridical measures as far beyond a matter of aesthetic principles or concrete forms; rather, he linked the preservation of Monte Cassino's cultural treasures as a major contribution to the Italian nation and, more broadly, the history of Western civilisation. Leccisotti recalled the 'deep emotion' evoked by these events, noting how

> both German embassies in Rome, the German Archaeological Institute, the Superintendence of archives and that of the Ancient Art of Latium, the General Direction of Antiquities and the Arts and that of the Academies and Libraries worked very hard to avoid the dispersion and loss of the treasures that had been removed.[163]

The whole salvage operation was an improbable success – an impressive exercise in diplomacy, secular and ecclesiastical collaboration, and logistics in the midst of war. For his role, Schlegel emerged in the aftermath of war as a 'hero of Monte Cassino'.[164] By his own account, Abbot Diamare even

---

160 Böhmler, *Monte Cassino*, p. 113.
161 See Becker, in *Il Bombardamento di Montecassino*, pp. 274–276.
162 'Lettera della Direzione Generale delle Belle Arti al Prof. Bartoli', in *Il Bombardamento di Montecassino*, p. 188.
163 Leccisotti, *Monte Cassino* p. 116.
164 'Italien hat Julius Schlegel nicht vergessen'. See also 'Julius Schlegel Dies'.

entrusted him with the earthly remains of Saint Benedict, making sure that the abbey's most prized reliquary reached its final destination in Rome. (Needless to say, the saint's purported move to the apostolic city casts further doubt on the later discovery of his tomb in 1950 (see Chapter 2).) Before Schlegel's final departure from Monte Cassino in December 1943, a special Mass was held at the high altar, during which the lieutenant colonel was presented with a manuscript which read (in translation from Latin) as follows:

> In the name of our Lord, Jesus Christ, to the illustrious and beloved Tribune, Julius Schlegel, who saved the monks and possessions of the holy monastery of Monte Cassino, these monks of Cassino give their heartfelt thanks and pray to God for his future well-being.
>
> Monte Cassino. In the month of November 1943.
> Gregorious Diamare
> Bishop and Abbot of Monte Cassino.[165]

As Leccisotti concluded: '[N]o possibility was overlooked to ensure the safety of the monastery, and any military use of it was firmly prevented so that legitimate hopes for the future could be entertained.'[166]

The abbey's material and spiritual treasures were one priority, the safety of its community another. The monks' evacuation from the mountain formed part of the same elaborate plan. On 16 October 1943, Captain Becker – speaking in French – told one of the monks that Monte Cassino would 'follow the same fate of S. Chiara in Naples and the churches of Rome'. 'It is painful,' he said, 'because your monastery is so beautiful and so important. *Mais c'est la guerre*. The order is to stop them here. They will never have Rome.'[167] The monks listened and had no choice but to obey the German command. 'In a way,' Leccisotti remarked, the situation

> seemed a repetition of what happened in the sixth century shortly after the death of St. Benedict. The community of Monte Cassino, forced into exile by the fortunes of war, arrived in Rome to find shelter in the sanctuaries of the city and protection of their most precious relics by the Apostolic See.[168]

---

165 Schlegel, in *Il Bombardamento di Montecassino*, p. 239.
166 Leccisotti, *Monte Cassino*, p. 116.
167 See Leccisotti in *Il Bombardamento di Montecassino*, p. 114.
168 Leccisotti, *Monte Cassino*, p. 116.

With the exception of Abbot Diamare, five fathers, five brothers, a priest, an oblate, some domestics, and three local families of farmers/refugees (approximately 150 in all),[169] the abbey was deserted. This group remained on the mountain until the fateful day early in 1944. On 14 February, one day prior to the bombing, the Americans distributed leaflets in Italian and English, warning of their impending attack.[170] 'Amici Italiani,' it began,

> ATTENTION!
>
> We have, until now, tried to avoid in any way the bombardment of the monastery of Monte Cassino. The Germans have taken advantage of this. Now, however, the fighting has drawn close to the sacred enclosure. The time has come when, reluctantly we are forced to aim our weapons at the monastery itself.
>
> We give this warning so that you may have the opportunity to save yourselves. Our warning is urgent. Leave the monastery. Depart immediately. Respect this warning. It is given for your own safety.
>
> THE FIFTH ARMY[171]

Three or four deadly waves of bombers arrived the following morning.[172] Having been given 'full warning', wrote Churchill, 'over 450 tons of bombs were dropped, and heavy damage was done'.[173] 'Monks and civilians alike were terrified.' For the next half an hour, 'the whole mountain quaked as though it were being shaken by some giant hand'.[174] Seven monks and one man from Cassino were buried alive during the second bombing raid, escaping through a small hole in the debris.[175] That anyone survived is a miracle. '[T]hanks to God,' recorded one monk, 'the entire small community

---

169 'Relazione sugli avvenimenti svoltisi nella badia di Montecassino (settembre–ottobre 1943)', in *Il Bombardamento di Montecassino*, p. 146. For the names of the twelve chosen monks of the community who remained, see Rosa, *Montecassino*, p. 65.
170 See also the apostolic delegate (Cicognani) in Washington's telegram to this effect in *Le Saint Siège et les victimes*, no. 56, p. 131.
171 'Relazione sugli avvenimenti svoltisi nella badia di Montecassino (settembre–ottobre 1943)', in *Il Bombardamento di Montecassino*, p. 91.
172 See Lt Col. Bradford Evans's account in Rosa, *Montecassino*, pp. 91–120.
173 Churchill, *Second World War*, vol. V, p. 442.
174 Böhmler, *Monte Cassino*, p. 168.
175 See Rosa, *Montecassino*, pp. 127–131.

is saved.'[176] '[A]s in the first destruction,' wrote Leccisotti, 'St. Benedict had obtained that the lives of his children be spared. On the day of the Octave of St. Scholastica, 17 February, he saw them cross unscathed the circle of steel and fire that surrounded their home.'[177]

The bombing continued for two more days.[178] Then, and only then, did the Germans move into Monte Cassino.[179] Deployed by the commanding officer of the German paratroopers, Rudolf Böhmler, about 70 men with three heavy machine guns and mortars occupied the debris. General Frido von Senger und Etterlin, commander of the German 14th Panzer Corps, later wrote how the bombing benefited their own position. 'It had, indeed,' he recorded in his memoir,

> become a far finer defence position than it would have been before its destruction, because as anyone who has had experience in street fighting – as at Stalingrad or at Cassino – is aware, rubble heaped upon basements and cellars form defences greatly superior to houses.[180]

In this way, he continued, 'the bombing had the opposite effect to what was intended'. Now the German Army could (and did) 'occupy the abbey without scruple, especially as ruins are better for defence than intact buildings'.[181]

The misinformation campaign continues here. Joseph Goebbels, the German propaganda minister, exploited the opportunity of Abbot Diamare's escape. Before he even reached the safety of Sant'Anselmo in Rome, the abbot was intercepted by the minister's agents. According to General Senger und Etterlin, 'the frightened old priest was accordingly brought to a radio station, kept waiting a long time without food, and finally induced to make another statement as prescribed by the radio columnists, which, however, was still in keeping with historical truth'.[182]

Abbot Diamare agreed to sign a document, stating without doubt that there was not – nor had there ever been – Germans inside Monte Cassino.[183]

---

176 Grossetti and Matronola, in *Il Bombardamento di Montecassino*, p. 94.
177 Leccisotti, *Monte Cassino*, p. 132.
178 'Annotazioni di Armando Carotenuto', in *Il Bombardamento di Montecassino*, p. 168.
179 For the question/controversy around possible German occupation of Monte Cassino before the bombing, see Blumenson, *Salerno to Cassino*, pp. 409–414.
180 Senger und Etterlin, 'Monte Cassino', p. 252.
181 Senger und Etterlin, *Neither Fear nor Hope*, p. 202.
182 Senger und Etterlin, 'Monte Cassino', p. 251. See also Senger und Etterlin, *Neither Fear nor Hope*, pp. 203–204; *Il Bombardamento di Montecassino*, p. 106
183 On this question, and its contemporary importance, see Mgr Tardini's notes in Blet et al., *Le Saint Siège et les victimes*, no. 69, pp. 141–144. See also nos 74–75, pp. 184–186.

According to this record, signed by the abbot and Lieutenant Deiber, and dated 15 February 1944, the neutrality of the abbey was never infringed by the German soldiers, who had long respected the sanctity of this site. Beginning in Italian, the document solemnly declared that:

> no German soldier has ever been stationed within the precincts of the monastery of Monte Cassino; that for a while three military police were on duty, with the sole object of ensuring that the neutral zone round the monastery was being respected. But these latter were withdrawn twenty days ago.

Added to this declaration was a brief German statement that 'there never has been and there is now no German soldier in the Monte Cassino monastery'.[184] Kesselring maintained the same claim, writing in his memoirs: 'Once and for all I wish to establish the fact that the monastery was not occupied as part of the line; it was closed against unauthorised entry by military police.'[185] General Senger und Etterlin also confirmed this position, adding that Kesselring 'had given express orders that no German soldier should enter the Monastery, so as to avoid giving the Allies any pretext for bombing or shelling the place'.[186] In his memoirs of the war, this general mentioned his good relations with the abbey, where he celebrated Christmas Mass in December 1943. He presented his visit on this occasion 'to confirm that no German soldiers were visiting the place once the fighting had broken out in the general area'.[187]

From the Germans' perspective, the abbey was 'neutralised'[188] by the Allied destruction. Kesselring's actions to protect it from the ravages of war were determined after a meeting with the German ambassador to the Holy See. He was approached by the Vatican to help protect the abbey, its treasures and library. In a statement issued on 18 February, he refuted any suggestion of German forces occupying the abbey; he deemed it a 'wicked lie' the assertion that 'the monastery had been transformed into "the strongest artillery fortress in the world"'. This account also confirms the free movement of Italian refugees into the monastery, noting that several hundred remained during the Allied bombing.[189] And, by his own account, the assertion was

---

184 Cited in Böhmler, *Monte Cassino*, p. 171. See also *Il Bombardamento di Montecassino*, p. 98.
185 Kesselring, *Memoirs*, p. 195.
186 Senger und Etterlin, 'Monte Cassino', p. 251.
187 Senger und Etterlin, *Neither Fear nor Hope*, p. 202.
188 Ibid.
189 Böhmler, *Monte Cassino*, p. 177.

'confirmed' by Abbot Diamare's statement, in addition to another such admission by the abbey's administrator, Don Nicola Clementi, and the Episcopal Delegate of the Administrative Department of the diocese of Monte Cassino, Don Francisco Salconio.[190]

By all accounts, the abbey was destroyed unnecessarily and with brutal military force. 'The result was not good,'[191] Churchill quipped in the aftermath. While it is possible to identify the culprits – the Allied Forces generally, the generals who pushed for the assault, others who ordered the bombing, and even some of the individual participants such as the American pilot Walter Miller, who later became known for *A Canticle for Leibowitz* (1959), a post-apocalyptic science-fiction novel set in a Catholic monastery, and the American who led the air attack, Lt Col. Bradford Evans of the US Air Force[192] – history has been kind to the abbey's aggressors.[193] Part of the reason, as we'll explore in Chapter 5, relates to the military necessities of war and the complexities introduced by the burgeoning philosophical, social, political, and legal argument for the protection of ancient and religious monuments. But another consideration concerns the abbey's seasoned experience with destruction and victimisation; Monte Cassino boasted a long history of martyrdom as a consequence of warfare, from which it always recovered. Its position was thus anything but neutral in the annals of time. As one historian noted about the abbey's role during the Italian campaign: it

> already had been converted into a fortress, and as the same vast unscalable walls that enclosed its spiritual purpose served also a secular intention, they were doomed to destruction as had been the earlier masonry that Lombards and Saracens had tumbled down.[194]

The lamentation following this particular destruction nevertheless stands apart from previous episodes. According to one monk's first-hand account, the abbey was stunned that others had forcefully decided its destiny.[195] Angelo Pantoni, a Cassinese monk (and engineer) forced to abandon the abbey in October 1943, recorded the extent of destruction upon his return to

---

190 Ibid.
191 Churchill, *Second World War*, vol. V, p. 442.
192 For a first-hand account (transcription), see Rosa, *Montecassino*, pp. 91–120.
193 Msr Tardini debated the question of responsibility in his notes (cf. Blet et al., *Le Saint Siège et les victimes*, no. 79, pp. 190–191.)
194 Linklater, *Campaign in Italy*, p. 173.
195 Fulvio De Angelis, in *Il Bombardamento di Montecassino*, p. 158.

the mountain in March 1945.[196] His journal entry is among the few accessible to scholars, as most other (unpublished) accounts remain part of the abbey's private collection. Section by section, cloister by cloister, Pantoni recounts the nature of destruction to the abbey's church, chapels, cupola, tomb, choir, crypt, kitchen, libraries, archive, collegium, seminary, etc. Performing the role of tour guide through a wasted landscape, his intimate knowledge of what stood before the fateful day is among the most powerful reminders of what was actually lost in the wake of destruction.

*

The fate of destiny ostensibly haunts and defines Monte Cassino. While the scale of death and destruction in the twentieth century was unprecedented, the experience of war on the venerable mountain was not; the religious community once again suffered displacement, trauma, and loss at the hands of external forces and aggressors. The monks who survived the bombing in February 1944 were no doubt aware of the footsteps in which they followed – history, or destiny, was unequivocally repeated. Yet like every prior episode of destruction, the abbey's tradition and heritage were not extinguished by war; its claims to historical continuity were never permanently severed. As time and a great deal of money would eventually tell, the obstacles posed by the abbey's complete physical destruction in February 1944 proved surmountable. While there is no denying that Monte Cassino 'fell victim to human inefficiency, political considerations and the brutalizing influences of war',[197] the abbey's triumphant resurrection soon followed its martyrdom.

Or so the dominant narrative suggests. This triumphalist vision of Monte Cassino is complicated by the arrangement and rearrangement of historical events over time, which connect the abbey's past to its present in a linear fashion. The various episodes of destruction (and near destruction) examined in this chapter reveal a familiar pattern of tragedy, loss, and perseverance. While the details recorded in medieval, early modern, and modern sources offer very little beyond the destructive act itself, the abbey's repeated experience across the centuries so clearly embodies the 'destruction tradition' framing this book's central argument. The manifestation of each destruction is largely uncontested in the written sources, a series of prescriptive 'truths' that proffer very little additional context in the historical record; each

196 Avagliano, 'Montecassino nella descrizione'.
197 Böhmler, *Monte Cassino*, p. 182.

episode is represented in classic empiricist fashion, in turn cementing the abbey's legacy through a recognisable process of description and narration.

But as we'll see in the following chapter, the abbey's recovery is an altogether different matter. These longer historical processes characterise Monte Cassino's identity with more definition than the physical violence that preceded them. Indeed, they *explain* the historical events in order to reveal their structure, coherence, and meaning. It is to this course of historical reconstitution, reconstruction, and representation that we must now turn our full attention.

4. *Floreat Semper:* Rebuilding, Stone by Stone

Abstract

This chapter examines the abbey's repeated recovery efforts. It asks two principal questions: why, after every episode of destruction between the sixth and twentieth centuries, was it deemed necessary to rebuild the abbey? And, how was this task successfully achieved? Such questioning necessarily considers the role of human agency, both individual and collective, in the overall enterprise. But it also counters the problem of historical determinism: the view, in this case, that the abbey's recovery was somehow inevitable or predetermined.

Keywords: founders; reconstruction; recovery; rebuilding; renovation; consecration

'Monte Cassino lives!'[1]

On 21 March 1947, three years after Monte Cassino's fatal destruction, Pope Pius XII issued an encyclical from Rome, *Fulgens Radiatur*, sub-titled 'On St. Benedict'. From the outset, he celebrated the brilliance of the saint's resplendent light, which shines 'like a star in the darkness of night […] a glory not only to Italy but of the whole Church'.[2] The focus on this solemn occasion then shifted to Benedict's role in the renewal and restoration of the Catholic Church in a post-war era. No better spokesman could be found in the aftermath of such devastation. For while 'all earthly institutions begun and built solely on human wisdom and human power, in the course of time succeed one another, flourish and then quite naturally fail, weaken and

---

1 Ibid.
2 Pope Pius XII, *Fulgens Radiatur*, c. 1.

crumble away',³ the abbey of Monte Cassino presented a powerful anomaly. Throughout the centuries of its long existence, 'through the hostile fortunes of time and circumstances', Benedict's mountaintop foundation remained steadfast and resilient. Suffering destruction on numerous occasions, its spirit nevertheless remained intact. The secret to its resurrection: the 'unfailing life and abiding strength [received] from on high', which was capable even amidst 'ruins and failures' to help sustain and fortify the Church.⁴

While the pope's message was overwhelmingly positive, the celebrations were comparatively sombre. On this feast day, which also marked fourteen centuries after 'that saintly man [Benedict] gained heaven',⁵ Pius XII issued a call to arms among his gathered brethren. 'When the recent war was raging and spread in a lamentable way to the shores of Campania and Latium,' he reminded his audience, 'it reached [...] the holy summit of Monte Cassino'.⁶ Despite his best efforts to persuade, exhort, and protest 'lest an immense loss be inflicted on religion, on culture and civilization', 'ruin and destruction' nevertheless 'came to that illustrious home of learning and piety which had survived the turmoil of centuries like a torch conquering darkness'.⁷ Affecting the whole region, '[p]ractically nothing else survived from the destruction except the sacred crypt in which the relics of the holy Patriarch are preciously kept'.⁸

The Second World War left an indelible mark on the abbey. 'At the present time,' the pope concluded, 'crumbling walls and rubble, which brambles pitifully overrun, stand where lofty monuments once met one's gaze; close by a small home for the monks has been erected recently'.⁹ But hope amidst 'such a mighty storm and universal upheaval'¹⁰ kept its spirit alive, sustaining its tradition, like so many times before. Why then, Pius rhetorically queried,

> may it not be hoped that with the help of all and especially the rich and generous, this very ancient Arch-Abbey be restored as soon as possible to its pristine glory? This indeed humanity owes to Benedict; for if today it glories in great learning, if it rejoices in ancient literary documents, it must mainly thank him and his hard working sons. We confidently trust,

3   Ibid., c. 2.
4   Ibid., c. 3.
5   Ibid., c. 32.
6   Ibid., c. 31.
7   Ibid.
8   Ibid.
9   Ibid., c. 32.
10 Ibid., c. 3.

therefore, that the future will happily realize Our hope and Our wishes. May this work be not only a task of restoration and reparation but also an omen of better times in which the spirit of the Benedictine Institute and its ever opportune teaching may flourish more and more.[11]

The abbey did flourish once again. Its recovery over the next two decades followed a familiar pattern in the community's history: a vigorous process of reconstruction, restoration, and resettlement reminiscent of past experiences. Monte Cassino's resurrection – its full-scale recovery in a material, spiritual, and symbolic sense – was not simply a matter of circumstance; rather, it was one of resilience, perseverance, religious justification, planning, and strong political will, support, and financing.

To examine the process historically requires a better understanding of the underlying and unifying motivations. To this end, this chapter asks two principal questions: why, after every episode of destruction between the sixth and twentieth centuries, was it deemed necessary to rebuild the abbey? And, how was this task successfully achieved? Such questioning necessarily considers the role of human agency, both individual and collective in the overall enterprise. But it also counters the problem of historical determinism: the view, in this case, that the abbey's recovery was somehow inevitable or predetermined. This extant configuration, or representation of events, fosters a false narrative of progress and triumph, which this book seeks to redress in its efforts to reveal the authentic history of Monte Cassino and the historical and cultural consequences of its destruction.

Restaurator ac renovator, fundator atque constructor

The history of Monte Cassino is fragmented. A history destroyed, a history resuscitated; an abbey destroyed, an abbey rebuilt. The fault lines are clearly visible. In their shadows lie a series of micro-histories or sub-plots from the late sixth century to the mid-twentieth century. These individual stories have been woven into a coherent narrative through a deliberate retelling of the abbey's death and subsequent resurrection in the wake of repeated destruction. Although the episodes of destruction examined the previous chapter rupture the abbey's timeline in a purely chronological sense, the historical representation of its recovery – how it is recorded and validated in the sources – sutures the temporal fragments together again. They make it whole. This reconstruction process is made possible through a series

---

11   Ibid., c. 32.

of proclaimed 'restorers and renovators', 'founders and builders'.[12] These historical figures are credited with the impulse and initiative to restoring the abbey's ancient glory, heritage, and tradition; their contribution and recognition provides a valuable framework for understanding Monte Cassino's impetus to recovery after every episode of destruction.

This linear vision of the abbey's past is not a modern construction; it existed, and was duly employed, already in the twelfth century. In his prefatory letter to Abbot Oderisius of Monte Cassino, Leo Marsicanus mentioned how the abbey's destruction and restoration would be among the treated topics in the *Chronicon*.[13] The works and deeds of distinguished men, he noted, and the overall memory of their collaborations, were well worth preserving. In his continuation of this monastic work, Peter the Deacon named four principal figures to whom many subsequent authors have attributed great progress and achievements.[14] The 'first founder' was of course Saint Benedict, whose monastic foundation atop the venerable mountain of Cassino provided an idealised model for the religious life. It became the objective and standard for future restorations; a reference point to which future founders could aspire, and against which their achievements could be continually measured.

The 'second founder' was Petronax of Brescia (c. 718–749/750). As we examined in Chapter 3, the Lombard attack on Monte Cassino c. 577 exiled the community of monks for over a century. The abbey was completely destroyed during the nocturnal event. Nothing remained intact or habitable. The monks fled, and no one officially returned until the first part of the eighth century.

The congregation's return to the venerable mountain resulted from a series of political actions, possibly initiated by the pope in Rome. Paul the Deacon tells us that a certain citizen of Brescia – 'spurred by the love of God'[15] – resettled the site c. 718.[16] Approximately 110 years after the abbey's initial destruction, a 'venerable man'[17] by the name of Petronax paid a visit to Rome. Meeting with Pope Gregory II (715–731), and encouraged by his exhortation to start a religious community, he then proceeded to the fortress of Cassinum, to dwell with 'the holy remains of blessed father Benedict'.[18]

12 *Chron. Cas.*, III. Prologus, p. 362.
13 Ibid., p. 5 ('Epistola Leonis').
14 Ibid., III. Prologus, p. 362.
15 Paul the Deacon, *Historia Langobardorum*, VI. 40, p. 178.
16 For the dating, see Hoffmann, 'Die älteren Abtslisten', pp. 242–247.
17 *Chronicon Vulturnense*, I, p. 151.
18 Paul the Deacon, *Historia Langobardorum*, VI. 40, p. 178.

The site of Monte Cassino was not completely vacant at the time. At some point after the Lombard sack, the mountain was repopulated by a small group of Christian ascetics, who nevertheless quickly came to recognise Petronax as their superior. 'Not long afterwards,' Paul's *History* relates,

> With the aid of Divine Mercy and through favour of the merits of the blessed father Benedict, after the lapse of about a hundred and ten years from the time when that place had become destitute of the habitation of men, he became there the father of many monks of high and low degree who gathered around him, and he began to live, when the dwellings were repaired, under the restraint of the Holy Rule of the Order and the institutions of the blessed Benedict, and he put this sacred monastery in the condition in which it is now seen.[19]

Writing almost two centuries after the event, Paul was in Monte Cassino when he did so. He went on to relate that, although Petronax was starting his community from scratch, he was given some aid by Pope Zacharias (741–752), who sent books and 'other things' pertaining to the utility of the abbey. Among the holy books bestowed on the new abbot, which were essential to the abbey's religious service, the pope allegedly returned the original monastic *Rule*, which Benedict had written with his own hand. The very same 'autograph' manuscript that accompanied the monks to Rome when they fled the Lombards; the one later destroyed by fire at Teano in 896.[20]

This contribution to the abbey's resurrection forged a relationship between the abbey of Monte Cassino and the apostolic see in Rome. Not only did the papacy play some role in re-establishing authority and governance, but, according to Leo Marsicanus, Petronax was accompanied on his mission by a group of monks from the Lateran community.[21] Another source from the nearby monastery of San Vincenzo al Volturno, the *Chronicon Vulturnense*, reports that this congregation – with an apostolic privilege supporting their mission – returned – 'cum regula et panis libra'[22] – that is, with the autograph *Rule* and the original piece of bread snatched by the monks who were fleeing the Lombard attack. The nature of this evidence has led to further claims (founded on a spurious bull) that Zacharias consecrated the basilica, acknowledged the presence of Benedict and Scholastica's bodies

---

19 Ibid., pp. 178–179.
20 *Chron. Cas.*, I. 44, pp. 114–115; I. 48, pp. 126–127.
21 Ibid., I. 4, pp. 22–23; *Chronicon Vulturnense*, I, p. 151.
22 *Chronicon Vulturnense*, I, p. 151.

beneath the altar, while confirming the inviolable possession of Monte Cassino's possessions.[23]

The story is a little suspect for a number of reasons. Its sequence of events raises questions on the probability of its outcomes. If Petronax truly sought to lead a monastic life, why was he not directed to one of 40 to 50 possible Roman monasteries?[24] On what basis would the pope receive this stranger from Brescia and recommend that he pursue the religious life on the ruins of Monte Cassino?[25] What convinced him to abandon his pilgrimage to Jerusalem, mentioned by the Volturno chronicler,[26] in favour of (re-)establishing a religious community? And who was he, exactly? The image above portrays him as a Roman soldier, not a man of God. The *Chronicon Vulturnense* mentions his election to the abbacy after his refounding the monastery, which suggests a transition from a temporal to spiritual lifestyle.[27] And one final consideration: what interest did the papacy have in refounding the abbey? Is it possible that the popes in Rome actively sought to renew the spiritual life on the venerable mountain, to resuscitate the spirit of Benedictine observance first animated in Gregory the Great's *Dialogues*?[28]

A more contemporaneous account provides some clues. It comes from Hunuberc of Heidenheim, who documented the pilgrimage of the future bishop of Eichstatt, Willibald. The young Anglo-Saxon came to Monte Cassino in 729, most likely en route to Rome, where he 'found only a few monks there under Abbot Petronax'.[29] Willibald's arrival towards the end of a ten-year pilgrimage bore little connection to Petronax's reputation. Rather, he was attracted first and foremost by the memory of Saint Benedict, which he sought to restore on the site of Monte Cassino.[30] Right away, this account presents a contrasting image to the richness, grandeur, and population of the religious community presented in Paul the Deacon's writings. It suggests a more likely scenario: that the abbey's restoration took some time, coming to fruition over the course of numerous decades.

The resettlement and return were certainly not immediate. Arriving on the mountain twelve years after Petronax, Willibald set about instructing

---

23   Bartolini, *Di s. Zaccaria papa*, no. 24, pp. 57–62 (*documenti*). See also pp. 259ff.
24   Estimate from a slightly later date in *Le Liber Pontificalis*, II, XCVIII (Leo III), pp. 22–25.
25   Ferrari, *Early Roman Monasteries*, p. 251.
26   *Chronicon Vulturnense*, I, p. 151.
27   Ibid.
28   See Wollasch, 'Benedictus abbas Romensis, pp. 126ff.
29   *Vita Willibaldi*, c. 5, p. 102.
30   Chapman, 'La restauration du Mont-Cassin', p. 78.

and reforming the religious community from within. 'Without delay,' his *Vita* further relates,

> he joined the community, for which he was so well fitted both by his great self-discipline and his natural aptitude for obedience. He learned much from their careful teaching, but he in turn taught them more by his outward bearing; he showed them not so much by words as by the beauty of his character what was the real spirit of their institute; and by proving himself to be a model of monastic virtue he compelled the admiration, love and respect of all.[31]

According to this account, Willibald endeared himself to the community, gaining valuable experience along the way as a sacristan of the church in his first year, a dean of the abbey in his second year, and a porter at various monasteries in the region over the following eight years. For ten years in all, then,

> the venerable man Willibald tried to observe, as far as possible, every detail of the monastic observance as laid down by the Rule of St. Benedict. And he not only observed it himself but led the others, whom he had brought over long distances by foot and by sea, to follow him in the traditional path of regular life.[32]

This contribution notwithstanding, the abbey's wholesale restoration is credited to Petronax. This attribution owes primarily to the later reconstruction of events in the Monte Cassino *Chronicon*. Drawing on earlier historical accounts, Leo Marsicanus accentuated the abbot's role as the central protagonist. His version of events represents the received grand narrative: the most popular, widespread, and digested account of the community's recovery in the post-Lombard era. Leo's representation of these eighth-century events situates Petronax – 'a very religious man' (*vir valde religiosus*) – as an agent of internal reform, and a catalyst for the abbey's future prosperity. Furthermore, it attributes the entire recovery process, which transpired over the next two and a half centuries, to a material restoration of the abbey's ancient fabric.[33]

---

31 *Vita Willibaldi*, c. 5, p. 102. See translation in Hunuberc of Heidenheim, 'The Hodoeporican of St Willibald', p. 172 (Latin from Acta SS. 7 July, vol. 29, c. III, pp. 509–510).
32 Ibid.
33 Bertolini, 'I Langobardi di Benevento e Monte Casino', p. 73.

Petronax played an important role in these developments. But the reality was a much more complex and less-solitary undertaking. It involved issues of governance, temporal and spiritual collaborations, financial and jurisdictional independence, in addition to the evolution of Benedictine customs and regulations. Under his abbatial leadership (c. 718–749/750), however, Monte Cassino began to flourish once again, owing in large part to its increasing landed wealth, the support of the papacy, and the patronage and alliances of political figures from Spoleto, Benevento, and the emerging Carolingian world north of the Alps.[34] As we've already seen (Chapter 2), the *Terra sancti Benedicti* was taking shape in this period, a significant growth in jurisdiction and revenues made possible by Duke Gisulf II of Benevento's generous donation in 744.[35]

The abbey's reputation was likewise gradually restored in this era. This claim is verified in part by the high-profile traffic to the mountain top by prominent figures like the Frankish mayor of the palace, Carloman (746/747), the Lombard King Ratchis (749), the famed abbot of Fulda, Sturmi (747), and Emperor Charlemagne (787).[36] As we saw in a previous chapter, it can also be witnessed through the abbey's construction achievements in the eighth and ninth centuries. Abbot Gisulf (796–817), for example, who 'came from the noble family of the Dukes of Benevento',[37] capitalised on the region's growing economy; he helped improve the abbey's wealth by taking Petronax's work and escalating the programme to one of 'grandeur'.[38] His ambitious building and decorating programme for the original site of Saint Benedict's foundation on the hilltop (*sursum*), and a new church and monastery at the base of the mount (*deorsum*) – known as San Salvatore – effectively established Monte Cassino's 'key structures as they were to last for centuries to come'.[39]

'As soon as he was made abbot', Gisulf

> began to occupy himself in planning how he could enlarge the limited quarters of the church and of the other facilities as well for the usefulness of brothers who lived there below. He was spurred to this task by the attractiveness of the place and by its abundant resources.[40]

---

34 See especially Falco, 'Lineamenti'.
35 *Chron. Cas.*, I. 5, pp. 25–28; *Chron. s. Ben.*, c. 21, pp. 479–480; Whitten, '*Quasi ex uno ore*', pp. 50–52.
36 Eigil, *Vita Sturmi*, c. 14, pp. 145–147; Rudolf of Fulda, *Vita Leobae abbatissae*, c. 10, p. 125.
37 *Chron. Cas.*, I. 17, p. 57.
38 Citarella and Willard, *Ninth-Century Treasure*, p. 49.
39 Ibid., p. 37.
40 *Chron. Cas.*, I. 17, p. 57.

Although Monte Cassino had come a long way since Petronax's arrival c. 718, much work remained to be done. The monks' 'dwelling on the mountaintop was confined, difficult and very toilsome, and inadequate for such a large number of brothers'. Tackling this logistical problem, Abbot Gisulf

> commissioned a brother named Garioald, who after him was in charge of this very place, to devote his full attention to this enterprise, and before where Abbot Poto [771–777] had built the little church of St Benedict, he should forthwith proceed to arrange the building of the necessary separate parts of the new monastery.

Obeying the abbot's command, therefore, Garioald filled 'with great masses of earth and with barriers of stone' an area once covered with 'water and rushes like a swamp'. There, 'on the site of the earlier small church, [he] built with quite beautiful workmanship a large basilica in honour of our Lord the Saviour'.[41]

The basilica itself is recorded in great detail.[42] This new monastic complex at the base of Monte Cassino was not built at the expense of the more ancient site above, which in Gisulf's time consisted of the Oratory of Saint John, where the altar of Apollo once stood, and where Saints Benedict and Scholastica (allegedly) lay buried; the church of Saint Martin, first built by Saint Benedict and later enlarged by Abbot Petronax; and the chapel of Saint Peter, donated to the abbey in 749 by King Ratchis.[43] Seeking to replace Saint Martin's as the abbey's main church, Abbot Gisulf set out to rebuild a new basilica of Saint Benedict. 'The same abbot', the *Chronicon* relates,

> acting no less energetically above, built there some decent housing; and the church in which the *corpus* of Saint Benedict was buried, because it was small, making it altogether larger and covering with lead the roof of cypress timbers, he embellished with *ornamenta* in gold as well as in silver. Furthermore, above the altar of Saint Benedict he placed a silver ciborium, adorning it in part with gold and likewise with enamels, while the remaining altars he covered with silver plates.[44]

Financial security soon followed this material expansion. By the mid-ninth century, Monte Cassino's treasury (*thesaurus*) consisted of '1,368.6

---

41 Ibid.
42 Ibid.
43 Citarella and Willard, *Ninth-Century Treasure*, p. 43.
44 *Chron. Cas.*, I. 18, p. 59.

ounces of gold, 9,422.3 of silver, 31,000 gold pieces, a large number of objects in silver and gold which with a silk vestment embroidered with gems were valued at 10,000 pieces of gold and a gold crown worth 3,000 gold pieces'.[45] The (estimated) state of its accumulated wealth is known from extant eighth- and ninth-century records, whose inventories kept track of various donations. It is further estimated from accounts of the treasure's surreptitious theft in 843–844 by Prince Siconolf of Benevento, who initially claimed it 'under the guise of a loan to pay his Spanish Agareni'.[46] In a series of visits to the abbey, he, his brother-in-law Maio, and his administrators (*gastaldi*) – Peter, Landenulf, Lando, Aldemarius – 'seized and carried away almost the whole treasure which kings of glorious memory like Charles and Pepin his brother, Carloman and Louis the sons of the same Pepin, and many more faithful kings and princes had brought here'.[47]

While the extent of the theft is likely overstated, it emphasises an important reality of the time: these (secular) actions did not bankrupt or derail the abbey. The economic vitality of the region, from which Monte Cassino directly prospered, continued into the following centuries. Meanwhile, the community's religious life continued in relative peace within its walls. That is to say, until the next attack on the abbey in the late ninth century.

Following this episode of destruction, the abbey's 'third founder' was Abbot Aligernus (948–985) – a Neapolitan and former monk of San Paolo fuori le Mura in Rome. The Saracen 'invasion' of Monte Cassino in 883 left the abbey destroyed and deserted once again, more than a century and a half after Petronax's resettlement. The murder of Abbot Bertharius at the altar of Saint Martin, in the church of San Salvatore, left the religious community without a leader.[48]

Recovery began almost immediately. Daily monastic routines were not interrupted for very long, as they became transplanted to a safer, temporary location south of the abbey. Erchempert noted in his *History of the Lombards of Benevento* that 'the monastery of the blessed Benedict, demolished earlier by the Saracens, [...] was begun to be rebuilt by order of

---

45 Citarella and Willard, *Ninth-Century Treasure*, p. 79.
46 *Chron. Cas.*, I. 26, p. 74, and *Chron. s. Benedicti*, c. 7, p. 473. See textual comparison and translation in Citarella and Willard, *Ninth-Century Treasure*, pp. 86–90.
47 Ibid.
48 See also Peter the Deacon, *Ortus et vita*, c. 28, p. 51: 'Bertharius abbas nobilis carne, nobilis spiritu, in monasterio Domini Salvatoris iusta altarium sancti Martiri pro fide Christi a Sarracenis capita trancatus est. Sepultus vero est sursum in monasterio Casinensi. Passi sunt autem cum eo et alii multi, undecimo calendas Novembris.'

the venerable abbot Angelarius in the month of August of the year 886'.[49] The Monte Cassino *Chronicon* also mentions Angelarius's assumption of abbatial duties (883–889) in the wake of Bertharius's martyrdom. His first action was practical: to build a small dependent cell (*cella*) at Teano for the exiled community 'in honour of the blessed father Benedict'.[50] There, situated 50 km south of Monte Cassino, they remained for the next 30 or so years.

This particular location offered the monks good strategic value. From this new residence, there remained 'the possibility of keeping an eye on the devastated house, which was nearby, and this kept alive the hope of returning'.[51] During the monks' exile following the Saracen attack, southern Italy was reconquered by the Byzantine general Gregorius. This renewed political influence from the Eastern Empire, which challenged the entrenched protectorate established by Frankish rulers in the region, re-established Greek benevolence of Western monastic dependencies. Emperor Leo VI, for example, was the first to grant a privilege to the monks of Monte Cassino at Teano (951), which amounted in the most practical terms to a tax exemption.[52] This was followed by a number of other privileges by the *catapani*, the Byzantine administrators in Italy.

The safety of the monks' temporary abode was nevertheless thwarted by a fire in 896, which destroyed the famous autograph manuscript of Benedict's *Rule*.[53] Almost two decades later, an offer from the Lombard princes of Capua, Landulf I and Atenulf, saw the monks of Monte Cassino resettle in 915 to the rich plains of Campania during the abbacy of John (913–934) – at his instigation.[54] There they remained, under the protection of the rival princes to Benevento, until their eventual return to the Apennines in the mid-tenth century.

At Capua, the monks became city dwellers. This cosmopolitan lifestyle clashed with the traditional discipline of Benedictine customs, thrusting the community into the temporal world and its localised political life. There were consequences to this new arrangement. As Erchempert relates, when Atenulf 'acquired the authority for ruling as a *gastaldus*, everything which the Benedictine order possessed within the city of Capua he ordered to be taken away from the exiled brothers'.[55] These manoeuvres concerned Aligernus enough to dispatch Erchempert as his messenger to Pope Stephen

---

49 Erchempert, *Historia Langobardorum Beneventanorum*, c. 61, p. 259.
50 *Chron. Cas.*, I. 44, p. 115.
51 Leccisotti, *Monte Cassino*, p. 43.
52 *Registrum Petri Diaconi*, no. 149 (fol. 67v), no. 149, p. 455.
53 See Zeller, 'Montecassino in Teano', p. 123; Pohl, *Werkstätte der Erinnerung*, pp. 154–162.
54 Ibid., pp. 123–124, 128.
55 Erchempert, *Historia Langobardorum Beneventanorum*, c. 69, p. 261.

V in Rome 'to make a claim for our property which had been taken away'. The monk-cum-chronicler returned to Capua with a blessing and a privilege of immunity for his religious community, which succeeded in restoring most of what Atenulf had seized by force.

That the monks reflected on their situation is evident from contemporary historical records. Both Erchempert's *History* and the *Chronica sancti Benedicti Casinensis* were written by monks of Monte Cassino, as critical responses to the unfavourable political circumstances in Benevento. It was during this period of Capuan exile that serious efforts were made to reassert and (re)compose the community's identity.[56] This was achieved in large part by producing what is now one of the abbey's oldest surviving manuscripts, written in Beneventan script and today preserved in the Monte Cassino archives (Codex Casinensis 175). Attributed to Abbot John I's 'vision and industry',[57] this codex contains some of the most fundamental histories and liturgical texts from the abbey's early history (sixth–ninth centuries), such as the *Rule of Saint Benedict*, Paul the Deacon's commentary on the *Rule*, and the *Chronica sancti Benedicti Casinensis*. Its composition served to fashion and transmit a history of the abbey, which greatly influenced the later writings of Leo Marsicanus.

The monks made the most of their predicament. Similar to their experience at Teano, they swiftly set about establishing a more suitable and permanent home. Under Abbot John, they built a monastery dedicated to Saint Benedict, large enough to accommodate 50 monks.[58] Even with this more suitable abode, the move to the Capuan court-city sacrificed the monks' independence, subjecting them to the authority and whims of lay princes.[59] The situation reads like a classic case of exploitation or political opportunism. Luigi Tosti, the great nineteenth-century historian and monk of Monte Cassino, stated that 'while the monks were busy enjoying the newfound pleasures, the princes hastened to make themselves masters of the whole patrimony of St. Benedict'.[60] Fortunately, the situation was not permanent. Though a measure of control was certainly being exercised over the religious community, their relationship with the Lombard princes would in fact benefit them in their abbey's longer-term recovery process.

The monks eventually returned to Monte Cassino c. 950, approximately 67 years after the Saracen attack. The congregation was restored to its

---

56 Berto, 'Oblivion, Memory, and Irony', p. 48.
57 Citarella and Willard, *Ninth-Century Treasure*, p. 84.
58 Zeller, 'Montecassino in Teano', pp. 124–127.
59 Leccisotti, *Monte Cassino*, p. 46.
60 Tosti, *Storia della badia*, I, p. 86.

original site, but the returning community found their region 'neglected and destitute, as if desolate' (*neglectus ac destitutus et quasi desolatus*).[61] The Liri Valley was not unoccupied during their absence; the *gastaldi* of Aquino had profited in the interim, before the princes of Capua helped to repatriate much of the abbey's land. One of Abbot Aligernus's first tasks was to continue restoring Monte Cassino's possessions in the 'lands of Saint Benedict', which had been dispersed during the period of exile.[62] His efforts brought to fruition the work of his predecessors, namely Abbots John I, Adalbert (934–943), Baldwin (943–946), and Maielpoto (d. 948).[63] In so doing, he secured the assistance from the Byzantine governor, Marianus Argyrus, the *anthipatus patricius et stratigos Calabrie et Langobardie*,[64] who in December 956 granted him permission to 'travel the entire province of Langobardia [est. 891/892] and to reclaim all former possessions of the monastery'.[65]

None of this reclamation was possible, however, before the abbey itself was restored. A functioning, physical abode on the mountain of Cassino was necessary before the comforts of Capua – whatever their advantages – could be traded. Aligernus's epitaph suggests his active role in this building activity; securing the final addition of new roof beams made the abbey habitable once more,[66] thereby enabling the monks' return.

Repopulation was also high on the agenda. During Aligernus's abbacy, many immigrants were attracted to the surrounding region to help cultivate wine and grain. In 966, a *castellum* was established with 30 men – a fortified village, whose foundation defined the settlement structure and economy of the region for many subsequent centuries.[67] This rapid resettlement around Monte Cassino was realised through agriculture and the families sustaining its production; filling the region with people in turn contributed to a period of economic prosperity, which would directly influence the abbey's ongoing construction and reform programmes for centuries to come. This recovery was made possible by the stability reintroduced in the post-Saracen world, an enjoyment or returning of peace that the Volturno chronicler defined

---

61 *Chron. Cas.*, II. 1, p. 166.
62 On the question of disputed land ownership in the *Terra sancti Benedicti*, monastic return, and legal culture, see Whitten, 'Quasi ex uno ore'.
63 Fabiani, *La Terra di S. Benedetto*, I, p. 47.
64 *Chron. Cas.*, II. 2, p. 171.
65 Ibid.; *Registrum Petri Diaconi*, no. 153 (fol. 69r), p. 464.
66 Anonymous, *Abt Aligern*, no. 121, pp. 344–345. See also Bloch, 'Monte Cassino's Teachers and Library', pp. 574, 603–604.
67 *Chron. Cas.*, II. 3, pp. 171–172.

by 'all the churches of the villages being full', and 'no fear or apprehension of war'; in other words, the 'cessation of devastation'.[68]

By the eleventh century, Monte Cassino had reclaimed its 'worldwide prestige'.[69] This status is attributed to a number of intersecting factors, the Byzantine connection in southern Italy being strong among them. Yet by the early 1020s, Byzantine rule on the peninsula ended with the intervention of Emperor Henry II of Germany. This new relationship with the Salian dynasty drew the abbey of Monte Cassino closer to imperial (German) rule. The election of Theobald as abbot in 1022, for example, resulted entirely from Henry's intervention; the monk-elect was the emperor's own nomination, a candidate that he could trust 'to safeguard the imperial interests in the abbey against Capua and Byzantium'.[70] The former abbot, John II, preferred by many, was passed over on account of his advanced age. Not all the monks agreed with Henry's role in the election process, but ultimately a vote saw the older and higher-ranking monks approve the choice.[71]

Yet imperial intervention did not stifle the abbey. Compromises were certainly made. The emperor proceeded to shower Monte Cassino with various gifts, in veneration for Saint Benedict. With such high patronage and protection, Monte Cassino once again entered a period of relative peace as well as financial and political stability. As we saw in the previous chapter, these were the favourable conditions into which Desiderius assumed the abbacy. His tireless devotion to the abbey's restoration, renovation, and artistic/intellectual aggrandisement more than explains his attribution in the *Chronicon* as Monte Cassino's 'fourth founder'. Yet he was certainly not the last. As the remainder of this chapter suggests, two more names can be added to the more common list of 'restorers and renovators', 'founders and builders'[72]; one belongs to the fourteenth century, while the second comes from the more recent events of the twentieth.

Two Birds

The great earthquake of 1349 shattered Monte Cassino's peace and prosperity. Striking the entire Latium-Abruzzi-Molise-Campania region during the

---

68   *Chronicon Vulturnense*, I, p. 231.
69   Bloch, *Monte Cassino*, I, p. 12.
70   Ibid., p. 16. See also Loud, *Church and Society*, pp. 29–30.
71   *Chron. Cas.*, II. 42, pp. 245–247.
72   Ibid., III. Prologus, p. 362.

hours of Mass, no building remained standing. The whole Kingdom of Naples was affected. The abbey, many surrounding villages and homes, were completely destroyed by its magnitude. Numerous casualties lay buried beneath the rubble. Once again, the surviving monks of this religious community found themselves at the beginning of a long and gruelling road to recovery.

The physical process of rebuilding was overwhelming. Yet for the historical narrative of Monte Cassino, this episode of natural destruction represents another temporary hiatus from the mountain top. It did not obliterate the religious significance or symbolism of the 'towering mountain', whose connection to Saint Benedict and his monastic *Rule* remained strong. Nor did it diminish the saint's importance. But it certainly contributed to a period of instability in the religious community, by virtue of destroying its primary place of worship. In order to resume devotional practice and realise the congregation's full-scale return to the mountain, the Cassinese community was at the mercy of external benefactors and the political whims of the time. Just like previous examples, the abbey was not rebuilt by the monks alone.

Fortunately for the community, there were many willing helpers in this time of crisis. Angelo II della Posta (1357–1362) – known as 'reformator et reparator monasterii Casinensis'[73] – rebuilt the abbey's dormitory and refectory 'as quickly as possible'.[74] This achievement naturally provided the monks of Cassino a place to live, eat, sleep, and worship. Before his efforts were realised, the abbot-bishops of Monte Cassino – Guiglielmo II of Rosières (1346–1353), Francesco d'Atti (1353–1355), and Angelo I Acciaiuoli (1355–1357) – had managed only to recover some of its lost assets.[75] Their vision for the abbey's recovery was overshadowed by one figure in particular. The greatest restoration work in the post-earthquake era must be attributed to Pope Urban V (1362–1370), the former abbot of Saint-Victor at Marseilles and Monte Cassino's unofficial 'fifth founder'.

Urban V has rightfully earned his reputation for restoring the abbey to its former glory.[76] It was through his initiative 'that the work of recon-

---

73 Gattola, *Ad historiam*, I, p. 853; Gattola, *Historia abbatiae*, II, p. 508.
74 Leccisotti, *Monte Cassino*, p. 69.
75 Dell'Omo, *Montecassino*, p. 59.
76 See Baluze, *Vitae papae Avenionensium*, vol. 1, p. 737: 'Memoratus etiam Urbanus papa, anno [MCCC]LXX currente, volens quod in monasterio Cassinensi, in quo, ut supra memoratum est, religio monachorum nigrorum, ex institutione et ordinatione beati Benedicti suum quasi sumpsit exordium, vigeret precipue, essentque religiosi in ipso vitam exemplarem ducentes, quemadmodum alias extiterant; postquam de episcopali dignitate ipsum ad abbatialem reduxit, tria fecit. Primo, quia erat quasi col[l]apsum in edificiis, que propter terre motum erant pro

13. Portrait of Pope Urban V, by Henri Auguste César Serrur (1794–1865).

struction was resumed in earnest when he personally took charge of the abbey in the summer of 1365'.[77] In truth, his efforts really began a few years

---

majori parte diruta, ipsum fecit reparari et reedificari, et in hoc voluit exponi proventus ipsius, quamdiu vacavit. Secundo, advocavitet collegit monachosreligiosos et devotos de diversis aliis monasteriis in quibus sciebat vitam monasticam melius et strictius observari, quos ibidem instituit, et ordinavit perpetuo residere, amotis abinde pluribus vagabundis et insolentibus qui vitam secularem potius quam regularem erant ibisoliti observare. Tertio, deliberavit eidem in abbatem preficere aliquem, qui, juxta regulam prefati beati Benedicti vivens, ad sic vivendum prefatos monachos suo exemplo alliceret et etiam compelleret, ubi ad contrarium eos inclinatos inveniret.'

77   Bloch, *Monte Cassino*, I, p. 483.

prior, shortly after becoming pope. Writing from Avignon, he noted in 1363 (28 May) how the ancient monastery was completely destroyed and the community disrupted by an earthquake.[78] Lamenting the state of affairs in 1365 (writing from Benevento this time), Urban commented further on the temporal state of the church, its refectory, *claustrum*, and other buildings, which he contended were already in a miserable condition at the time of the natural disaster. In addition to rebuilding the monastery from scratch, therefore, the pope was proposing a spiritual reform of the monastic life at Monte Cassino, which he deemed a necessary first step towards its material remedy and reparation.[79] The opportunity for rebuilding the abbey presented the opportunity for internal reform – two birds with one stone. A similar sentiment was expressed on 20 November 1366, when the pope emphasised once again the necessary reparations towards reinstating the pastoral care, devotional offices, and the abbey's buildings.[80]

The extent of Urban's grief is conveyed in his papal bull *Monasterium Cassinense* (15 February 1369).[81] In it, he expressed his disbelief that the church and the monastery had been left in a state of disrepair for 20 years, noting once again the dismal state of internal (religious) and temporal (external or material) affairs, which barely permitted the monastic observance in accordance with Benedict's *Rule*. To fix the problem, he ordered that all Benedictine monasteries contribute one-sixtieth of their revenue (*sexagesimam omnium fructuum*) to the abbey's restoration.

With this mandate, the pope invoked the ancient, celebrated abbey, which he considered as 'the prototype, even materially', of the Western monastic tradition. In this way, 'almost like a canon and a model in the life of the Church, it must be preserved and defended from tampering'.[82] Urban tackled the problem of external influence by abolishing the episcopal see, reserving 'for himself for several years not only the title but also, in the true sense of the word, the office of Abbot of Monte Cassino'.[83] This reorganisation of internal administrative structures complemented his wider

---

78 *Documenti Vaticani*, no. 3, p. 54: 'propter ipsius vetustatem et terremotus totaliter dirupta et destructa existat eiusque reparatio iam inchoata opere non modico sumptuoso sine fidelium auxilio perfici et consummari non possit.'
79 Dell'Omo, *Montecassino Medievale*, pp. 127–230; *Documenti Vaticani*, no. 7, p. 59. See also Pantoni, 'Descrizioni di Montecassino', p. 544.
80 Gattola, *Historia abbatiae*, II, pp. 509–510. See also Picozzi, 'Gli abati commendatari', pp. 118–119.
81 Ibid., pp. 520–522. Printed also in *Documenti Vaticani*, p. 27.
82 *Documenti Vaticani*, p. 28.
83 Leccisotti, *Monte Cassino*, p. 70.

initiatives for spiritual reform. The pope's message was repeated in a flurry of correspondence from Montefiascone between May to August 1370.[84] In a bull issued on 10 May 1370, Urban promised yet again to restore the abbey to its pristine condition, populating it with a hundred monks.[85] Writing to Abbot Andrea I of Faenza (1369–1373) on 17 August, he promised to send a further 40 monks to assist with bolstering the abbey's regular observance.[86]

By the time that Pietro IV of Tartaris (1374–1395) was elected abbot, Urban's rebuilding programme had already achieved significant results. For his zeal and determination, the pope 'remains in the history of Cassino as that of one of the most strenuous defenders of the legacy of St. Benedict, whose survival he made possible'.[87]

It would be wrong, however, to characterise the abbey as flourishing in the first century following the earthquake. Historians describe the fourteenth and fifteenth centuries as a 'crisis of the modern age',[88] a statement referencing its period of *commenda* (1454–1504), which reoriented its political-institutional-administration focus. By this epoch's end, as we've seen, the abbey was thrust into the middle of a succession dispute over the Kingdom of Naples. Yet, even as it wrestled back control of its lands, Monte Cassino continued to benefit from the generosity of its patrons, and a steady flow of pilgrims and prominent visitors.

Thus began 'a long period of calm and peaceful prosperity'[89] at Monte Cassino. Leccisotti defined this period of 'vigorous recovery' as 'one of the most notable periods in the life of Monte Cassino'.[90] With more attention devoted to the restoration of buildings, and the reestablishment of payments and patrimony, the monks began dedicating themselves 'fearlessly and with renewed zeal to their own religious lives and to peaceful pursuits'.[91]

---

84 *Documenti Vaticani*, nos 44–59, pp. 103–120.
85 *Monasterium Casinense*, 1370, maggio 10, in Leccisotti, 'Montecassino agli inizi', p. 76: 'Nos igitur, qui dictam regulam fuimus a nostra iuventute professi [...] merito reputantes indignum, quod tam celebre monasterium, quod aliorum fuit inicium ac forma, sic dirutum et desolatum non absque quadam monachorum professorum regulae dicti Sancti verecundiae nota remaneat, et unde monasticae sanctitatis regulae praefatae primordium, et constructionis aliorum monasteriorum forma processit [...] praefatam ecclesiam et monasterium super suis fundamentis, quae illesa consistunt [...] providimus in statum pristinum reparanda, et reintegrandum ibidem numerum centum monachorum.'
86 *Documenti Vaticani*, no. 59, p. 120.
87 Ibid., p. 47.
88 Titular reference from Dell'Omo, *Montecassino nel Quattrocento*.
89 Leccisotti, *Monte Cassino*, p. 79.
90 Ibid.
91 Ibid.

This decorative fervour, which began with Abbot Ignazio Squarcialupi (1510–1516, 1520–1521, 1524–1526) and perpetuated under Abbot Angelo de Faggis (1559–1564), culminated in Pope Benedict XIII's consecration of its main church (begun almost a century earlier and completed in the Neapolitan style from the designs of Cosimo Fansaga) on 19 May 1727.[92] In one of the illuminated choir books commissioned during the abbot's rule, Monte Cassino was compared to 'flowers in spring': its soul was 'rising again with Christ', its small ship 'conquered the waves of the times and gave new wings to hope'.[93]

The following two centuries evoke a similar and continuous state of progress. Pilgrimage traffic increased, especially in the Holy Years of 1600, 1625, and 1650; the abbey reacquired its criminal jurisdiction, which it had lost in the fifteenth century; the building work initiated in the sixteenth century continued apace into the eighteenth century.[94] Visitors well into the twentieth century marvelled at its grandeur and eloquence, virtues characterised by its decorative features from the Beuron school; its Doric arcades and ancient columns dating to the eleventh century; its Desiderian bronze doors; its decadent plasterwork, woodwork, gilding, inlaid marble, Florentine mosaics; and its monuments/tombs of figures such as Pietro di Medici.[95] The eighteenth-century archivist of Monte Cassino, Erasmo Gattola, has preserved some priceless images in his history of the abbey. This architectonic, architectural, and artistic footprint from the post-earthquake years remained more or less intact until that fateful morning in February 1944, when 'four groups of stately Flying Fortresses passed directly overhead and a few moments later released their bombs on Monastery Hill'.[96]

A Mass of Ruins

The destructive fury of the Second World War is not difficult to imagine. In fact, there is much to help us remember. The war's devastating effects on the abbey of Monte Cassino in particular are well-documented in contemporary photographs, black-and-white videos, newspapers, diary/journal entries,

---

92 For a good summary of architectural developments in this period, see Cigola, 'L'Abbazia di Montecassino', esp. pp. 45–46. See also Cigola, *L'Abbazia Benedettina*, esp. pp. 75–93; Fratadocchi, *La ricostruzione*, pp. 25–36.
93 Minozzi, *Montecassino*, p. 52.
94 For architectonic argument, see Giovannoni, 'Rilievi ed opere'.
95 Cigola, *L'Abbazia Benedettina*, pp. 27–50.
96 Clark, *Calculated Risk*, p. 319.

14. Bombing of Cassino Monastery and town, May 1944, by Peter McIntyre. Oils on canvas. Archway Archives (New Zealand, Wellington Office), R22504008.

memoirs, magazines, military and other official reports, and first-hand histories from a number of different perspectives.[97] 'What squalor!', wrote Leccisotti, the abbey's famed historian and archivist. 'This destruction was the last in order of time,' he continued, 'but certainly the first for the intensity and extent of its violence. This time, the objective had been more important, the instruments of destruction more powerful and the will to carry it out more determined'.[98] The outcome was the near annihilation of the ancient Benedictine abbey, which in one fell swoop was reduced to a pile of rubble.

Monte Cassino was almost unrecognisable in the aftermath. 'From the devastated plain,' continued Leccisotti's contemporaneous record,

> where all former lush vegetation had disappeared, to the torn-up summit, the abbey offered a stark sight of its present condition. In the place where the monumental, solemn cloister had once been, one could now see vast and deep chasms, running down to the underlying wells.[99]

In short, 'there were few things that could even be clearly distinguished' amidst the 'mass of ruins where everything was reduced to shapeless rubble and dusty debris'.[100] The luminescence of Monte Cassino was cast violently

---

97 See, for example, the film collection at https://www.archivioluce.com.
98 Leccisotti, *Monte Cassino*, p. 145.
99 Ibid., pp. 145–146.
100 Ibid., p. 146.

into the 'shadows of death'; 'gleams of light', however, 'began to appear in the darkness'.[101]

Three days after the aerial attack, Cardinal Ildefonso Schuster (archbishop of Milan) expressed his grief to the abbot and his community. As Mariano Dell'Omo has recently shown, the archbishop's fondness for Monte Cassino dates to the late 1920s, well before the outbreak of war.[102] His impression of the abbey, and friendships formed with its abbots, contributed in no small part to its material reconstruction and spiritual reform decades later.[103] Schuster believed 'in God and resurrection', equating the abbey's first destruction and subsequent recovery with the current state of affairs in the twentieth century; just as Monte Cassino was resurrected after the Lombard sack in the sixth century, 'so it will be again this time',[104] he wrote. When the future abbot, Ildefenso Rea (then abbot at SS. Trinità di Cava), visited the fresh ruins in late May 1944, he was rendered 'almost dazed' by the sight. 'Almost nothing remained of the ancient abbey,' he stated. '[O]nly very little was still standing.'[105]

Efforts to revive the 'weak spark'[106] of Monte Cassino soon followed. The dangers of malaria did not prevent a small group of monks from gathering in the crypt in order to resume devotional work and prayer. There they remained for the next year or so, practicing the liturgy over the tomb of Saints Benedict and Scholastica, which had miraculously escaped destruction. (A bomb had fallen mere yards away but failed to explode.[107]) German prisoners of war were enlisted in clearing the extensive rubble; Italian and Polish soldiers provided logistical assistance, communications, and security; the Italian Corps of Engineers helped to restore a water supply and road access, and eventually electricity. The monks also did as much as they could, clearing more than 900,000 cubic yards of rubble.[108] According to a monk who survived the attack, interviewed 40 years later, 'we began to recover what we could from the rubble. [...] Until 1948, we did only that'.[109]

Clearing the remnants of destruction was only the first step. A more strategic and organised approach was soon constructed to help realise the

---

101 Ibid., p. 148.
102 *Ildefenso Schuster-Ildefonso Rea*, pp. 39–53.
103 Ibid., pp. 52–55.
104 Cardinal Ildefonso Schuster, in *Il Bombardamento di Montecassino*, p. 195.
105 Ibid., p. 198.
106 Leccisotti, *Monte Cassino*, p. 147.
107 According to Archbishop Guido Maggiori, in Avagliano, 'Montecassino "com'era e dov'era"', appendix III, p. 157.
108 Kamm, '40 Years Later', p. 2.
109 Ibid.

objectives. Under Abbot Gregorio Diamare's leadership, a *commissione ministeriale* was established with the Minister for Public Works, Meuccio Ruini, 'to study a general plan for the reconstruction of the abbey of Monte Cassino and to determine the directives to follow in its realisation'. By his 'wise and vigorous hand',[110] it was later claimed, he sought to re-establish the vision outlined by Alfanus of Salerno, who immortalised the 'venerable mountain' as the 'new Sion' that guides all faithful.[111] And so, 'with a significant gesture, it was decided to make Monte Cassino, a symbol of Italian life, the first step in the great task of national reconstruction'.[112]

Progress was slow at first. One year after its destruction (15 March 1945), the abbey's first official stone was laid by Italy's Prime Minister, Ivanoe Bonomi. The occasion was marked by the presence of eight ministers, undersecretaries, ambassadors, and the president of the Vatican's 'Pontifical Commission for Sacred Art', His Excellency (Monsignor) Giovanni Constantini.[113] A small structure was then built on the site, in order to provide more suitable accommodations for the monks. In the meantime, until this small abode's completion and consecration (dedicated to Saint Joseph) on 19 March 1946, some of the remaining monks established a residence at Casalucense so that they might observe more fully the Benedictine *Rule*; the abbot remained in Rome at Sant'Anselmo, while the other displaced monks were accommodated at San Paolo Fuori le Mura, Farfa, Perugia, and Assisi.

A second phase of construction followed under the newly elected abbot of Monte Cassino, Ildefonso Rea (1945–1971).[114] In an oft-cited statement, he pleaded on 18 January 1946 (in a letter to Cardinal Ildefonso Schuster) for the abbey's reconstruction "as it was, where it was" (*dov'era, com'era*).[115] This now famous motto invokes his belief in a long and important tradition, a continuity of heritage, history, and architecture grounded in Benedict's original foundation. It is a modern, mid-twentieth-century expression of the abbey's unchanging identity; a bold statement on the infallibility of the

---

110 Lentini, 'Montecassino tra rovina e risurrezione'.
111 Alfanus of Salerno, *I carmi*, 32, p. 173; see also *I carmi*, 15, p. 139.
112 Leccisotti, *Monte Cassino*, p. 149. See also Lentini, 'Montecassino tra rovina e risurrezione'. On the committee's origins, see Fratadocchi, *La ricostruzione*, pp. 61–62.
113 For fuller details on the committee's organisation, see Fratadocchi, *La ricostruzione*, p. 57.
114 On Rea's character, vision, and achievements, see especially D'Onorio, 'L'Abate Rea e la ricostruzione', p. 6.
115 'Costituzione dei Comitati', p. 5; *Ildefonso Schuster – Ildefonso Rea*, no. 109, p. 169. See also Fratadocchi, *La ricostruzione*, p. 63, and Avagliano, 'Montecassino "com'era e dov'era"', p. 141; Lentini, 'Montecassino tra rovina e risurrezione'.

idea of Monte Cassino, which had weathered numerous storms before this one. In short: a call to arms for a universal and swift recovery, which in some respects defied the realities of the post-war European theatre.

This project signified more than just a material restoration of buildings. According to Leccisotti, Abbot Rea – acting also as the head of the *commissione ministeriale* – aspired to knit together 'traditions that were over a thousand years old'.[116] To Cardinal Schuster (18 January 1946), he asked for his prayers in helping him 'gather the missing of Israel and reconstitute this spiritual organism'.[117] Over the radio on 15 February 1946, he explained his hope that Monte Cassino would rise again 'as an expiatory monument of the devastating violence of war, a temple of peace, from which St Benedict once again would launch his appeal, his motto for future generations: Peace...!'[118] This vision for the abbey was echoed the following year in Pope Pius XII's encyclical *Fulgens Radiatur* (1947), in which its long and continuous history was forcefully repeated and invoked (see Chapter 6). As the abbot mentioned in a letter to Cardinal Schuster (31 March 1952), he firmly believed that the 'resurrection' of Benedict's house (*sua casa*) was entirely the saint's own doing.[119]

But the abbey was not rebuilt on rhetoric alone. The planimetric and altimetric relief plans of the Cassinese monk Angelo Pantoni, an architect by trade, were invaluable to restoring the abbey's architectonic footprint as faithfully as possible.[120] A copy of these plans was deposited at Rome in 1939; their preservation, a matter of good timing and fortune, was heralded as one of the abbey's many miracles of war.[121] Because the Italian suppression act of 1868 rendered the abbey state property – but more so because of the state's recent law on the protection of cultural property ('Leggi Bottai', no. 1089, 1 June 1939) – the Ministry of Public Works (Minestero dei Lavori Publici), first under Undersecretary Gennaro Cassini (then Umberto Tupini (1947–1950) and Salvatore Aldisio (1950–1953)), was entrusted with the restoration work. Under Constantini, the Vatican handled (or oversaw) the budget and planning. But the Ministry of Public Works retained operational control and final spending approval, since the funds for each of the eight

---

116 Leccisotti, *Monte Cassino*, p. 152.
117 *Ildefonso Schuster – Ildefonso Rea*, no. 109, p. 169.
118 Rea, 'Pro Montecassino', p. 4.
119 *Ildefonso Schuster – Ildefonso Rea*, no. 167, p. 232. See also Avagliano, 'Montecassino "com'era e dov'era"', p. 147.
120 For insight into his first-hand and intimate archaeological knowledge of Monte Cassino, see Pantoni, *Le vicende*.
121 Kamm, '40 Years Later', p. 2.

proposed restoration sections (or lots) were provided by the Italian state.¹²² The government was directed in its endeavours by a United Nations General Assembly resolution (no. 28, 2 February 1946)¹²³ which recognised the need for expedient and efficient resources in the work reconstruction in its affected countries. It was strengthened by the new Republic's constitution, which 'promotes cultural development', and 'safeguards natural beauty and the historical and artistic heritage of the nation' (Article 9).

State interests notwithstanding, Pantoni assumed the responsibility for executing the project. He was assisted on his mission by the 'technical competency' and 'artistic sensibility'¹²⁴ of another architect named Giuseppe Breccia Fratadocchi (1898–1955).¹²⁵ Hundreds of specialist craftsmen were employed to repair and reproduce the stone, marble, wood, and iron; a group of young and notable architects from the Roman firm Castelli were engaged in the initial years; the contracting firm of Serafino Gravaldi and Antonio Jacovitti was hired to oversee the logistical operations, while the abbot bore personal responsibility for issuing contracts.¹²⁶ Even the landscape was transformed in the process, with the works executed by the Ministry of Agriculture and Forests.¹²⁷ The mountain of Cassino,

> completely ravaged by the enormous amount of explosives rained on it, was completely restored and given back its green cover by the Ministry of Agriculture and Forests, while the 'land of St. Benedict' once again was dotted with its hundred white churches and ecclesiastical buildings.¹²⁸

The fidelity of reconstruction would have been impossible without the contributions and overall patronage of contemporary artists, societies, government agencies and funds, national banks, and other benefactors, both public and private, secular and ecclesiastical.¹²⁹ Emblematic of postwar national reconstruction efforts, the Italians took the lead with Monte Cassino, despite reported promises of outside financial assistance from the

---

122 For an estimate of costs, see Fratadocchi, *La ricostruzione*, appendix II and IV. For a map of the lots, see p. 81.
123 See United Nations General Assembly, 'Reconstruction of Countries Members'.
124 'Tre anni di ricostruzione', p. 17.
125 See Dell'Omo, '1944–1964', appendix IV, pp. 183–184.
126 Fratadocchi, *La ricostruzione*, p. 58 and p. 85. See also 'Tre anni di ricostruzione', p. 17.
127 'Tre anni di ricostruzione', p. 19.
128 Leccisotti, *Monte Cassino*, pp. 158–159.
129 See, for example, the results of Cardinal Schuster currying favour with the Banco Ambrosiano, in *Ildefonso Schuster – Ildefonso Rea*, no. 123, p. 186.

likes of the American President, Franklin Roosevelt.¹³⁰ In a lengthy footnote on the subject, Leccisotti bitterly remarked that

> no foreign government has contributed to the work of reconstruction, in fact, even the sums collected, directly or indirectly under the name of Monte Cassino, e.g., by the association of the 'Sons of Italy' in the United States of America, have been used for different purposes.¹³¹

Presumably, he is referring to the financial backing that came to the Italian government from the United Nations Reliefs and Rehabilitation Administration. Whatever the case, Leccisotti is overlooking the paltry gift of shoes received from the Americans in 1946. In letter published in *The New York Times* (3 February 1946), the 'vicar general of the ruined abbey', Dom Faustino M. Le Donne, sincerely hoped that 'in the future distributions of clothing and other articles the monks of Montecassino will always be considered'.¹³²

The reconstruction began officially on 24 June 1947, the liturgical feast day of Saint John the Baptist.¹³³ Its success relied on Abbot Rea's fundraising efforts and abilities. Appealing to Benedictine communities and the Catholic world more broadly, he formed a 'Committee of High Patrons' (*alto patronato*) composed of 'very eminent Cardinals, who with the prestige of the Roman purple and with the veneration that they collect in the world, honour and foment the work of reconstruction'.¹³⁴ Among its members were the archbishops of Milan, Naples, Hungary, Toledo, Toronto, and Sydney.¹³⁵ An international sub-committee (*comitato internazionale*), led by the Grand Master of the Sovereign Military Order of Malta, Prince Ludovico Chigi-Albani, combined ecclesiastical and secular forces.¹³⁶ With the support of two other committees (the Comitato Centrale Effettivo and the Comitato Nazionale Italiano), the overall campaign for rebuilding Monte Cassino was publicised through 'the press, conferences, concerts, radio, special holidays, the collection of donations, raffles, the publication of books, etc.'.¹³⁷

---

130 Kamm, '40 Years Later', p. 2. On America's contribution to the rebuild (none), see Rosa, *Montecasino*, pp. 213–219.
131 Leccisotti, *Monte Cassino*, p. 175, no. 5.
132 'Monks Thankful for Aid', p. 7.
133 For details, see 'Tre anni di ricostruzione', pp. 16–19.
134 'Costituzione dei Comitati', p. 5 (no. 1).
135 Ibid., p. 6.
136 Ibid. See also Michel, 'Reconstructing the National Narrative', pp. 264–265.
137 Ibid.

With such legislative, labour, and financial assistance, the abbey was restored over the course of two arduous decades. The archaeological and scientific examinations considered in Chapter 1 form an important part of the recovery process, providing powerful justification for rebuilding the resting place of Monte Cassino's joint-founders, Saints Benedict and Scholastica. The impetus for rebuilding was greater than the desire for the cenobitic life alone; it was driven by the constant observance of religious life, and the symbolism of Monte Cassino as a pathway to heaven and 'a beginning to the reconstruction of Italy'.[138]

To the outside observer, the abbey's reconstruction progress appeared swift. So noted an American reporter who, present when the Polish Army captured 'Monastery Hill' in May 1944, returned for a reappraisal of the battle site in June 1949. At the time of its initial destruction, this man was surprised to witness 'how much of the Abbey had survived the persistent forty of our bombardments'.[139] Walls were still standing, two main courtyards appeared unscathed, saintly frescoes remained unharmed on the chapel walls. On his return five years later, however, the entire abbey 'looked already substantially rebuilt, and there are no jagged walls to be seen'.[140] The once treacherous route to the mountain summit, moreover, took only 20 minutes by car, compared with the eight to ten hours of his previous experience. Considered of 'essential importance',[141] the road was improved and widened at various points, providing advantages on the road and panoramic sides.

The mountain top was described as 'one of the busiest scenes in all Italy'. Its plateau was occupied by 'hundreds of labourers and stonemasons' who 'chipped away incessantly with hammer and chisel'.[142] Impressed by the progress of rebuilding, which had 'risen to one story in most parts', the American reporter marvelled at the 'greatest preliminary task' of removing more than 400,000 cubic yards of rubble. The central cloister, formerly 'buried in dust and debris', was nearly complete. The refectory was also finished, as was the framework of the church and the Sanctuary. The cost of reconstruction was estimated at one million British pounds 'for the restoration of the buildings' and five million 'for the artistic work'.[143] More impressive still was the 'infinite patience' with which the workers 'have

138 Ibid., p. 5.
139 Gander, 'Return to the Battlefields', p. 38.
140 Ibid., p. 39.
141 'Tre anni di ricostruzione', p. 18.
142 Ibid.
143 Ibid., p. 40.

delved into the ruins to find pieces of the numerous statues. It is the world's biggest jig-saw puzzle'.[144]

One contemporaneous British traveller offers a similar perspective. Visiting the abbey in the early 1950s, the English travel author Donald Hall was surprised by what he encountered. He noted the constant sounds of buzzing saws, hammers and chisels 'working on stone and the plaintive song of Italian masons made antiphony with the music of Matins from the chapel'.[145] The restoration work had come a long way, but he 'did not believe they could have got very far in rebuilding the pile of rubble left in 1944'.[146] Expecting a 'half-ruin' on his approach, he instead found 'a great façade of honey-coloured stone' that 'rose eyeless 30 feet from the bare rock before a row of windows showed the first floor that was entered from the higher level of the cloisters within, so long was the building that from the archway at one end it seemed to run almost to a point'.[147] Shown the abbey's most precious possession – the bones of Saints Benedict and Scholastica – he was then led into the small reconstructed chapel for Mass, which was overfilled by a congregation of monks and local townspeople.

Amidst the renovation chaos, religious life continued on the venerable mountain. The refectory and cells were more or less complete; pilgrims flocked to the mountain summit to view the sacred bones of Saints Benedict and Scholastica[148]; various anniversaries of the destruction, feast days, dedications, celebrations, and visitations were recorded between 1948 and 1950.[149] The library, moreover, '660 feet long with windows watching space', was entirely reconstructed and fitted with fireproof steel shelves. Although it remained empty for the moment, the pride of Monte Cassino's intellectual heritage was generously assisted by donations to restore its collection from the British Museum, the publisher Blackwell, the Bodleian Library in Oxford, Leeds, the Dean of Winchester, Cambridge, and other organisations. The collection removed in late 1943 before the abbey's destruction – 'some 40,000 parchments, collections of Papal Bulls, diplomas of emperors, kings and princes, together with the capsulae containing hundreds of thousands of paper records had not yet returned from Rome'.[150] Their preservation in the months leading up to the bombing, however, as Julius Schlegel remarked,

144 Ibid.
145 Hall, *Eagle Argent*, p. 16.
146 Ibid., p. 2.
147 Ibid., p. 3.
148 'Pellegrini alle sacre ossa'.
149 'Notiziario di Montecassino'.
150 Hall, *Eagle Argent*, p. 8.

played into the idea that its cultural heart would be restored, that it would once again become a 'monument to peace'.[151]

The basilica too was nearing the end of its construction. Though it would never rival Desiderius's original work from the eleventh century, the objective was to rebuild and decorate it according to its seventeenth-century predecessor. Piles of rubble had been replaced with coloured marble and ornate decorations. 'Staring at it,' observed Hall, 'I was awed only by its fabulous costs, and disturbed by such expensive ugliness in a world of want.' It might have been the intention, he continued, 'to preserve a sense of continuity, by presenting everything as though it had never been destroyed'.[152] This observation illustrates precisely the central intention underlying post-war reconstruction: to resuscitate a crumbled heritage by restoring the abbey to its former glory, 'as it was, where it was'.

This particular rebirth was the last in a long chain of destructive fury. Restoration was officially completed in 1964, 20 years after the Allied bombing. Elaborate plans were soon put in place to mark the occasion; the ceremony was an event of significant public standing.[153] On the one hand, it signalled the return of peace to the abbey, but also within Italy more generally. 'Here,' Pope Paul VI said in his homily, 'peace appears equally real and alive, here it appears active and fertile to us. Here its capability, extremely interesting, to reconstruct, to be reborn, to regenerate is revealed.' 'These walls speak,' he continued.

> It is peace that made them revive. It still seems incredible that the war acted against this Abbey, incomparable monument of religion, culture, art, civility, one of the proudest and blindest gesture of its fury, so we can't believe it is true when today we see this magnificent building revived, almost wanting to pretend that nothing happened, that its destruction was a dream and we can forget the tragedy that had made a pile of ruins. Brothers, let us cry with emotion and gratitude. [...] [W]e cannot not deplore that civil men had the boldness to use Saint Benedict's grave as a target of atrocious violence. And we cannot contain our joy seeing today that the ruins have disappeared, that the holy walls of this Church have arisen, that the austere building of the ancient monastery has a new image. God bless the Lord!'[154]

---

151 Schlegel, in *Il Bombardamento di Montecassino*, p. 237.
152 Hall, *Eagle Argent*, p. 11.
153 For some interesting details about the day's schedule, programme, and attendees, see *L'Osservatore Romano*, 25 October 1964, pp. 1–3.
154 Pope Paul VI, 'Consecrazione della chiesa'.

On the other (but related) hand, the consecration represented a significant spiritual renewal.

> [It] marks not only another victory of life over death, but if confers a divine chrism to this new resurrection, the sigh of that hand 'which destroys and revives, which brings pain and consoles'. It is, once more, the charismatic recognition of the validity and vitality of the work of Benedict.[155]

Marking the culmination of its revival, the pope concluded with an expression of gratitude 'to those who merit in this huge reconstruction'. In particular, he extended his compliments to 'the abbot, his collaborators, to the benefactors, to the technicians, to the labourers and workmen'. A 'special acknowledgement' was also granted to 'the Italian Authorities, who took care of means and implementation when needed, so that peace would triumph over war'.[156]

'In this way,' Paul VI concluded, Monte Cassino

> has become the trophy of all the hard work done by the Italian people for the reconstruction of this beloved town, torn to pieces from one end to the other, and immediately revived in a more beautiful and modern way by divine assistance and the virtue of its inhabitants.[157]

With these words, the abbey becomes almost immortal, representing far more than a material object. Destruction and its aftermath are vivid expressions its cultural, political, and religious identity – how it views itself and, in turn, is viewed by others. 'Where before there was nothing but a mountain of ruins and rubble,' wrote one soldier-cum-historian,

> the walls and roofs of the immortal House of St Benedict have today been resurrected. Unbroken in spirit and full of courage, the Benedictines have rebuilt their monastery; fresh branches are growing from the evergreen tree-trunk that is the ancient symbol of Monte Cassino, and once more the time-honoured motto resumes its age-old significance: *Succisa virescit!*[158]

*

---

155 Leccisotti, *Monte Cassino*, p. 172.
156 Pope Paul VI, 'Consecrazione della chiesa'.
157 Ibid.
158 Böhmler, *Monte Cassino*, p. 182.

This twentieth-century revival was by no means a *fait accompli*. As the third and final section of this book demonstrates, its success harks back to earlier achievements in promoting the abbey's reputation, historical significance, and cultural value to an increasingly international audience. The state of the abbey in the twenty-first century speaks to the overall success of this initiative, whose processes began in earnest during the late nineteenth.

Before this historical era, rebuilding and reconstituting the abbey was seemingly taken for granted – a process of reconstruction that inevitably followed its destruction. Well-versed in recovery efforts since the early Middle Ages, the monks of Monte Cassino followed a recognisable pattern for reanimating their abbey, striving on every occasion to re-establish their severed connection to Saint Benedict and the 'towering mountain' on which his community was founded – a dislocation caused almost entirely by external (human) interference.

As the final two chapters of this book demonstrate, however, the stimulus for recovery was not exclusively determined by the religious community. Interrogating this reality in the nineteenth and twentieth centuries explains the abbey's inherent identity and tradition, effectively substantiating its coherence, meaning, and value in the modern ecclesiastical and secular world.

Part III

Preservation and Valorisation

5. The People's Patrimony: Defining Historical Value

Abstract

In the contemporary world of nineteenth- and twentieth-century politics, Monte Cassino's patrimony passed from the monks of the abbey to the sovereign nation state; as ideological claims over the abbey's (universal) heritage became more pronounced with the threat of imminent disaster, however, its heirs became the wider world. Recognition of its value became formalised as external interest in its preservation increased; as an object deemed worthy of protection, the abbey came to signify not only a united Europe, but an emblem of Western civilisation. This chapter traces the development of this idea, paying particular attention to its emergence and uniqueness in the nineteenth and twentieth centuries. It argues for Monte Cassino's role in this era as an etic symbol of continuity capable of transcending national and international borders – an order of ideas whose interrogation reveals a process of consecration and institutionalisation.

Keywords: patrimony; unification; Gladstone; Tosti; preservation; protection; veneration; historic monuments

'History is European. [...] [I]t is quite unintelligible if treated as merely local.'[1]

On 31 July 1866, Mr John Hubbard rose in the House of Commons to address 'certain circumstances relating to the great Benedictine monastery of Monte Cassino'. He was concerned, first and foremost, with the preservation of this distinguished seat of learning. Its monks 'were not what we supposed the inhabitants of convents generally to be'; they 'were men of family, education, and independence', he said, 'who in their retirement guarded literary

---

1 Morley, *Life of Gladstone*, I, p. 164.

treasures of great value, and whose learning had been of advantage to the whole of Europe'.[2] Moreover, they 'had taken a warm interest in the progress of Italy', whose government had recently issued a 'statute for the suppression of Ecclesiastical Corporations'. The House wished to gather more information on the matter, to discern whether the Italian government might make an exception to the law of suppression, or to find out whether institutions like Monte Cassino might be preserved without violating the sovereign decree.

The cause for concern was not merely political. Religious institutions like Monte Cassino were centuries old and distinguished. As such, it was asked, have they not 'acquired the sympathy and respect of the civilized world?' The answer from within the House was a resounding 'yes'. Sir George Bowyer added that the question was 'one interesting to civilization and science, and apart from all religious, political, and party feeling', he continued, 'he would press upon the Italian government not to destroy so ancient and influential a seat of learning as that referred to'. To do so, he intimated, would be an absolute 'disgrace to the civilisation of Europe as that which it was feared was contemplated'.

The House was in full agreement. Her Majesty's Government should use its influence to prevent such a tragedy. Obviously, as Mr Charles Newdegate said, foreign intervention must be careful not to interfere with Italy's internal affairs. It was hard for him to imagine that the Italian government 'was so lost to the traditions of its own people as to be guilty of anything like the destruction or desertion of its own monuments of art or literature'. He suspected that British interference in these affairs would be tantamount to insult. After all, who better and more competent to judge the matter than the government of King Victor Emmanuel, whose experience with the monastic orders surely outranked that of the English?

The question of foreign interference was quickly laid to rest. The political dangers of meddling in the affairs of other states were self-evident. No governmental imposition was imagined or condoned. Mr Beresford Hope rather simplified the question to one of diplomatic influence: 'to prevent the destruction of those beautiful monuments of art such as Monte Cassino by the Italian Government'. The House was once again in full agreement: the abbey was worth preserving.

Lord Stanley then presented the strongest evidence. To his knowledge, based on the known communication of his predecessor, the Earl of Clarendon (acting as the British plenipotentiary and foreign secretary), the issue had already been raised with the Italian government. The latter, he was

---

2   Hansard, HC Deb, 31 July 1866, vol. 184, c. 1841.

informed, was powerless to modify the law passed by the Italian parliament, though discretionary power allowed for the preservation of Monte Cassino's library and 'monuments of antiquity' in its possession. But the gist of the communiqué was clear enough: Her Majesty's Government 'ought not to further interfere'.

Fortunately for the history of Monte Cassino, Mr William Gladstone – then Chancellor of the Exchequer – objected. The preservation of this great abbey, the future Prime Minister contended, was 'a matter which went far beyond the limits of Italy, and one in which other countries were greatly interested'. His argument cut through the diplomatic pretensions of modern nation states to the significance of historical precedence and cultural responsibility. To him, the matter was of universal concern, regardless of political, religious, or national affiliation. 'When Monte Cassino and other similar institutions were first founded,' he said,

> Italy was just beginning to abdicate her position of supremacy of the civilised world, and in fact it was the mother of civilisation, by which all had been nurtured and enriched, and therefore we had almost the same interest in what took place in connection with the institution as the people of Italy had.

Gladstone's message was concise and clear. The entire House agreed to his motion for a liberal interpretation of the provision, which would 'preserve the library, archives, and monuments of the institution of Monte Cassino and other similar institutions in Italy'. This political action represents a culture of preservation on the cusp of legal articulation. It demonstrates an international level of commitment to protecting ancient monuments – their material and cultural property – which became adopted by many nation states in the late nineteenth and early twentieth centuries. It introduces the notion that history is universal and democratic; that it belongs to the people; and that its value profited from an age of increasing historical consciousness.

That Monte Cassino needed saving was not implicit. It was a question subject to intense scrutiny and public debate; it required a certain validation, which in turn contributed to the abbey's growth as an international cultural symbol. In the contemporary world of nineteenth- and twentieth-century politics, Monte Cassino's patrimony passed from the monks of the abbey to the sovereign nation state; as ideological claims over the abbey's (universal) heritage became more pronounced with the threat of imminent disaster, however, its heirs became the wider world. Recognition of its value, it will be argued, became formalised as external interest in its preservation increased;

as an object deemed worthy of protection, the abbey came to signify not only a united Europe, but an emblem of Western civilisation. This chapter traces the development of this idea, paying particular attention to its emergence and uniqueness in the nineteenth and twentieth centuries. It argues for Monte Cassino's role in this era as an etic symbol of continuity capable of transcending national and international borders – an order of ideas whose interrogation reveals a process of consecration and institutionalisation.

Between Religion and Civilisation

The background to the above British motion concerns Italian reunification. It signifies a much deeper relationship between two nations, formed well before the Italian kingdom of early 1861. The 'Italian Question' had long occupied the British government; its sympathies for Italian independence and nationalism were rigorously debated within Parliament, as a matter of foreign policy concerning the great concert of European powers (France, Austria, Piedmont, and the Papal States). The outcome, contemporaries argued, mattered a great deal not just to England, but to Europe and the world more broadly. Indeed, in a lengthy letter to the Earl of Aberdeen, William Gladstone treated the 'laudable sentiments of national independence' as inseparable from the 'sacred purposes of humanity'.[3] In this public tract, which earned him both praise and criticism at home and abroad, he labelled the Neapolitan government 'an outrage on religion, upon civilisation, upon humanity, and upon decency'.[4] The 'miseries of Italy', he argued in Parliament ten years later, 'have been the danger of Europe'. 'The consolidation of Italy,' he strongly believed, 'her restoration to national life [...] will add to the general peace and welfare of the civilised world a new and solid guarantee'.[5]

An advocate for Italian unification, Gladstone's political philosophy had been evolving since his travels to the peninsula in the 1830s.[6] As he told John Morley towards the end of his life: 'I was brought up to dislike and distrust liberty; I learned to believe in it. That is the key to all my

---

3   Gladstone, *Two Letters*, p. 41.
4   Gladstone, *Gleanings of Past Years*, IV, p. 3.
5   Hansard, HC Deb, 7 March 1861, vol. 161, c. 1579.
6   For a good contemporary summary of his beliefs, see 'Mr Gladstone on Italy', and also see Gladstone, 'Italy in 1888–89'. More modern appraisals are: Schreuder, 'Gladstone and Italian Unification', pp. 475–501; Dickens, 'William Gladstone'.

changes.'[7] Fearing revolution and its negative consequences, he fought tirelessly to preserve liberty, law, and social justice in an ordered civil society, views famously expressed through the publication of his letters to Lord Aberdeen in 1851,[8] and in his *An Examination of the Official Reply of the Neapolitan Government* in 1852.[9] The central message of providence and moral improvement is epitomised by his desire 'to harmonise the old with the new conditions of society, and to mitigate the increasing stress of time and change upon what remains of the ancient and venerable fabric of the traditional civilisation of Europe'.[10] The very idea, he contended, 'appertains to the sphere of humanity at large', and therefore deserves 'the consideration of every man who feels a concern of the well-being of his race, in its bearings on that well-being'.[11]

Gladstone's policy of peace through moderation and reform found expression in unification.[12] Yet this constitutional triumph did not end the threat to liberty and freedom, especially as it concerned the Roman Church. As we saw in a previous chapter, Italy's 1866 suppression act (no. 3066) targeted religious institutions that did not perform educational or liturgical functions. Those monasteries that did not provide cure of souls were repossessed by the Italian state and their properties sold for profit. Monte Cassino, receiving something like a special (though not exempt) status, was allowed to continue its operations despite the mandate. Its community of monks was permitted to remain as caretakers within the monastic walls, in recognition of the monastery's exalted historical and cultural status. It was already considered an exemplary model. Yet these privileges notwithstanding, the 'most distinguished members of the celebrated Benedictine convent of Monte Cassino', Gladstone later wrote to the Earl of Aberdeen,

> have for some time been driven from the retreat, to which they had anew given the character of combined peace, piety, and learning. Several of them were in prison [and] [...] others not in actual confinement, but trembling, as a hare trembles, at every whisper of the wind.[13]

7 Morley, *Life of Gladstone*, III, pp. 474–475.
8 Gladstone, *Two Letters*.
9 Gladstone, *An Examination*.
10 Gladstone, *Gleanings of Past Years*, IV, p. 113 (Examination of the Official Reply).
11 Ibid.
12 See especially Schreuder, 'Gladstone and Italian Unification', pp. 500–501; Zumbini, *W.E. Gladstone*.
13 Gladstone, *Two Letters*, p. 57.

Gladstone's political experience shaped his conceptualisation of religion – a position described as 'liberal Catholicism'.[14] In promoting tolerance, private conscience and agency, he became a champion of religious freedom, providentialism, and integrity. For these personal and political reasons, the abbey of Monte Cassino occupied a special place in his defence of liberty and authority. As he argued to Parliament in July 1866, the abbey's preservation was bigger than Italy or Italian politics; it bridged any divide between his own Anglican beliefs and the Catholic beliefs of the Italian (Roman) Church.

This seed of thought was planted on his first visit to Monte Cassino in 1832. It sprouted into a lifelong friendship with the abbey's celebrated historian, Dom Luigi Tosti, which lasted until the late 1890s.[15] In a letter written from London in 1860, the first year of their correspondence, Gladstone recalled his first impressions of the Benedictine house, which he greatly admired. But he also took the opportunity in this letter to invoke God's help in securing Italy's 'ultimate and proper consummation'. To his mind, this is where the famed Italian abbey and its faithful congregation could assist with a much bigger humanitarian cause of the times. 'To you, and to such as you,' he wrote to his good friend, 'we must look as her proper instruments in His hand for restoring the broken concord between Church and country, between religion and civilisation'.[16]

Aware of the changes around them, the monks played a willing part in this mission. They became engaged in an industrious contemplation of their own predicament. 'The work of progress is corruptible,' Tosti warned, 'if not sprinkled by the mystical salt of the religion of the past'. And so, while the 'drama of human civilisation' was unfolding all across Europe, the monks continued to chant the psalmody, 'because the impetus of progress is tempered by the wisdom of the ancients'. In the transformational world of nineteenth-century politics, the presence of Saint Benedict's tomb atop the mountain presented a constant. But even this 'most splendid signal of gathering and rest for the tired Christian generations' was in desperate need of restoration; Tosti actively petitioned to restore the sepulchre and to decorate it with rich arts and materials. (Gladstone willingly contributed some money from his own personal bank account.) In the past, he stated, the pilgrim would visit the tomb of the saints 'to find the way that led to Heaven'. By the second half of the nineteenth century, they paid the saints

14 Butler, *Gladstone*, p. 234.
15 See Leccisotti, 'D. Luigi Tosti'.
16 Cited in Inguanez, 'Lettere di Gladstone', letter 1, p. 163.

15a and 15b. Dom Luigi Tosti (1811–1897) (a) and William Ewart Gladstone (1809–1898) (b).

a visit 'also to remember the journey that our fathers made to pass on to us the treasure of so much civilization'.[17]

Monte Cassino was the guardian of this 'treasure'. As a religious house of significant historical and spiritual credentials, the abbey assumed the responsibility of its survival, as rightful heirs and custodians of a long and rich tradition. This connection between Benedictine observance and the future of humanity was more than mere rhetoric; such a claim emerged shortly after foundation in the sixth century and was perpetuated throughout the Middle Ages.[18] Already in the late eleventh century, Pope Urban II (1088–1099) referred to the abbey as a 'blessing not only for the apostolic see but also for the whole of Italy'.[19] The 'grace of God' and 'the merits of Saint Benedict' were ostensibly critical to his appraisal, demonstrating a belief in the abbey's cultural value that has been reinforced through the centuries.

Such claims found their greatest expression in the nineteenth and twentieth centuries. The imminent threat to Monte Cassino's autonomy in the Risorgimento inspired a series of powerful political defenders. The level of support must have been surprising to the 30 or so monks living

17 Letter to Gladstone, cited in Leccisotti, 'Aspirazioni all'unità dei Cristiani', p. 116.
18 Dell'Omo, *Montecassino Medievale*, p. 60 and pp. 136–139.
19 Pope Urban II, *Epistolae*, no. 245, col. 512.

at the abbey.[20] After the 1866 Italian parliament, Tosti marvelled at the demonstrative concern for its survival among international allies. 'When the news spread through Europe,' he wrote

> a large number of scholars rallied around the abbey, fearing that the policies of the Italian fisc might permanently damage the cause of civilisation and historical studies. There was great commission in the academies of France, England, and Germany, and innumerable pleas were heard to preserve the seat of scholarship, to which for so many centuries travelled the learned men of Europe. The Chancellor of the new German empire manifested this wish to the Italian minister; the French academy expressed similar entreaties, and in England not only scholars, like those of the Archaeological Society, but all those who had read in the history of European civilisation the name of Monte Cassino, pressed the leaders and Parliament with the force of public opinion to open private negotiations with the Italian authorities on behalf of the abbey. And it was joy, indeed, to see how this small piece of Italian soil fired the enthusiasm of so many feared people for its preservation. Among them we gratefully want to remember the names of Gladstone, Clarendon, Stanley, Forbes, Russel, Pertz, Saint Marc Girardin, and Dantier.[21]

The Society of Antiquaries of London (est. 1751) can be added to the list of advocates.[22] Writing to Lord Clarendon, the society's president, Lord Philip Stanthorpe (Viscount Mahon), lamented the loss of antique and august traditions as a consequence of the Italian suppression law. On Monte Cassino, in particular, honoured for so many centuries and 'celebrated by the whole world', he implored governmental intervention (both English and Italian) in preserving the abbey. As justification, Stanthorpe mentioned how 'its fame is spread to every country, and its words penetrated to the ends of the world'. The 'memory of its glorious past' was represented up to the present through a continued tradition of education, archival collection, diocesan administration, liberal sentiment, and generous hospitality, which in turn had spawned immense admiration, benevolence, and respect.[23]

20   Estimate from Iannetta, *Henry W. Longfellow*.
21   Tosti, *La biblioteca dei codici manoscritti*, II, pp. 291–292 (translation in Leccisotti, *Monte Cassino*, p. 99).
22   On the formation of this society, see especially Levine, *Amateur and the Professional*, pp. 49–51.
23   Cited in Tosti, *Storia della badia*, IV, pp. 46–47.

A report of a meeting of the Archaeological Institute in May 1866 sheds light on the level of intervention. Its members were inspired by a letter in the *Daily News* (dated 26 February), written by one of the Masters of Eton College, Mr Oscar Browning. According to the institute's report, published in *The Archaeological Journal*, it claimed the influence of Monte Cassino on 'students of archaeology and all friend of literature, in consequence of the services which it renders to learning, and which it has rendered for 1500 years'. "'If we are saved,'" said a monk to Mr Browning, "'it will be by the public opinion of Europe'".[24] A Florentine contact named Bartholomeo Cini reportedly inquired from the Italian government into the possibility of an exemption, only to learn that no such leniency was possible. He was assured by the Minister of Public Instruction, however, that the 'great services formerly rendered to civilisation by Monte Cassino' would not be forgotten. The 'monument may be preserved', he continued, by 'establishing in it some school or other institution' so that the glory of the Benedictine order could be continued.

The abbey is recognised here as 'an ornament and an honour to Italy'.[25] Yet despite its historic prestige, there was a genuine fear at the time that 'this singularly valuable and meritorious establishment' might be swept away. Summoning its intimate experience with destruction, Tosti defiantly declared that the abbey 'will remain standing [...] as the tree of a shipwrecked vessel' and 'as a sign of a great submersion and of a greater resurrection'.[26]

But further assurances were sought on the international stage, beyond the assumed influence of divine providence and intervention. With the Archaeological Institute's backing, an appeal was launched with a 'sympathising interest on the brave struggles of that highly cultivated people'. Putting aside the general objections to the 'suppression and spoliation of all monastic houses in Italy', the matter of national interests was raised:

> a ground common to all present – to every Englishman, in fact – standing together upon which they might warrantably upraise a loud entreating cry in behalf, if not of the possessions of the Benedictine Order, at least of Monte Cassino, which ought to be now, as much as it had once been, dear to every Englishman.

---

24 The Marquess Camden, 'Proceedings at Meetings of the Archaeological Institute', p. 153.
25 Ibid.
26 Cited in Leccisotti, 'Aspirazioni all'unità dei Cristiani', p. 117.

The speaker (Dr Rock) reminded them of the debt owed to Monte Cassino – the shared heritage imparted on the West from this venerable mountain. He suggested that

> if Monte Cassino did not send forth those devoted men who towards the end of the sixth century brought Christianity, with all its softening, elevating, civilising influences to this, for the most part, then heathenish island, Monte Cassino undoubtedly was the cradle that nursed those masters who taught the self-denying band sent by St. Gregory the Great to evangelise the Anglo-Saxons. Those forefathers of ours soon forsook the rites of Woden for a belief in the Gospel, and, laying aside their superstitious songs, learned to sing the hymns of the Church to the music of Rome, and after the just found notation of her England-loving pontiff. That was not all: our land quickly became fruitful in great and good and holy men, and took and kept a high place for learning, zeal, and civilisation among the nations. Through those same countrymen of ours the ages that have been miscalled dark became, as far as this country was concerned, the ages of learning, progress, and jurisprudence – in fact, of light. Few are the large towns in England in our own days that have not grown out of some Benedictine monastery, around which our fathers had built their houses for instruction and protection, and were taught the various arts that sweeten life. Many were the men who were trained in learning within those cloistered walls; many were the worthies who went forth, like those of old from Monte Cassino, to scatter blessings on their path.[27]

This relationship between past and present was taken as common knowledge; its historic connections were treated with great pride. '[W]e ought not to overlook the fact,' he went on, 'that Monte Cassino was one at least of those fountains which helped to enrich our native land with moral worth, and enable one of her great sons to convert the German race to Christianity, and another to become the restorer of learning all over Gaul'.[28] To Benedict, therefore, 'ought we to be deeply indebted for much that we enjoy in our present civilisation, and that freedom which we so warmly love'.[29] For these reasons, and for the fact that Monte Cassino extended its hospitality to countless English guests over the centuries, the appeal was unanimously supported.

27 The Marquess Camden, 'Proceedings at Meetings of the Archaeological Institute', pp. 153–154.
28 Ibid., pp. 154–155.
29 Ibid., p. 154.

Lord Clarendon responded. Because the matter concerned the internal affairs of a foreign government, as we've already seen, great diplomatic tact was exercised through Her Majesty's Minister at Florence. These representations on behalf of Monte Cassino earned some assurances of its preservation. Declared a national monument by the Italian government, the abbey was spared destruction and received a promise of maintenance from the state. 'The archives, library, and monuments of the Abbey remain intact in the building,' as one of the institute's honorary members wrote, 'and Abbate Tosti will be appointed the *custode*, for the benefit of all scholars'.[30]

Monte Cassino survived the cull, thanks in large part to foreign intervention and developing historical awareness. Though limited in its capacity, religious, educational, and intellectual life nevertheless continued on the venerable mountain. When Henry Wadsworth Longfellow visited the abbey three years later (March 1869), very little appears to have changed. The famed American poet, professor and chair of Romance languages and literature at Harvard University spent one night at Monte Cassino, where he visited the abbey's hallowed archives, and met and conversed with the abbot, the historian (Tosti), and other monks

> [...] late into the night,
> Till in its cavernous chimney the wood-fire
> Had burnt its heart out like an anchorite.

As one of the monks present during his visit later noted, Longfellow's 'admiration and wonder' came to him above all 'from the religious and holy atmosphere of the monastery, from its antiquity, its historical traditions, its multitude of literary and artistic treasures gathered and preserved here from centuries past'.[31] Inspired by the ancient abbey, 'the alma mater of so many Benedictine saints, scholars, and learned laymen, throughout the fourteen long centuries of its beneficent influence upon Latin civilised life and Catholic Christianity',[32] Longfellow composed a poem ('Terra di Lavoro') as testimony to its splendour. Most striking is the poet's ability to capture the peace residing within the abbey's walls, seemingly unperturbed from recent political events, almost unchanged over fourteen disruptive centuries; despite the most recent blow dealt to

---

30 Ibid., p. 300.
31 Iannetta, *Henry W. Longfellow*, pp. 32–33.
32 Ibid., p. 40.

the abbey by the introduction of new legislation limiting its autonomy, there is a timelessness noted by many of its visitors that reflects Monte Cassino's fundamental identity. Waking up in his convent cell, Longfellow wrote, he observed a 'scene'

> On which Saint Benedict so oft had gazed, –
> The mountains and the valley in the sheen
> Of the bright sun, – and stood as one amazed.
>
> Gray mists were rolling, rising, vanishing;
> The woodlands glistened with their jewelled crowns;
> Far off the mellow bells began to ring
> For matins in the half-awakened towns.

The silence which reigned in the abbey is juxtaposed by the 'conflict of the Present and the Past':

> The ideal and the actual in our life,
> As on a field of battle held me fast,
> Where this world and the next world were at strife.
>
> For, as the valley from its sleep awoke,
> I saw the iron horses of the steam
> Toss to the morning air their plumes of smoke,
> And woke, as one awaketh from a dream.[33]

There is a sense in this final poetic verse that the inertia which had long sustained Monte Cassino was nearing its end; that the industrial and commercial achievements, growth, and progress of the world outside the abbey walls were slowly – and inevitably – creeping inside the cloister. Longfellow's poem reads as a harbinger of things to come in the following century; as a snapshot of shared experiences, it also serves to preserve the abbey as it was in the late 1860s. Its narrative captures the beauty, serenity, and history of Monte Cassino in the late nineteenth century, which more than 70 years later would collapse under the destructive fury of modern warfare.

---

33   Longfellow, 'Terra di Lavoro'.

Kultur über alles

'History repeats.'[34] When this adage appeared in a 1944 *New York Times* editorial, it was already a cliché. But its title was still rather poignant under the circumstances. International media coverage on the Battle for Monte Cassino was intensifying; the stakes were high and the human, material, and fiscal investments were waning rapidly. The Allied Forces in southern Italy, with their sights on Rome, were waylaid south of the Gustav Line, struggling to fight their way up (or past) 'Monastery Hill' (see Chapter 3). Concern for its survival amidst constant fighting spurred international outcry to save the abbey from destruction. While many undoubtedly appreciated the abbey's deep historic roots, the paper's readers were reminded that Monte Cassino had faced worse challenges and destruction in its long institutional history.

Concerted efforts were made to avoid another such disaster. But at what cost? There was general agreement on both sides of the Gustav Line that the abbey should be spared. Heated political debates ensued over the priceless cultural, religious, and architectural value attributed to Monte Cassino on the one hand, and the importance of life in besieging and defending it on the other. The mutual desire to preserve the great abbey was balanced alongside the potential loss of life. The wish to preserve the former intact was never meant to sacrifice the latter, though the balance weighed heavily on the minds of those planning and fighting the battle.

The basis of this moral tension was not without precedent. As nineteenth-century British politicians and diplomats debated, the abbey of Monte Cassino was more than just bricks and mortar. It was a reminder of past civilisations, cultures, and peoples; a physical embodiment or specimen of continuous tradition. Its material presence housed a memory of the past, one kept alive in spirit through its art and architectural treasures. In this way, the abbey represented a shared identity, whose resilience across numerous centuries contributed to the preservation and idealisation of Western civilisation.

This view promotes a past with which one bears a seamless relationship; a connection or familiarity that renders the present familiar. It likewise fosters the notion that cultural treasures like Monte Cassino are the people's patrimony – humanity's inheritance, to which all are entitled, for which all are responsible, and for which all must be held accountable. This notion of transnational heritage reflects the enduring appeal of history beyond

---

34   Clark, 'History Repeats', p. 12.

national and denominational borders; and in practical terms, its inherent meaning derives in large part from the protection and survival of material remains, which forge the tangible connection between past and present. Saving the abbey from destruction thus became a matter of great political and public urgency, precisely because of a fundamental (and growing) belief in its cultural value. Remembrance of past experience was constitutive in this respect, the projection of historical and religious significance onto this Italian mountain site and its surrounding landscape.

The idea of 'saving the tangible past',[35] however, is a relatively recent phenomenon. National and international regulations intended to minimise the impact and unnecessary damage of war give witness to 'the idea that cultural property constitutes universal heritage'.[36] Rules around moveable and immovable property had been developing since the early sixteenth century, demonstrating 'an emergent consciousness which inspired the earliest domestic examples of historical preservation'.[37] Many important lessons were learned from the French revolutionary wars, whose wake left countless examples of wartime plunder and pillaging by armed forces. Denouncing these activities at the time, the constitutional bishop and revolutionary leader Abbé Grégoire wrote three commissioned reports on what he dubbed revolutionary 'vandalism'.[38] Desiring to 'pass on' France's artistic, archaeological, and architectural 'inheritance to posterity',[39] he marvelled at the respect for monuments in Italy, where 'the nation's objects, which, belonging to no one, are the property of all'.[40] In a series of letters published in 1796, furthermore, Antoine Quatremère de Quincy argued that the arts and science of Italy 'belong[ed] to all of Europe, and were no longer the exclusive property of one nation'[41]; their richness derived from their belonging 'to the whole universe'.[42]

Such patrimonial expressions were increasingly prevalent by the mid-nineteenth century. In his *Civilization of the Renaissance in Italy*, Jacob Burckhardt wrote that the 'age in which we live is loud [...] in proclaiming

35 Lowenthal, *The Past Is a Foreign Country*, p. 385.
36 O'Keefe, *Protection of Cultural Property*, p. 1.
37 Ibid., p. 8.
38 Abbé Grégoire, 'Rapport sur les inscriptions des monuments publics', in Grégoire, *Oeuvres de l'Abbé Grégoire*, II, p. 149. See also his 'Second rapport sur le vandalisme' (pp. 321–332) and 'Troisième rapport sur le vandalisme' (pp. 337–357).
39 Abbé Grégoire, 'Rapport sur les destructions opérées par le Vandalisme', in Grégoire, *Oeuvres de l'Abbé Grégoire*, II, p. 268.
40 Ibid., p. 277.
41 Quatremère de Quincy, *Lettres à Miranda*, p. 88.
42 Ibid., p. 123.

the worth of culture, and especially of the culture of antiquity'.[43] In May 1872, the Italian Minister of Public Instruction put it this way:

> The state has a supreme interest in using all vigilance and care for the proper custody of the precious monuments of art and of antiquity: its intervention is accordingly justified in all that concerns this great patrimony of the nation. From this exalted interest is derived the principle that the state alone can give permission for restoration, removals, and works of repair; that the state in the same way has not only the day of preserving the monuments so that they shall be of service to the progress in education of the studious, but also the duty of repressing and punishing all attempts at vandalism.[44]

This draft act on the conservation of art and monuments aspired 'absolutely to prevent the monuments of antique civilisation and the masterpieces of Italian art, in whosesoever possession they might be, being in any way injured or destroyed'.[45]

Meanwhile, the first international compilation on the law of war – the (Francis) 'Lieber Code' (1863) – declared that moveable property should never be sold, given away, privately appropriated, 'wantonly destroyed or injured'.[46] Draft International Regulations on the Laws and Customs of War – known as the 'Brussels Declaration' (1874) – declared that 'all necessary steps must be taken to spare, as far as possible, buildings dedicated to art, science, and charitable purposes [...] on condition they are not being used at the time for military purposes' (Article 17).[47] The Laws of War on Land (1880) – known as the 'Oxford Manual' (Article 34)[48] – repeated this provision, as did the Hague Rules of the First Peace Conference in 1899 (Hague Convention II, Article 27).[49] Taking its cue from the Brussels Declaration in particular, the Second Peace Conference of 1907 (Hague Convention IV) took these provisions one step further, adding specific reference to protecting 'historic monuments [...] provided they are not being used at the time for military purposes'.[50]

---

43 Burckhardt, *Civilization of the Renaissance in Italy*, p. 181.
44 Mariotti, *La Legislazione delle belle arti*, p. 314; translation from Brown, *Care of Ancient Monuments*, pp. 5–6.
45 Ibid.
46 Lieber, *Instructions for the Government of Armies*, articles 34–36, pp. 13–14.
47 'Project of an International Declaration' ('Brussels Declaration').
48 'Laws of War on Land' ('Oxford Manual').
49 'Convention (II) with Respect to the Laws and Customs of War' ('Hague Convention II').
50 'Convention (IV) respecting the Laws and Customs of War' ('Hague Convention IV').

Further developments along these lines followed the First World War. After devastating aerial bombardments of cultural sites like the Louvain Library and Rheims Cathedral, Sub-Commission III (Responsibility for the Violation of the Laws and Customs of War) of the Preliminary Peace Conference at Paris (1919) listed as a war crime the 'wanton destruction of religious, charitable, educational and historical buildings and monuments'.[51] The interwar years witnessed the 1923 Hague Draft Rules of Aerial Warfare (never adopted), which similarly sought to take 'all necessary steps [...] to spare as far as possible buildings dedicated to public worship, art, science, or charitable purposes [and] historic monuments [...] provided such buildings, objects or places are not at the time used for military purposes' (Article 25). With support from the governing board of the Pan-American Union, moreover, a Treaty on the Protection of Artistic and Scientific Institutions and Historic Monuments – known in short as the 'Roerich Pact' or 'Washington Pact' – was introduced in 1935.[52] Its concern for the 'advancement of the Arts and Sciences, in the common interest of humanity', whose institutions 'constitute a treasure common to all the Nations of the World'[53] were ideals advanced in the Preliminary Draft International Convention for the Protection of Historic Buildings and Works of Art in Times of War (1937).

Attitudes towards the abbey of Monte Cassino were influenced by these attempts to protect the world's art and monuments. German efforts in late 1943 to remove priceless artefacts from the abbey are a poignant example of genuine efforts at preservation – a successful commitment to safeguarding the remains of the past, well before the formation of international agencies and governing bodies. Ultimately, however, this goodwill and burgeoning desire was unable to keep pace with the vicissitudes of war, whose intensification consumed the monks' lives between November 1943 to late May 1944. During this time, the world outside the Terra di Lavoro was watching with increasing consternation, as impending fears escalated over Monte Cassino's potential destruction.

This international concern resuscitated old debates about protection. Echoing sentiments of nineteenth-century British politicians during the Risorgimento, the Allied Supreme Commander in Europe, General Dwight D. Eisenhower, expressed his admiration for Italy: '[It is] a country which has contributed a great deal to our cultural inheritance, a country rich in monuments which by their creation helped and now in their old age

---

51   Article 20 in *History of the United Nations War Crimes Commission*.
52   'Treaty on the Protection of Artistic and Scientific Institutions' ('Roerich Pact').
53   Chklaver, 'Projet d'une Convention'.

illustrate the growth of civilisation which is ours. We are bound to respect those monuments as far as war allows'.[54] An earlier cable from General Marshall to Eisenhower (dated 1943) noted how 'protection of [her] artistic and historic monuments [...] is a subject of great concern to many institutions and societies'. But 'declaring open the cities in which most of the treasures exist' was impractical. Appealing to the Italian people by means of radio, leaflets, 'and any other means available', therefore, General Marshall sought to remove all 'moveable works of art' from harm's way. Destruction of 'immovable works of art' was also to be avoided, 'insofar as possible without handicapping military operations'.[55] To assist with the identification, the US War Department circulated a document known as 'The Ancient Monuments of Italy', which included a thorough list of towns/cities, aerial photographs, coordinates, and instructions intended to avoid unnecessary destruction.

There were practical limits, however, to the protection available. The lives of fighting men, it was fiercely argued, should take precedence over ancient buildings. But as Eisenhower acknowledged, 'the choice is not always so clear-cut as that'.[56] The situation was morally and historically complex. At Cassino, the enemy 'relied on our [Allied] emotional attachments to shield his defense'. (Writing after the war, German General Senger und Etterlin remarked that 'nobody would want to sponsor the destruction of a cultural monument of this kind merely to gain a tactical advantage'.[57]) So despite a desire to protect, necessity could sometimes dictate and justify complete annihilation of 'some honored site'.[58] It was the imperative of high commanders, he repeated on more than one occasion, to 'spare without any detriment to operational needs' whatever monuments could be spared.

A similar debate was taking place in the House of Lords. On 9 February, one week prior to Monte Cassino's destruction, the Bishop of Chichester asked His Majesty's Government to 'make a statement as to their policy regarding the bombing of towns in enemy countries, with special reference to the effect of such bombing on civilians as well as objects of non-military and non-industrial significance in the area attacked'.[59] 'At the outbreak of the war,' he noted

> in response to an appeal by President Roosevelt, the Governments of the United Kingdom and France issued a joint declaration of their intention

---

54 Eisenhower, 'Historic Monuments'.
55 'Cable from General Marshall to General Einsenhower'.
56 Eisenhower, 'Historic Monuments'. See also Blumenson, *Salerno to Cassino*, p. 397.
57 Senger und Etterlin, *Neither Fear nor Hope*, p. 202.
58 'Memorandum from General Dwight D. Eisenhower'.
59 Hansard, HL Deb, 9 February 1944, vol. 130, c. 737.

to conduct hostilities with a firm desire to spare the civilian population and to preserve in every way possible those monuments of human achievement which are treasured in all civilized countries. At the same time explicit instructions were issued to the Commanders of the Armed Forces prohibiting the bombardment, whether from the air or from the sea or by artillery on land, of any except strictly military objectives in the narrowest sense of the word. Both sides accepted this agreement.[60]

The prelate referenced in his motion the Washington Conference on Limitation of Armaments (1922) concerning the rules of conduct around aerial warfare. Citing Articles 22 and 24 in particular, he addressed the issue of bombardment affecting and injuring non-combatants. Citing the Hague Convention of 1907, furthermore, he nevertheless acknowledged 'that there are recognized limits to what is permissible'.[61]

The debate intensified the following week (16 February), when the former archbishop of both York and Canterbury – Lord Cosmo Gordon Lang of Lambeth – put forward a motion on the preservation of historical and art treasures.[62] Their cultural value in the theatre of war prompted a lengthy discussion, intended to advise His Majesty's Government about what measures could be taken. The lord was speaking mainly 'of Italy as a country rather than as a nation with its somewhat chequered political history'.

> As a country Italy has inspired not only the interest and admiration of all who have known her, but love. I do not suppose there is any country in the world that has been the object of such love for centuries as Italy. Indeed, its monuments of the great past, its architecture, its sculpture, its pictures are among the noblest expressions of the human spirit.[63]

Rome (and the Vatican) epitomised the argument. The eternal city was 'the object of veneration by millions of our fellow Christians in all parts of the world'. As the Bishop of Chichester argued one week prior,

> the history of Rome is our own history. Rome taught us, through the example of Christ, to abolish human sacrifice and taught us the Christian

---

60 Ibid., c. 738.
61 Ibid.
62 Title: "To call attention to the importance of preserving objects of special historical or cultural value within the theatres of war and to ask His Majesty's Government what measures they have taken or propose to take for this purpose."
63 Hansard, HL Deb, 16 February 1944, vol. 130, c. 814.

faith. The destruction would rankle in the memory of every good European as Rome's destruction by the Goths or the sack of Rome rankled.[64]

Viscount FitzAlan of Derwent agreed that such an attack 'would be deplorable, not only on religious grounds but also on grounds of culture'. For this or any other centre of religious culture, it was necessary to take 'every precaution to avoid any such thing occurring'.[65] Any bombing in the city 'might very well do irreparable damage to great works of art'.[66] On 19 May 1943, Pope Pius XII made an appeal to President Roosevelt for the protection of Rome's 'many treasured shrines of Religion and Art – precious heritage not of one people but of all human and Christian civilisation'.[67]

'But Rome does not stand by itself': the ravages of war threatened, damaged, and destroyed many 'wonderful creations' and 'expressions of the human spirit'. As Lord Lang saw it, this reality gave rise to two extremes. 'On the one hand,' he argued,

> there are those who ask impatiently, and rather contemptuously: 'What is the worth of these dead stones and dead pictures in comparison with the life of one single soldier?' But these things are not dead. They are always alive; they have, as has been truly said, the quality of enhancing life, of giving fresh vitality to the mind and spirit of successive generations. And it must not be forgotten that they are part of that humane civilization which it is one of our aims, in this war, to protect against barbarians.

'On the other hand,' Lord Lang continued,

> there are those who, in their zeal for history and art, tend to forget the inexorable necessities of war. Just because the issues involved in the war are so great, just because it is being waged for the whole of civilization and not only for this aspect of it, just because from all the enslaved and oppressed countries a cry for liberation is rising, it is impossible to sanction anything that would seriously hinder the one essential thing – that the enemy, who is prepared to bring all this evil on the world, should be defeated rapidly and completely. It must never be allowed, for one moment, to be supposed by the enemy that if he chooses to occupy any

---

64 Hansard, HL Deb, 9 February 1944, vol. 130, c. 743.
65 Ibid., c. 747.
66 Hansard, HC Deb, 12 November 1942, vol. 385, c. 114.
67 Pope Pius XII, 'Pope Pius XII to President Roosevelt', II, p. 917.

of these centres of history or of art and to use them as posts for his own operations, he will be allowed to remain immune from attack.[68]

The 'crucial instance' was Monte Cassino. Famous as the central home of the Benedictine order, 'renowned through all these centuries for its scholarship and devotion', and revered as the custodian of priceless manuscripts and books, the abbey 'should be spared'. Referencing the Americans' tireless work in the realm of restoration and restitution, supported by President Roosevelt's American Commission for the Protection and Salvage of Artistic and Historic Monuments in War Areas – known in short as the 'Roberts Commission' (approved on 20 August 1943)[69] – Lord Lang asked whether a similar commission might be appointed by his own government.

Lord Latham did not share his colleague's sympathies. 'No one,' he argued, 'can justify adding to the dreadful toll in this war by one single life in order to save a building.' After a passionate defence of the common man and his home, he regretted that he could not 'subscribe to this doctrine of "Culture [sic] über alles."' Adopting the restoration view 'that there is no wealth but life – life, with all its powers of love and joy and admiration' – the very purpose of the current conflict – Lord Latham argued that 'nothing must be permitted to interfere with its prosecution or to delay securing final victory at the earliest possible moment'.[70]

Viscount Samuel then acknowledged the 'widespread public discussion' surrounding this topic. For most, it was a question of sacrificing the lives of its soldiers, sailors, and airmen – of risking victory in a battle or campaign – all because of a building. 'It was believed,' he continued, 'that many precious manuscripts belonging to the learned Benedictine Order had been sent for safe refuge to this monastery and that they might also be destroyed'. It therefore became 'the duty of the Germans occupying the place to remove them to safety as soon as they were in real danger of being subject to the swaying tides of battle'.[71] Citing Eisenhower on the central question, he reminded the House of the incalculable 'loss to the cultural treasures of mankind when the Goths, the Vandals and Saracens swept over Roman civilization'. In other words, it was imperative for the British government to 'consider whether similar consequences are to follow now the war is creeping up through Italy'.

---

68 Hansard, HL Deb, 16 February 1944, vol. 130, c. 815.
69 For a full account, see the 'Records of the American Commission' ('Roberts Commission').
70 Hansard, HL Deb, 16 February 1944, vol. 130, c. 822.
71 Ibid., cc. 824–825.

The potential consequences are interesting to note. Concern was expressed about

> the reputation of this country and this nation for caring, and caring deeply, for matters of art and culture should not be lightly cast aside even under the exigencies of war. When we look back on these years from the years that are to come and to the history of this war, we want to take pride in the victory that will have been won by the steadfastness and valour of this nation without any feeling of regret and without having to make any apology for disasters that may have fallen upon our human heritage through carelessness or neglect in the course of the campaign.[72]

Countering loud protests in what became a distorted debate, Lord Geddes remarked that everyone

> without exception, deplores the loss of great churches, great pictures, and all the other cultural possessions of Europe. We all hate to think that that is going on, but that it not the predominant hatred in our minds. The thing that we hate most and fear most is not that these material creations of the human spirit, as the noble and most reverend Lord calls them, should be lost. Our greatest fear is that the greatest creation of the human spirit – the whole of the Christian civilization of Europe – should be lost. That is a thing of the spirit and not of the material. Its preservation, as the guiding force of Christendom, must depend upon our victory and upon the victory of all who think and fight with us. If we are to allow that great heritage, that great creation of the human spirit, to be destroyed, of what value are these material creations of the human spirit? They are gone. They are milestones, indeed they are caddis cases, of the evolution of our Christian civilization. Yet we do not want to use any expression here that would discourage in any way whatever or limit the initiative of our commanders, soldiers, airmen, and sailors in winning that victory which we know to be essential, which we know we cannot do without, without which we know, if we were not to win the war, there would be no value left in any of the cultural monuments of Europe for our time and probably for any time.[73]

Finally, towards the sitting's end, the Lord Chancellor (Mr John Simon) returned to 'the actual case of Monte Cassino'. He offered some detailed

---

72   Ibid., c. 827.
73   Ibid., c. 843.

information on the material stakes, which he thought might provide the House with a more sobering perspective. 'In the first place', he stated,

> the buildings themselves are of small importance. Most of them date from the nineteenth century. They are decorated with frescoes by German artists. The great church inside the abbey is of the late seventeenth and early eighteenth centuries. I believe the objects of most interest artistically in the church are its bronze and silver doors. The most important feature of the monastery is the library, which contained over ten thousand printed volumes, some of them extremely rare, and thousands of manuscripts. Early in the war the Italian authorities sent to Monte Cassino for safety the finest objects from the National Museum at Naples, including a unique collection of bronze statues and busts from Herculanæum and Pompeii, all the treasures from the convent of Montevergine near Avellino, and all the objects from the San Martino Museum at Naples – ivories, majolicas and a number of other things. I hope I shall not be suspected of not being a thorough-paced supporter of bombing; when I say that it would be a misfortune if those things were to perish.[74]

But these items were 'no longer at Monte Cassino', he suggested. Relying on reports from three of four German newspapers, the Lord Chancellor assured the House that the abbey's 'treasures of art and antiquity' were already at a safe distance.[75] (As detailed in Chapter 3, German efforts in late 1943 were successful in moving and protecting as much of the abbey's material artefacts as possible.) In the absence of its treasures, Monte Cassino was no longer the famed repository of ancient knowledge and continuator of Western tradition; it became a religious monument of more material proportions, certainly not insignificant but one whose cultural esteem had been temporarily transferred to safer locations. What Europe and Western civilisation more broadly stood to lose by its destruction was thus tempered by a measured concern for its artefacts, which as we've already seen was a matter for both sides in the war. From this perspective, the question of aerial bombardment and preservation was now open to serious consideration.

The tenor of this debate recalls an important view, one generally accepted: Monte Cassino represented far more than a material construction. To General Eisenhower, it symbolised 'to the world all that we are fighting

---

74 Ibid., c. 857.
75 Ibid., cc. 857–858.

to preserve'.[76] Both before and after its destruction, the abbey came to signify a pinnacle example for moral contemplation of modern warfare and the hazards on civilian life and welfare. Speaking at a Metropolitan Museum of Art luncheon in April 1946, he referred to the ideals for which the 'materialism and destructiveness of war' were fought; contact in foreign lands with 'mankind's vast heritage of culture' holds the potential of awakening the common soldier 'to the permanent value of beauty as expressed in architecture, sculpture, painting, and folk-arts'. The threat to, and destruction of, this past, he contended, 'has served only to increase their respect and veneration for civilisations of the past'.[77]

Bringing home 'the value of the monuments of the past'[78] took time. The post-war decades witnessed intensifying measures in this cultural realm. Thanks to the creation of organisations like UNESCO, the International Council on Monuments and Sites (ICOMOS), the International Centre for the Study of the Preservation and the Restoration of Cultural Property (ICCROM), among others, international efforts for protection, preservation and restoration of cultural property – landscapes and sites – widened significantly. UNESCO's 'Convention for the Protection of Cultural Property in the Event of Armed Conflict with Regulations of the Convention 1954',[79] for example, as well as its charter on 'Protection of Mankind's Cultural Heritage' (1970),[80] present major steps in this direction. The emphasis on appreciating cultural formation, and safeguarding its heritage, dominate the field of discussion, giving rise to explanations on the importance of humankind's relationship to the past. '[M]an needs continuity', it was increasingly argued, because any disunity in the 'chain of human evolution' might perilously lead to a 'real breach in our cultural history'.[81]

Historic monuments like Monte Cassino were well poised to bridge the historical divide. They were deemed 'representative of the way man lives: they form the background to his daily life and reflect the social and psychological conditions of their time'. 'The art of building', moreover, was considered 'an expression of the society in which they have emerged'. Buildings that have survived the society which produced them were of greatest concern 'because of their value as witnesses to the culture and history of the past'. On this point, the modern attitude differs from that of

76 Eisenhower, 'Preservation'.
77 Eisenhower, 'Notes for Use at Luncheon'.
78 UNESCO, *Protection of Mankind's Cultural Heritage*, p. 22.
79 UNESCO, 'Convention for the Protection of Cultural Property'.
80 UNESCO, *Protection of Mankind's Cultural Heritage*, p. 22.
81 Ibid., p. 25.

'our for[e]bears, who had little hesitation in destroying old monuments in order to substitute new edifices which were more in accordance with their needs or even merely with their tastes'. 'When they showed some respect for certain famed buildings,' it was written

> they yet looked on them simply as manifestations of faith, marks of power or wealth, artistic masterpieces or merely curiosities. Today, on the other hand, it is because of their value as irreplaceable evidences of bygone ages and vanished societies that we are striving by all appropriate means to preserve our monuments.[82]

The stakes of this debate were not lost on those blamed for Monte Cassino's destruction. For this reason, the controversial question of its necessity continues to occupy military historians. On the one hand, General Freyburg's insistence on bombing the abbey represents the strongest 'realist' argument for protecting the human element: life over material culture, whatever the cost. Providing some nuance to the moral dilemma, General Senger und Etterlin later wrote that the New Zealanders 'suffered heavy losses' during the attack on Monte Cassino. 'Were they to run the risk of still heavier losses', he asked, 'in order to avoid destroying the abbey? Were the people of New Zealand to be asked to pay for the preservation of the monastery with the lives of their own sons?'[83] The answers are implicit.

Dissenting voices from the 'idealist' camp nevertheless abound. General Clark considered the bombardment as a mistake. 'The official position was best summed up', he suggested, 'in a State Department communication to the Vatican's Undersecretary of State on 13 October 1945, saying that "there was unquestionable evidence in the possession of the Allied commanders in the field that the Abbey of Monte Cassino formed part of the German defensive system'.[84] As Clark went on to say, however, as 'one of the Allied commanders in the field and the one in command at Cassino, [...] there was no evidence the Germans were using the Abbey for military purposes'.[85]

A retired British Army officer, Major-General J.F.C. Fuller, wrote that 'the bombing of the abbey was not so much a piece of vandalism as an act of sheer tactical stupidity'.[86] All the bombing did, he said, 'was to turn the Abbey

---

82 Ibid., p. 23.
83 Senger und Etterlin, *Neither Fear nor Hope*, p. 205.
84 Clark, *Calculated Risk*, p. 457.
85 Ibid.
86 Fuller, *Second World War*, p. 272.

from a building into a fortress, because the defence of a rubble heap mixed with ruins is an easier and more comfortable operation than the defence of a building'.[87] Writing on 16 February 1944, US Army Major General Fred L. Walker, commander of the 36th Infantry Division, claimed that Monte Cassino

> was a valuable historical monument, which should have been preserved. The Germans were not using it and I can see no advantage in destroying it. No tactical advantage will result since the Germans can make as much use of the rubble for observation posts and gun positions as of the building itself. Whether the Germans used the building for an observation post or for emplacements makes little difference since the mountain top on which the building stands can serve the same purpose. If I had had the decision to make I would have prevented its destruction. I have directed my artillery not to fire on it to date.[88]

According to Rudolf Böhmler, moreover, commander of the XIV Panzer Corps and a former Rhodes Scholar at Oxford, 'no matter how one twists and turns the facts, there is no justification for this senseless piece of destruction'.[89] Few would dispute its outcome as a political and intelligence blunder, but Böhmler makes an even grander connection. 'The destruction,' he argued, 'was an irreplaceable loss to the whole of the Christian world'.[90]

The Vatican heartily agreed. When Pope Pius XII first heard of the abbey's destruction, he reportedly said: 'If they had wanted, Monte Cassino could have been saved. It would have needed good-will only and consideration not of my person but of the Catholic world'.[91] According to Berlin radio, the American chargé d'affaires at the Vatican, Harold H. Tittmann Jr, told the Cardinal Secretary of State, Maglione, 'that the monastery could be rebuilt and that the United States would interest itself financially'. Though lacking any authority, the estimates of material loss were given at 200,000,000 lire (equivalent to two million US dollars). But the financial value of destruction misses the main point, which the cardinal is said to have addressed. According to the broadcast, he responded that 'even if you rebuild it in gold and diamonds, it still isn't the monastery'.[92]

87 Ibid.
88 From General Walker's Diary, 16 February 1944 (cited in Blumenson, *Salerno to Cassino*, p. 413.)
89 Böhmler, *Monte Cassino*, p. 180.
90 Ibid.
91 'Pope Bitter, Berlin Declares'.
92 Ibid.

On this finer point, the monks of Monte Cassino would have disagreed. The views expressed in this broadcast evoke an 'anti-restoration' theory of more modern tastes: the belief that destruction severs the monument from past societies, never to be recovered; that a monument's spirit – and the spirit of its original builders, craftsmen, and artisans – cannot be resurrected from the depths of destruction. If they fall to ruins, '*We have no right to touch them.* They are not ours. They belong partly to those who built them, and partly to the generations of mankind who are to follow us. The dead still have their right in them.'[93] As John Ruskin further argued in his influential work *The Seven Lamps of Architecture* (1849), restoration 'means the most total destruction which a building can suffer: a destruction out of which no remnants can be gathered; a destruction accompanied with false description of the thing destroyed'. 'Do not let us deceive ourselves in this important matter,' he contended. '[I]t is *impossible*, as impossible as to raise the dead, to restore anything that has ever been great or beautiful in architecture'.[94]

This was not the view supported by the abbey, however, as its community began compiling historical evidence and every available expertise for its wholesale reconstruction. Restoration in this case was more than mere symbolism; in ideological terms, it served to foster a timeless unity between the present and past, which was fundamental to preserving the abbey's identity. There was no room for nostalgia, because in the most practical sense, the abbey aspired to resume its functional role as a leading Benedictine house. While the building's memorial function was doubtless important, so too was returning the community as quickly as possible to full religious observance.

The abbey's past was ultimately deemed recoverable. In rebuilding, the Ruskin-like concern for a building's authenticity and integrity was balanced against the theory espoused by his contemporary, the French architect, Eugène-Emmanuel Viollet-le-Duc, who wrote that 'to restore a building is not to preserve it, to repair, or rebuild it; it is to reinstate it in a condition of completeness which could never have existed at any given time'.[95] According to this more radical restoration theory, a priori principles of aesthetics were privileged over rigorous historical evidence.[96]

This theoretical antagonism (interventionist versus non-interventionist)[97] explains the opposition to the architectural plans presented by the

---

93   Ruskin, *Seven Lamps of Architecture*, vol. 8, p. 245.
94   Ibid., p. 242.
95   Violet-le-Duc, *On Restoration*, p. 9.
96   Spurr, *Architecture and Modern Literature*, p. 150.
97   Choay, *Invention of the Historic Monument*, p. 102.

Vatican's Pontifical Commission for Sacred Art, which initially proposed that the abbey be reconstructed in a 'progressive' style (i.e., using modern techniques) 'where it was, in its ancient perimeter, around the elements that still remember the great founder'.[98] Writing a passionate letter on 23 July 1945 to Monsignor Giovanni Constantini, president of the Pontifical Commission, Abbot Rea of Monte Cassino expressed his greatest fear that, if the reconstruction programme continued in the proposed fashion, the abbey would become little more than a magnificent monument to its fourteen centuries of life. He, or his brethren, could not condone this course of action.[99] The abbot proposed an alternative approach: a *pro memoria* method for conserving the status quo ante, with due diligence to decorative styles and historical records.

This difficult task was ultimately realised. Abbot Rea delivered on his promise to rebuild the abbey, 'As it was, where it was' (*com'era e dov'era*).[100] But this was a maxim that required repeated justification and hard evidence over the course of many years. As head of the *commissione ministeriale*, the abbot mounted a considered defence that aimed to resuscitate the history of Monte Cassino through the reconstruction process.[101] Presenting rigorous historical, planimetric, and architectural documentation in support of a faithful restoration, the committee addressed in detail: the character of reconstruction; institutions/agencies called upon to finance and carry out the work; a general technical programme; planning, management, and surveillance; and a system for executing the work.[102] And after successful lobbying to the Italian Ministry of Public Works, the abbot was successful in his mission to restore the abbey according to its true historical character.[103]

*

The fruits of this impassioned plea stand atop the mountain today. But there is one important difference: no longer an isolated Benedictine house on the mountain summit overlooking the Liri Valley, the abbey's newest incarnation – for better or worse – became enveloped in the wider wartime recovery efforts of a grieving Italian nation. On 2 April 1949, when President Luigi

98 Fratadocchi, *La ricostruzione*, appendix 1, p. 177.
99 Archivio Apostolico Vaticano, Fondo Commissione Centrale per l'Arte Sacra in Italia, A.G. Busta 272/2, fascicolo 55 (cited in Fratadocchi, *La ricostruzione*, p. 61).
100 For a personal side to this commitment, see Avagliano, 'Montecassino "com'era e dov'era"'.
101 See ibid., p. 155.
102 Fratadocchi, *La ricostruzione*, appendix II, pp. 178–181. See also 'Relazione della commissione'.
103 Ibid., p. 53.

Einaudi of the Italian Republic awarded it the Gold Medal for military valour, the abbey became 'part of the foundation myth on which post-war Italian society was built'.[104] It was now the people's patrimony. In the aftermath of war, Einaudi said, the abbey's 'harsh Calvary, its long martyrdom, its immense ruins were, in the passion of the people for independence and the liberty of the homeland, like an altar of pain for the triumph of justice and of the millenarian Italian civilization'.[105]

As a national monument and property of the state since the late nineteenth century, Monte Cassino was hailed as the cultural symbol of national suffering and renewal. As we'll see in the final chapter of this book, it transcended both contemporary religion and politics to represent a universal human experience. Incorporated into a much longer 'destruction tradition' spanning centuries, the abbey became recognised in the modern world as far more than the spiritual home of Benedictine monasticism; its coherence, meaning, and value were transformed into a 'symbol of the destruction that had been overcome'.[106]

---

104 Michel, 'Reconstructing the National Narrative', p. 322.
105 Einaudi, 'Visita', p. 31.
106 Melville, 'Montecassino', p. 324.

6. A New Europe: Erasing the Destruction

Abstract
Monte Cassino became a fitting symbol for post-war recovery efforts. Its lived experiences account for the abbey's role in the second half of the twentieth century as the binding agent and promoter for a unified Europe. This chapter makes sense of this unique designation by examining the way(s) in which the abbey's fractured past has been harnessed into this synthetic vision. It asks how Monte Cassino's 'destruction tradition' – that evolving narrative and shared reality from the Middle Ages to the present day – served as an instrument for promoting the abbey's faith and prosperity well into the twentieth century. It shows how the abbey's cumulative experiences with death and resurrection were transformed into a secular and religious rhetoric of hope, unity, and essential European identity.

Keywords: identity; unity; Europe; historiography; representation; culture; memory; civilisation

'Monte Cassino Never Dies.'[1]

The English travel writer Donald Hall was enamoured by Monte Cassino. The abbey dazzled him 'with fickle brilliance',[2] even before he drew near its summit. 'For nearly a millennium and a half,' he wrote, 'men have been halted by that watch-tower of religion and culture rising above the crossroads, Lombards, Saracens, Normans, Spaniards, Frenchmen, Germans, and then again Germans with Englishmen and their allies in hard pursuit'.[3] Their fascination with the Benedictine house was 'usually angry and gnawed by a frustration which they resolved by destroying, looting and all manner of

---

1   'Il terzo anniversario della distruzione di Montecassino'.
2   Hall, *Eagle Argent*, p. 2.
3   Ibid.

nastiness directed at the object in their path'. Their reasons for doing so were varied:

> [W]hether they were pagans who disliked Christians or Christians who disliked monks, a desire for loot or just a natural bent for destruction, the ultimate devastation being in the name of the Western civilisation of which the monastery was a beacon, a very knotty point.[4]

This modern representation of the abbey's victimisation is common but not universally shared. When Hall asked one of the monks about the most recent destruction in the Second World War, he was reportedly told: 'We hardly ever speak of it here. [...] For us it is already only an incident in our history'.[5] This striking interpretation of the abbey's near annihilation in February 1944 is not altogether surprising given the longer tradition of destruction and rebuilding examined throughout this book. But its unique perspective nevertheless demands further context and explanation. For the monks of Monte Cassino, their abbey was the 'cradle of Western religious life' from where 'the civilising influence of the religion of Christ descended to penetrate through all directions in the West, softening the harsh customs in the formation of new people'.[6] It was 'the starting point of the spread of Benedictine monasticism',[7] which became 'an essential part of the great heritage common to the peoples of Europe'.[8] For these core reasons, the abbey has always been regarded as more than a 'fake, cold, [...] artistic mass of stones'; it was 'the realisation of an ideal among the noblest and most fecund in results that humanity ever had'.[9]

Historically speaking, the abbey's 'eternal value' always prevailed against its transgressors. Supporting this claim is the enduring belief that Monte Cassino 'cannot perish',[10] that new life can always be transplanted, that 'following the ruin came the resurrection'.[11] Its 'exceptional mission' was entrusted to God as a destiny of human civilisation. That destiny, wrote one former monk, 'was to be accomplished through alternations of splendor and desolation. Like all great Christian institutions, it was to be its salutary

---

4   Ibid.
5   Ibid., p. 15.
6   Cited in Leccisotti, *Monte Cassino*, p. 200.
7   Ibid.
8   Leccisotti, 'Il contributo Benedettino', p. 268.
9   Ibid.
10 Iannetta, *Triumph of Life*, p. 8.
11 Ibid., p. 10.

fruits through sufferings.'[12] These 'sufferings' were defining qualities in the abbey's historical and religious identity; as this final chapter suggests, they formed essential building blocks in the making of a 'new Europe' whose 'furrows' could be filled with the 'life-giving sap'[13] of Benedict's teachings. Whereas '[e]mpires and kingdoms have fallen, philosophical and artistic systems have faded away, people and nations have disappeared', the 'ideal of Benedict has survived, hewn from the rock of his mountain, now covered with woods, now barren, now crowned with peaceful silvery olives, now savagely devastated'.[14]

Such sustained views project Monte Cassino's continuous and linear past. They reveal a unique tradition uninterrupted by the vicissitudes of time or the destructive forces of medieval, early modern, and contemporary warfare and its associated destruction. They reinforce a fate predicted by Benedict himself, who prophesied that his 'entire monastery' and everything that he provided for the community would 'fall into the hands of the barbarians'.[15] The sixth-century saint might be excused for failing to mention exactly how many times his abbey would in fact have to endure such a fate.

Such was the 'brilliant light of St. Benedict' – the subject of Pope Pius XII's 1947 encyclical *Fulgens Radiatur*. 'Like a star in the darkness of night,' he wrote,

> Benedict of Nursia brilliantly shines, a glory not only to Italy but of the whole Church. Whoever considers his celebrated life and studies in the light of the truth of history, the gloomy and stormy times in which he lived, will without doubt realize the truth of the divine promise which Christ made to the Apostles and to the society He founded 'I am with you all days even to the consummation of the world'.[16]

By this reasoning, the destructive fury unleashed upon the venerable mountain could never vanquish its spirit or tradition. 'At no time in history', the pope continued, 'does this promise lose its force; it is verified in the course of all ages [...] under the guidance of divine Providence'.[17] Ultimately, it was divine Providence which assigned to Monte Cassino its universal mission,

---

12   Ibid., pp. 16–17.
13   Rea, 'Pro Montecassino', p. 2.
14   Leccisotti, *Monte Cassino*, p. 311.
15   Vogüé, *Grégoire le Grand: Dialogues*, II. 17, p. 192.
16   Pope Pius XII, *Fulgens Radiatur*, c. 1.
17   Ibid.

under Benedict's guidance, for disseminating Christianity and culture to the West.

What hurt the abbey only made it stronger – or so it was repeatedly suggested. For

> when enemies assail the Christian name more fiercely, when the fateful barque of Peter is tossed about more violently and when everything seems to be tottering with no hope of human support, it is then that Christ is present, bondsman, comforter, source of supernatural power, and raises up fresh champions to protect Catholicism, to restore it to its former vigour, and give it even greater increase under the inspiration and help of heavenly grace.[18]

Monte Cassino seemed destined to assume this role. The fourteenth centennial of Benedict's death (1947) presented a timely reminder of its restorative function in this historical narrative. The saint emerged from a 'dark century when the position and fate of civilization as well as of the Church and of civil society was in danger of collapse'.[19] Monte Cassino was thus founded in a post-Roman world 'weakened and corrupt from within', one laying 'in mighty ruins in the West'. Very early on, as we've seen, the abbey's peace was 'shattered by the invasions of the northern tribes'. Yet hope, help, and protection for the safety of humanity could always be found, as a ship to guide what was left of its treasures through the 'mighty storm and universal upheaval'.[20] Because at its helm stood Saint Benedict, the spiritual and historical stalwart for the abbey's 'renewal and restoration'[21] – 1,400 years after his passing.

The return of peace and harmony in the twentieth century made this resurrection possible. The abbey was just the first piece of a much larger puzzle, but an important one nonetheless. Pius XII's encyclical heralded a recovery process for humanity, which was initiated in the immediate aftermath of war.

As we've seen throughout this book, Monte Cassino was all too experienced with such matters. Its religious community knew the road to recovery could be pursued through 'peace, harmony and earnest work'. 'From renascent barbarism, from destruction and ruin', it sought once

---

18 Ibid.
19 Ibid., c. 2.
20 Ibid., c. 3.
21 Ibid., c. 4.

again to lead the faithful 'back to benign influence human and Christian, to patient labor, to the light of truth, to a civilization renewed in wisdom and charity'.[22] This time, however, many others outside the abbey began placing their hope and trust in its capacity to realise this outcome; they believed with Abbot Rea of Monte Cassino that 'the unity and peace of our spirits, a sure pledge of the material and spiritual unity of our holy and beloved Italy', could be recovered on the ruins of this 'ancient abbey', 'in the Alleluia of the Resurrection'.[23] Marvelling at the success of its resurrection decades later, Abbot Martino Matronola (1983–1994) reflected on how the abbey was once again full of peace, not affliction; he encouraged others to 'remember that date of misfortune only to remind men and peoples that war is horrid and peace is beautiful'.[24]

This familiar representation of loss and recovery made Monte Cassino a fitting symbol for post-war recovery efforts. Its lived experiences account for the abbey's role in the second half of the twentieth century as the binding agent and promoter for a unified Europe. This chapter makes sense of this unique designation by examining the way(s) in which the abbey's fractured past has been harnessed into this synthetic vision. It asks how Monte Cassino's 'destruction tradition' – that evolving narrative and shared reality from the Middle Ages to the present day – served as an instrument for promoting the abbey's faith and prosperity well into the twentieth century. It shows how the abbey's cumulative experiences with death and resurrection were transformed into a secular and religious rhetoric of hope, unity, and essential European identity.

Golden Chain

Monte Cassino has always championed its own historical narrative. The abbey boasts a long and continuous tradition across fourteen centuries of existence, demonstrating a capacity and competency for building, protecting, and venerating its past.[25] The main arc of this narrative is sustained by a 'golden chain'[26] of historiography: a linear vision of the past that begins with

---

22 Ibid., c. 18.
23 Avagliano, 'Montecassino "com'era e dov'era"', appendix II, p. 154.
24 Matronola, 'Pensieri di pace'.
25 On the ninth- and tenth-century textual influence, see especially Pohl, *Werkstätte der Erinnerung*, pp. 152–179.
26 Leccisotti, *Monte Cassino*, p. 196.

'the common father and master, Benedict, and his virgin sister, Scholastica'.[27] The saint's immediate disciples, and every subsequent abbot, are themselves links in the long and unbroken chain. Referring to the memory of this abbey and its preservation through the vicissitudes of time, the twentieth-century Cassinese archivist-cum-historian Tommaso Leccisotti outlined its role in fostering the abbey's identity. From Benedict to the current abbot, the 'flame of holiness'[28] grew brighter with every subsequent phase of recovery. The long list of contributors to this campaign has been preserved as faithfully as possible by the 'jealous, pious diligence of contemporary historians and chroniclers'.[29] But it is true, Leccisotti admitted, that 'Cassinese historians have always preferred to devote themselves to events of national interest, caring little or nothing at all about the relations of Monte Cassino with the outside world'.[30] This insular focus was partly explained by the disappearance of 'so many memories'.[31] Yet the past never truly dies. It is sometimes forgotten, just as it is often remembered.

The history of Monte Cassino is a past mediated through written representation. It is a 'remembered past', whose experiences and memories have been shaped over centuries by monks living inside the cloister walls. The many episodes of destruction which punctuate its long existence do not detract from this sense of purpose, value, and identity.

The question is more about *how* the remembering is done. It is tempting to view the abbey's representation of its continuous past as a myth or legend. But the monks' interpretation is more than a 'pious illusion'.[32] Their version represents a firm recognition of intrinsic historical value and knowledge, with a different critical apparatus. 'Historical men,' Nietzsche contended, 'do not know how unhistorical their thoughts and actions are in spite of all their history, and how their cultivation of history does not serve pure knowledge but life'.[33] The configuration of Monte Cassino's past was merely formulated towards different ends; its construction was founded on a deep-seated belief in Benedict's eternity and spiritual transcendence, his restorative and unifying power.

This interpretation raises the possibility of religious dogma: that Monte Cassino's engagement with its own past – its representation over centuries

27 Ibid.
28 Ibid., p. 197.
29 Ibid., p. 198.
30 Ibid., p. 201.
31 Ibid.
32 Nietzsche, *Use and Abuse of History*, p. 42.
33 Ibid., p. 10.

– is a reinscribed form of knowledge. It would be wrong, however, to call it a falsification. It is rather an intimate representation told from the inside: a manifestation of truth that belongs most resoundingly to the Cassinese monks. They are the judges, lawgivers, and witnesses to their abbey's past. The remembrance and configuration of this past both authorises and authenticates it. Its history has been recorded, interpreted, and validated from the Middle Ages to the present day, contributing to a continuous tradition that greatly informs our modern understanding.

The experience and ordering of time shed some light on this historical construction. The French historiographer François Hartog described our relation to time as 'the way in which a given society approaches its past and reflects upon it'.[34] Drawing on the philosopher Paul Ricoeur, he described the 'degrees of historicity' in human communities as being formed by 'the modalities of self-consciousness that each and every society adopts in its constructions of time and its perceptions'.[35] This construction of historical time contributes to the 'construction of a self-image continually enriched by genealogical data',[36] both textual and iconic.

Applying this notion to our present subject, Monte Cassino's unique relationship to temporality brings the past into the future with little or no discernible separation. Its anthropological essence comes from its referential connection between time and memory.[37] The abbey's identity – the construction of its self-image and purpose – takes shape (or is conceived) in a world where time does not pass in any traditional sense: an atemporal dimension where the Cassinese (emic) representation trumps the historian's (etic) interpretation. It is a distinct realm of knowledge wherein Monte Cassino's past is not treated as an object of study with sufficient historical distance. Rather, its long history is collapsed, offering an objectivist view that presents an unproblematic description of historical events and their causal effects. The end result is a 'regime of historicity' whose inherent meaning and value is determined most authoritatively by the religious community that inhabits it.

The modern historian takes a more direct view. S/he posits, by contrast, 'that a sense of time is generated by the distance, and tensions, between the space of experience and the horizon of expectation'.[38] Yet the representation

---

34 Hartog, *Regimes of Historicity*, p. 9.
35 Ricoeur, *Memory, History, Forgetting*, p. xvi.
36 Choay, *Invention of the Historic Monument*, p. 139.
37 Ibid., p. 7.
38 Hartog, *Regimes of Historicity*, p. 17.

of Monte Cassino's past is unique precisely because of its projected symmetry between experience and expectation; the absence of any visible tensions eliminates the question of historical distance. The result is suspended historical time, 'as though there were nothing but the present'.[39] That is to suggest an immediacy with the present which abstracts the past: a 'dialectical movement that simultaneously assumes and transcends' the abbey's 'original historical signification, by integrating it into a new semantic stratum'.[40] In this sense, recalling and retelling the abbey's past is not a critical, interpretative, or argumentative exercise; its authentic purpose serves instead to observe, record, and validate the sequence of events, which in totality link the 'golden chain' together.

On a basic level, this interpretation is reminiscent of universal history: a past, firmly grounded in Saint Benedict's sixth-century foundation, and one that is always future-oriented. The abbey might be destroyed, but its 'centuries-old tradition [...] remained well-defined and in logical relation with the future'.[41] This relationship between the past and future presents its own 'chronosophy' – what Hartog described as 'a mixture of prophecy and periodization'[42] – which in this case produces a linear and continuous vision. By this reasoning, Monte Cassino's 'golden chain' of historiography is a dominant narrative driven and framed by experiences of destruction, 'restoration', and 'vital recovery'.[43] These experiences define almost every period of the abbey's existence, providing clear boundaries for historical categorisation and explanation.

This emic interpretation originates with the abbey's representation in medieval sources. After brief mention in Gregory the Great's *Dialogues*, Monte Cassino came to be regarded with a certain prestige from both inside and outside the abbey. Paul the Deacon's *History of the Lombards* 'played a decisive role in merging outside expectations and self-perceptions'.[44] It did so principally by introducing the narrative of restoration under Abbot Petronax in the eighth century[45], signalling the abbey's second period of growth after foundation; this method and periodisation influenced later writers, who adopted similar 'before' and 'after' taxonomies in their records of Monte Cassino's destruction and its aftermath. There was religious life

39 Ibid., p. 18.
40 Choay, *Invention of the Historic Monument*, p. 75.
41 Leccisotti, *Monte Cassino*, p. 146.
42 Hartog, *Regimes of Historicity*, p. 11.
43 Leccisotti, *Monte Cassino*, pp. 196–197.
44 Pohl, 'History in Fragments', p. 357.
45 Paul the Deacon, *Historia Langobardorum*, VI. 40.

and observance before and after the Lombard attack, before and after the Saracens, the Normans, the earthquake, etc.

The abbey's own (internal) record begins slightly later, in the late ninth and early tenth centuries (c. 867–920) with the anonymous *Chronica sancti Benedicti Casinensis* (copied into the first part of Codex Casinensis 175).[46] Comprising short historiographical, liturgical, and chronological texts in no apparent or logical order, the *Chronica* was composed by multiple authors during the monks' exile at Capua, during the abbacy of John (915–934). The inclusion, ordering, and interpretation of historical events in this source recount the events between the Lombard invasion of the late sixth century and the Saracen attack of the late ninth. In annalistic style, the author of the second section elaborates on the first, criticising the Lombards of past and present, 'passing on to the posterity the reasons'[47] for the Saracen destruction of Monte Cassino in 883. Heavily annotated and used, the *Chronica*'s texts give 'important clues to the concerns of the monastery in the tenth century'.[48] Prior to its composition, moreover, the abbey

> had no Benedictan [sic] tradition of its own and owed whatever monastic practices and manuscripts it possessed to outsiders, such as the Anglo-Saxon Willibald (who served as a model of monastic life) or Pope Zacharias (who donated a manuscript of the *Rule*).[49]

By situating the abbey's place in the medieval world, this written representation made an important contribution to Monte Cassino's self-identity.

The *Chronicon monasterii Casinensis* differed slightly in its approach. But its contemporary representation of the abbey was no less effective, fostering an even stronger sense of identity. First written by Leo Marsicanus, and continued by Peter the Deacon in the early twelfth century, the chronicle informed – and continues to inform – subsequent histories of the abbey. We might reasonably view it as the first systematic collection of documents, which together shaped the abbey's patrimonial expression. As noted in a previous chapter, Leo marshalled the events of the abbey's destruction and recovery between the sixth and eleventh centuries into his larger monastic narrative, striving to preserve the works and deeds of distinguished men.[50]

---

46 Pohl, *Werkstätte der Erinnerung*, pp. 85–95.
47 Berto, 'Oblivion, Memory, and Irony', p. 61.
48 Ibid.
49 Pohl, 'History in Fragments', p. 357.
50 *Chron. Cas.*, p. 5 (Epistola Leonis).

He divided his work into three sections, which he outlined in his prefatory letter to Abbot Oderisius: (1) from the Lombard destruction to Abbot Petronax's restoration, followed by the second destruction under Abbot Bertharius and subsequent restoration under Abbot Aligernus (including the period of exile at Teano and Capua); (2) from the early ninth century to the second half of the eleventh, spanning the industrious building activities of prominent abbots like Richerius; and (3) Abbot Desiderius's own contributions and achievements to the entire monastic complex and surrounding lands as the so-called 'other Solomon'.[51] Peter the Deacon's continuation of this chronicle drew on the four principal figures of Benedict, Petronax, Aligernus, and Desiderius, to whom many subsequent authors have attributed great progress and growth.[52] Abbot Desiderius's *Dialogues* and Peter the Deacon's *Ortus et vita* are also important sources for preserving and transmitting as precise a memory as possible.[53]

The 'concretization of memory and oral traditions in writing'[54] define Monte Cassino in the central Middle Ages. The Desiderian era in particular (eleventh century) served to consolidate the abbey's historical narrative by memorialising and commemorating its past, particularly through the enlargement of the abbey's scriptorium and the construction of a new library; through the production and preservation of texts like the Monte Cassino *Chronicon*, the abbey's entire existence was (re)organised into an eleventh-century framework; this version of the past shaped its 'archival memory',[55] effectively determining 'what records of the past future generations might access and, to a considerable extent, how they might interpret these records'.[56] This heuristic product not only defined Monte Cassino's coherence and continuity over the first 500 years, but it contributed directly and purposefully to constructing monastic identity. In this respect, we might more accurately define the material outcome as 'imaginative memory', which connotes a creative flair to the process of historical construction, but one consciously believed and remembered by its creator(s) and the wider Cassinese community.[57] As Amy Remensnyder has argued, the constitutive power of imaginative memory holds the potential to create and situate

---

51 Ibid., pp. 8–9.
52 Ibid., III. Prologus, p. 362.
53 Leccisotti, *Monte Cassino*, p. 196.
54 Boynton, *Shaping Monastic Identity*, p. 16.
55 Geary, *Phantoms*, pp. 81–114.
56 Ibid., p. 84.
57 On this concept, see Remensnyder, *Remembering*, pp. 1–2.

meaning, to 'establish and reaffirm the cohesion of a group',[58] to authorise and shape the symbolic boundaries of a religious community in relation to the world around it. Ultimately, the *Chronicon* offered the first such glimpse into how this Benedictine religious community viewed itself in accordance with the historical events which determined its fate.

This substantial medieval record served the abbey's historical representation for more than half a millennium. A new historiographical standard emerged only in the eighteenth century, as the shape and organisation of Monte Cassino's archive helped to secure its status as the lifeblood of the abbey. Its rich resources – preserved and enlarged, as we've already seen, over many centuries – informed Erasmo Gattola's *Historia abbatiae Cassinensis* (two volumes, published in 1733) and *Ad historiam abbatiae Cassinensis accessiones* (two volumes, published in 1734).[59] Archivist from c. 1687 until his death in 1734 (a position interrupted between 1722 and 1725/1726), Gattola wrote the abbey's first true comprehensive or universal history.[60] His palaeographic and diplomatic approach to the unedited source material was more critical than his predecessors', drawing on the contemporary spirit for Italy's antique valour and profound cultural influence within Europe; he did not simply narrate the facts but relied on a more critical analysis of the documents available to him in the archives. In his methods, Gattola was deeply persuaded by the likes of the Italian historian L.A. Muratori[61] as well as the burgeoning philological tradition advanced by his friends and colleagues, the French Maurist monks Michele Germain and Jean Mabillon (among others).[62]

The material outcome of this approach is worth noting. Gattola's *Historia* 'is not a continuous history of Monte Cassino, but an elaborate presentation of certain aspects of the development of the abbey, according to the centuries of its existence'.[63] Not only did he possess an erudition and scholarly ability for weaving together this singular Benedictine house with a broader historical context, but he also broke the mould of a 'severe and jealous archivist'[64] to

---

58 Ibid., p. 3.
59 See Bloch, *Monte Cassino*, I, pp. xxi–xxii. See also Leccisotti, 'L'archivio di Montecassino', pp. vii–xlii.
60 On Gattola's prefecture, see especially Leccisotti, *I Regesti*, II, pp. ix–xlii.
61 Muratori, *Epistolario*. See especially Leccisotti, 'Il contributo di Montecassino'.
62 Raimondi, 'I padri maurini', pp. 430–431. For a list of correspondence between Gattola and Maurist monks, see Ettinger, 'La Corrispondenza dei Benedettini Maurini'. For the reprinting of unedited letters, see Petrella, 'Lettere inedite del Mabillon'. See also Tosti, *Storia della badia*, III, pp. 314–317; Leccisotti, *I Regesti*, II, pp. xxxiii–xxxvi.
63 Bloch, *Monte Cassino*, I, p. xxii.
64 Leccisotti, 'L'archivio di Montecassino', p. xli.

liberate the secrets of his archive for the general public. Utilising numerous unpublished texts at his disposal – namely charters, diplomas, privileges, and letters – Gattola sought to place Monte Cassino within the civil, social, economic, jurisdictional, and cultural life of Italy in the eighteenth century. Abandoning the chronological narrative employed by Leo Marsicanus, Peter the Deacon, Don Onorato Medici di Napoli (*Annali casinensis*), and Placidi Petrucci (*Romani libri quinque chronicorum casinensis monasterii*), Gattola was therefore more than a mere continuator of the abbey's past. His contribution to the knowledge of Monte Cassino and its dependencies has rarely been surpassed; this enormous achievement served also to preserve in printed form so much historical material that would otherwise be unknown outside the abbey.

Gattola's methodological influence pervades most modern representations.[65] Three publications from the last two centuries illustrate this point by simple virtue of their content, organisation, and reception. Luigi Tosti's *Storia della badia di Montecassino* (1843),[66] Tommaso Leccisotti's *Monte Cassino* (1947),[67] and Mariano Dell'Omo's *Montecassino: Un'abbazia della storia* (1999)[68] evoke the spirit of Gattola's historical representation. All three authors share a common heritage as excellent historians of the abbey; as such, they are legitimate heirs to – and promoters of – a rich historiographical tradition. (As Cassinese archivists, moreover, both Leccisotti and Dell'Omo were (and are) custodians of the abbey's intellectual splendour.) And all three books adopted a similar written format and applied strategy: they begin with a chronological survey of the abbey's long history, organised into phases of destruction and renewal. This first (empirical) section is then customarily followed by a celebration of the abbey's spiritual, artistic, and scientific-intellectual achievements.[69]

Common to all these works is their familiar representation of destruction and recovery. While the secular tendency might be to interpret these events as sharp breaks in the continuity of Monte Cassino's historical narrative – a rupture in the abbey's timeline – their representation is more self-contained and referential; the 'golden chain' of historiography frames our modern understanding of this abbey, evoking its inner coherence and

---

65 For its influence on his successors, see Jallonghi, 'D. Ottavio Fraja Fangipane'.
66 For a look at Tosti's process, see Leccisotti, 'D. Luigi Tosti'.
67 For his broader contribution to scholarship and preservation, see Dell'Omo, 'Tommaso Leccisotti e Montecassino'.
68 Dell'Omo, *Montecassino*.
69 For Fraja's contemporary reflection of Tosti's work, see *Giornali*, 18 July 1835 (cited in Leccisotti, *I Regesti dell'Archivio*, vol. X, p. xxxiv).

self-consciousness. The written sources comprising this unique historical vision 'are not simple reflections of past realities, but ways to create a new past for the present'. 'This was a continuous process,' as Walter Pohl suggested, 'in which successive generations appropriated and shaped their history, and thus also their identity'.[70]

The coherence to this narrative belongs exclusively to the Cassinese monks who fashioned it. From the early Middle Ages to the present day, the abbey's 'destruction tradition' has been incorporated into the longer story of its existence. In the aftermath of the Second World War, amidst the abbey's material ruins, a new edition of that past was considered urgent and necessary. With the publication of Leccisotti's book in 1947 (the first of many Italian editions), great hope was placed in resuscitating Monte Cassino's 'lost beauty and its eternal meaning'[71]; its dissemination was intended to 'help to bring to life and a sense of reality to the abbey's long and noble history'.[72] 'Updating' the abbey's history, Abbot Diamare saw in this work 'the means to encourage and strengthen the resolve of his tired and scattered monks, but he also wanted to stimulate to the work of reconstruction all people of good will'.[73] As the remainder of this chapter suggests, this enduring representation assumed a critical role in contemporary efforts to unite a broken Europe. In this grand enterprise, the solitary religious community of Monte Cassino and its patron saint served as exemplars; both were visible and historical reminders of a deep past, universal purpose, future hope and promise.

Spirituality and Civilization

The word 'PAX' is inscribed above Monte Cassino's main gate. Its meaning has served the monastic community for centuries. In the prologue of his sixth-century monastic *Rule*, Saint Benedict invited every person who climbed the hill of Cassinum to 'seek peace and to follow him' (Psalm 34:14).[74] Turning away from evil towards a spiritual life of obedience and humility became the hallmark of the religious life. Fourteen centuries later, on the occasion of the abbey's reconsecration in 1964, Pope Paul VI celebrated peace

---

70   Pohl, 'History in Fragments', p. 349.
71   The words of Giorgio Falco, quoted in the foreword to Leccisotti, *Monte Cassino*.
72   The words of Armand O. Citarella, quoted in the preface to Leccisotti, *Monte Cassino*.
73   Leccisotti, *Monte Cassino*, p. 151.
74   *Rule of Saint Benedict*, 'Prologue', verse 17, pp. 416–417.

16. Exterior of the Abbey of Monte Cassino.

'as a resurrected light, after whirlwinds of war had blown out the holy and benevolent flame'.[75] 'It is not by chance,' Pope Benedict XVI noted in a 2009 homily, that the word 'is used to greet pilgrims and visitors at the entrance of this Abbey [...]; it rises like a silent warning to reject every form of violence in order to build peace: in families, in communities, among peoples and throughout humanity'.[76]

'Peace' in this context is both a harbinger and a reminder. In the Christian tradition it implies Christ himself, who is peace. It is confirmed at baptism, upon entry into the Christian community. It is attainable between man and God, symbolising harmony of the body and soul, and faith to the eternal law. In the Benedictine tradition, it embodies a core eremitic value or principle: a spiritual goal, desire, and way of life. Historically (and temporally) it signifies the end of Christian persecution. According to Augustine of Hippo, peace is the 'tranquillity of order',[77] which refers to earthly peace in the earthly community – that is, the peace of all things.

Its meaning found renewed expression in the twentieth century. Monte Cassino had become its modern embodiment, custodian, and shepherd; peace could be found on the venerable mountain 'as envied treasure in its safest custody'. Pope Paul VI addressed the abbey's contemporary significance in his homily celebrating its reconsecration. He spoke directly to the brothers of the Holy Church, who felt 'the history that passes, the civilization that is generated and described, the Christianity that is tired and affirms itself'.[78] He reminded them of the 'generating virtue of peace', which in the case of Monte Cassino appeared to be 'just as true as it is alive', 'active and fruitful'.[79] There it revealed itself 'in its extremely interesting capacity for reconstruction, rebirth, regeneration'.[80]

The abbey's capacity for renewal was written on its walls:

> It is peace that made them rise again. As it still seems incredible to us that the war has had against this Abbey, an incomparable monument of religion, culture, art, civilization, one of the proudest and most blind gestures of its rage, so it does not seem true to see today the resurrected majestic building, almost as if it wanted to delude us that nothing happened, that its destruction was a dream and that we can forget the tragedy

---

75 Pope Paul VI, 'Discorso', in *Pacis Nuntius*, p. 9.
76 'Homily of His Holiness Benedict XVI'.
77 Augustine of Hippo, *De civitate Dei*, 19. 13, p. 679.
78 Pope Paul VI, 'Discorso', in *Pacis Nuntius*, p. 10.
79 Ibid., pp. 10–11.
80 Ibid., p. 11.

that had made it a heap of ruins. Brothers, let us cry with emotion and gratitude. By duty of our office with Pope Pius XII, of venerable memory, we are well informed witnesses of what the Apostolic See did to spare this fortress not of arms but of the spirit, the grave outrage of its destruction. That pleading and sovereign voice, defenseless vindication of faith and civilization, was not heard. Montecassino was bombed and demolished. One of the saddest episodes of the war was thus consumed.[81]

Paul VI was present to celebrate the abbey's reconstruction, not to allocate blame. He praised and blessed the many workers, collaborators, technicians, and benefactors who contributed to the gargantuan feat. He commended the authorities, who also played their part by lavishing care and various resources. As a direct consequence of this concerted industry, financial, philanthropic, and artistic support, the abbey had

> become the trophy of all the immense effort made by the Italian people for the reconstruction of this beloved country, terribly torn from one end of its territory to the other, and immediately, by divine assistance and by virtue of its children, immediately risen more beautiful and younger.[82]

But the abbey's contemporary and future history was not based on material construction alone. 'No, of course [not]'. Benedict was at the centre of it all. 'It is his spiritual mission, which finds its headquarters and its symbol in the material building, which qualifies it for it. It is his capacity for attraction and spiritual irradiation, which populates his solitude of energies, which world peace needs.' The Church and the world, 'for different but convergent reasons, need St. Benedict to come out of the ecclesial and social community, and surround himself with his enclosure of solitude and silence'. He

> returns to help us recover our personal lives; that personal life, of which today we have longing and anxiety, and that the development of modern life, to which we owe the exasperated desire to be ourselves, suffocates while awakens it, disappoints while it makes it conscious.[83]

The world needed the values possessed by this abbey. So the pope argued. It was no longer possible for Monte Cassino to exist in isolation from the

---

81 Ibid.
82 Ibid., p. 12.
83 Ibid., p. 13.

secular world, as Benedict intended upon foundation in the early sixth century. The times had changed, though the spirit of this abbey could still offer guidance in the modern world; its historical experience and resilience in the face of multiple adversaries fostered a continuous tradition between the past and the present. In this way, the pope believed, the abbey

> touches the existence and the consistency of this old and always vital society of ours but today so much in need of drawing new sap from its roots, from which it drew its vigour and its splendour, its Christian roots, to which St Benedict gave so much and nurtured its spirit. And it is such a beautiful fact that it deserves memory, worship and trust. Not because we should think of a new Middle Ages characterized by the dominant activity of the Benedictine Abbey; now a completely different face gives our society its cultural, industrial, social and sports centres; but for two leaders who still desire the austere and gentle presence of St Benedict among us: for the faith, which he and his order preached in the family of peoples, especially in that which is called Europe; the Christian faith, the religion of our civilization, that of the holy Church, mother and teacher of the people; and for unity, to which the great monk solitary and social educated us brothers, and for which Europe was Christianity.[84]

'Faith and unity'. These were the virtues most represented by the famed abbey. What better qualities, the pope asked, 'could we desire and invoke for the whole world, and especially for the large and elected portion, which, we repeat, is called Europe? What [is] more modern and more urgent? And what [is] more difficult and contrasted? What [is] more needed and more useful for peace?' It is for these reasons, the homily concluded, that Saint Benedict was proclaimed 'patron and protector of Europe' (*patrono e protettore dell'Europa*).[85]

This very accolade was the subject of Pope Paul VI's apostolic letter *Pacis Nuntius* (24 October 1964), in which he exalted Saint Benedict as a 'Messenger of peace, creator of union, master of civilization, and above all a herald of the religion of Christ and founder of monastic life in the West'.[86] Recalling his progress with the Cross, book, and the plough in the wake of the Roman Empire, a period of darkness across Europe, 'devoid of civilization and spiritual values', it was Benedict who showed 'a constant and assiduous

---

84 Ibid., p. 15.
85 Ibid.
86 Pope Paul VI, *Pacis Nuntius*, p. 17.

commitment to give birth to the dawn of a new era'.[87] Through the laws of Christ, which 'gave consistency and development to the systems of public and private life', and by teaching humanity through divine worship, liturgical and ritual prayer, Benedict

> cemented that spiritual unity in Europe by virtue of which peoples divided on the linguistic, ethnic and cultural levels warned to constitute the one people of God; a unity which, thanks to the constant effort of those monks who followed this illustrious master, became the distinguishing feature of the Middle Ages.[88]

This exemplary unity was 'unfortunately broken up into a tangle of historical events'.[89] With his book and his culture, however, Saint Benedict 'saved the classical tradition of the ancients with providential solicitude, at the moment when the humanist heritage was dispersing, transmitting it intact to posterity and restoring the cult of knowledge'. With his plough, he 'succeeded in transforming deserted and wild lands into very fertile fields and in pretty gardens; and uniting prayer to material work, according to his famous motto "ora et labora", he ennobled and elevated human fatigue'. It was for these initiatives of loving care, order, and justice, Paul VI contended, that his predecessor (Pius XII) 'greeted St. Benedict [as] "father of Europe" (cfr. *A.A.S.* loc. mem.)'.[90]

This pope was determined to follow the same course as his predecessors.[91] Doing so meant receiving the full assent of the 'Cardinals, Archbishops, Bishops, Superiors General of Religious Orders, Rectors of Universities and other distinguished representatives of the laity of various European nations to declare St. Benedict Patron of Europe'.[92] Taking the opportunity of Monte Cassino's reconsecration in 1964, he sought by solemn proclamation to exalt the saint who made the abbey famous, to fulfil his vows, and 'with the light of Christian civilization [...] to dispel the darkness and radiate the gift of peace'. By virtue of his apostolic power, he marked the occasion of his historic visit to the mountain by constituting and proclaiming Saint Benedict as 'the principal patron of the whole of

87 Ibid.
88 Ibid., pp. 17–18.
89 Ibid., p. 18.
90 Ibid.
91 For a record of postulator letters (dated June 1946–October 1964), see *Pacis Nuntius*, pp. 96–104.
92 Pope Paul VI, *Pacis Nuntius*, p. 18.

Europe, granting every honour and liturgical privilege, due by right to the primary Protectors'.[93]

The 'most auspicious event'[94] was meticulously planned. Upon entry into the church on 24 October, Abbot Rea addressed the pope and the audience gathered inside.[95] He began by recalling the papacy's support during Monte Cassino's 'long existence', from Zachary in the eighth century to Benedict XIII in the eighteenth, which had kept the 'traces' of the abbey's passage alive.[96] From the days of the very first 'barbarian' attack, he contended, popes were active contributors to the community's 'new life'.[97] Speaking on this celebratory occasion, 20 years after Monte Cassino's most recent destruction, the abbot noted how 'the ancient history has been renewed, [it] is repeated even today, in its analogies, before our eyes'.[98] To commemorate the event, an inscription was written and engraved on white marble which summarised the history of the basilica and its papal consecrations, ultimately exalting Benedict's newly bestowed title as the 'patron of Europe'.[99]

The next pope to visit Monte Cassino stoked the flames of this tradition even higher. As the first Polish man ever to occupy the Holy See, Pope John Paul II paid his respects in May 1979 to this historic religious community and the thousands of Polish soldiers who died fighting there in the winter of 1943–1944. To this day, those killed during the Battle of Monte Cassino lie buried in a finely preserved cemetery, situated just below the 'Hill of St Benedict'. As the pope himself professed, his stop at the abbey 'takes on almost a symbolic meaning. Completely destroyed by the fury of war and reborn from its ruins, it [Monte Cassino] continues to be for Europe and for the world a centre of spirituality and civilization'.[100]

He then promptly turned his attention to outlining what he called 'a programme of life in the light of Monte Cassino and St. Benedict'. He asked his audience: 'What can it say to us, what does it want to say to us, this outstanding monument of religious spirit and of humanity?' By his count, the abbey had been destroyed three times throughout its existence. '[T]hree times it rose again from its ruins, remaining a mystical centre of inexpressible

---

93   Ibid., p. 19.
94   Ibid., p. 107.
95   For the complete list of attendees, see *Pacis Nuntius*, pp. 123–132.
96   Ildefonso Rea, in *Pacis Nuntius*, p. 114. For the longer tradition of papal visits and support, see especially pp. 41–48.
97   Ibid., p. 115.
98   Ibid.
99   Ibid., p. 139.
100 Pope John Paul II, 'Address of His Holiness' (18 May 1979).

value for Italy, Europe and the world.' Throughout its history, it had attracted the 'humble and the powerful, saints and sinners, mystics and the desperate', 'poets, writers, philosophers and artists', as well as 'defenceless and fugitive multitudes, exhausted and frightened, victims of the storms of the times, and they found refuge and comfort'.[101] 'Why,' he then asked, 'did these humble or important people flock to Monte Cassino?' Citing Dante's *Paradiso* (XXII 37–45), he answered that '[p]eople have always come and continue to come here to meet "the truth which lifts us so high", to breathe a different atmosphere, transcendent and transforming'. Invoking the abbey's past, he called for everyone to visit. 'Come', he said,

> to meditate on past history and understand the true meaning of our earthly pilgrimage! Come to regain peace and serenity, tenderness with God and friendship with men, to bring back hope and goodness to the frantic metropolises of the modern world, to the anguish of so many tormented and disappointed souls!

This was not a targeted tourism campaign but a critical reflection on contemporary society. More than three decades after the war's end, the 'voice of the times' was still filled with much anxiety and trepidation. Yet humanity was 'aiming more and more at unity', for a 'greater mutual knowledge among individuals and among peoples'. Europe was 'realizing its unity'. 'But listening to St Benedict,' the pope said,

> who was defined 'Father of Europe' by Pius XII and whom Paul VI decreed its heavenly Patron, the times are urging towards increasingly intense reciprocal understanding, which will defeat and overcome social inequalities, selfish indifference, arrogance and intolerance.

This was the true message of Christian faith (e.g., Matthew 5:1–12; Colossians 3:12–15) – the 'soul and the spirit of Europe'.[102]

The pope did more than simply reinforce the general message of his predecessors: he attempted to deepen the historic connection by explaining its relevance to the modern world. Benedict's voice, he argued, 'unites with the voice of the times'. He presented the unity of European peoples as being fulfilled through the peace of Christ: '[W]e hope that this will lead also to deeper awareness of the roots – spiritual roots, Christian roots – because,

---

101 Ibid.
102 Ibid.

if a common house is to be built, deeper foundations also have to be laid. A superficial foundation is not enough.' And that deeper foundation, he stated, 'always means "spiritual"' – that is, 'based on the spiritual foundation of the Benedictine tradition, of the Christian tradition, the Catholic one, which means universal'.

Monte Cassino remained the most visible embodiment of that spirit and its foundation. The fifteenth centennial of Saint Benedict's birth (21 March 1980) marked an occasion to unite these beliefs into a unified and powerful message for all Christian faithful. Meetings, conferences, publications, liturgical celebrations, musical concerts, exhibitions, and grand artistic works were part and parcel of the organised festivities.[103] The cycle of planned activities culminated on 20 September with the pastoral visit of Pope John Paul II, who issued a number of speeches to the people, clergy, religious, young people, and laity of Cassino. Similar to the celebrations in 1947 noted above, the festivities were held to remind the contemporary world about the teachings of Saint Benedict – 'may they long live and contribute to the revival of European unity'.[104] This was precisely the pope's message in this jubilee year, paying deep respects to a land 'profoundly marked by the memory and protection of the patriarch of the West'.[105]

The opportunity to restate this deep spiritual connection was not missed. In his message to the people of Cassino, the pope hoped that Benedict's celebratory year would bring 'a valid contribution to the renewal of ecclesiastical and human life in an authentically Christian sense'. Because, simply stated, 'Saint Benedict belongs to the history of the whole world'; he and his *Rule* marshalled in the 'advent of European culture and civilisation', crossing national and continental borders to 'spread through the whole world'. Like the evangelical doctrine on which it is founded, the 'whole institutional structure' of Monte Cassino, so strong as to challenge over fourteen centuries of history, converges to create the climate in which to put into effect those that the saint calls the 'instruments of good works'.[106] Speaking to the universal principles of love and the family, John Paul II suggested further that Benedict 'also invites us to transform the whole of humanity into a Christian family of peoples, based on the values introduced by the Rule in the historical ferment that created Europe's unity of faith'.[107]

---

103 For a good summary of events, see Dell'Omo, 'Cronaca delle celebrazioni cassinesi'.
104 Leccisotti, *Monte Cassino*, p. 189.
105 Pope John Paul II, 'Discorso di Giovanni Paolo II al clero'.
106 *Rule of St Benedict*, chapter 4.
107 Pope John Paul II, 'Discorso di Giovanni Paolo II al clero'.

Love and peace were two main Christian agents of unification. Their absence in times of war served as a sharp reminder of their valued necessity to humanity. The town of Cassino had been utterly destroyed during the Second World War. '[T]he glorious Benedict abbey, world center of piety, culture and art' was also 'barbarously razed to the ground. All the populous surrounding villages, fervent with honest work; all your beautiful fields, so fertile and luxuriant, reduced to a desolate moor, infested with malaria'. 'Why remember all this,' the pope asked, 'if not to shout from here to everyone, individuals and communities, that every war is always a fratricide; if not to proclaim the need, the security, the joy of peace?' Lumping together the town and mountain summit, the pope's speech praised the glory of their recovery:

> [N]ow reborn from its rubble for a gift of God, of the Assumption of Mary and of St. Benedict, and for the value of your intelligent work, must be today and tomorrow not a call to the death inflicted by wars, but a very strong and resonant invitation to the industrious and joyful life of peace.[108]

That life had a long and sometimes confused history. Such is the chaos of time and its relationship to memory. Addressing a group of dignitaries from various nations, the Italian Secretary of State, Agostino Casaroli, said: 'The soil we trample is marked, and almost oppressed, by centuries of history: a story that is inserted, and sometimes confused with that of Europe'. The reason for the confusion, he noted, was its connection 'to the person, first, and then to the spiritual heritage of a man'.[109] For this civil servant, this jubilee 'invites us to return, with the memory, to the times of the appearance of Saint Benedict on the Italian scene, and of Europe. Dark and difficult times, more oppressed by worry and fear, than open to hope'. He grafted the abbey's history onto the formation of Europe and the Christianisation of the West, a period which 'marks the starting point of that vigorous expansion of monastic life, throughout the West, which represents one of the most characteristic and richest phenomena of positive consequences of the historical period in which Europe was built'.[110]

Monte Cassino played an irrevocable role in this formation story. As an exalted religious house with a long European heritage, it 'pointed out to the peoples, with the example lived, before the enunciation of a doctrine, the

---

108 Ibid.
109 'Allocuzione del Segretario di Stato, Agostino Casaroli'.
110 Ibid.

path to the realization of what was and remains the profound aspiration of men'.[111] Its experience and triumph over loss and destruction offered a profound lesson in humility, a message both spiritual and civil that 'from the top of this hill, sacred to its memory, it still launches today in Europe, to the world'. 'Yes, to the world', the Secretary of State said, '[b]ecause the legacy of example and teaching left by St. Benedict is a universal good'. The abbey represented the light of his spirituality and the leaven of civilisation, 'of which he was the bearer and remains a symbol'. His message, moreover, 'on which so much responsibility continues to weigh on the world, for better or for worse', was especially relevant to the European continent. 'Here the fire that twice broke out,' he continued,

> involving so much of the globe, in the first half of our century. Here they have cradled so many movements of thought and action that have then spread far beyond its borders. Europe therefore has a special duty to be, in this age of new grave dangers, which seem to want to extinguish the hopes that arose after the end of the Second World War, an element of balance and peace.[112]

The latter responsibility did not belong solely to Europe. Benedict's message of peace, and his motto of 'ora et labora' could find wider application in the whole world – 'the robust fruit of the clear political vision and the decisive will of all men responsible for the fate of the peoples themselves'. His message 'anticipated the modern vision, laying the cornerstone of his rule of life – together with prayer – work'. This religious and moral message, it was contended,

> reminds us that the roots of peace go deep into the heart and conscience of man. There, where selfishness, indifference towards others, even hatred often reside, the feelings of fraternity, the co-responsibility of each with regard to the fate of the entire human family must be educated from childhood; to put it in Christian terms: love.[113]

The Italian Secretary of State spoke of 'a solemn commitment to history', to whose origins the whole of Europe was returning. Monte Cassino was a 'victim of the terrible destruction of the war,' but one which had 'once

---

111 Ibid.
112 Ibid.
113 Ibid.

again risen from its rubble: monument of fraternity and peace, symbol and triumph of the will to life, stronger than hatred and death, irrepressible as the hope of peoples'.[114] It therefore represented a 'luminous Christian tradition,'

> which is at the same time so frankly human, therefore open to the contributions of cultures different design, as long as they are faithful to the values of a genuine humanism: may Europe rediscover the essential reasons for its unity, which, despite the travail of this new phase of its multisecular history, marked by tensions and divisions that could seem irremediable, allow to guarantee its peoples a secure and fruitful peace: not in opposition to, but at the service of peace and cooperation among all the peoples of the world, for common security and common progress.[115]

*

Monte Cassino assumed a principal role in this mission. Or rather, it might be more accurate to conclude, this role was assigned to it. As an emblem and guardian of European heritage, the abbey was widely recognised with the Church for its capacity to rebuild Western culture and civilisation. Its symbolic potential for reinvigorating, rebuilding, and unifying in the post-war era evokes a secular and religious idealism thrust upon the Italian community from the nineteenth century onward: the scaffolding for a united, 'new Europe' – the authentic symbol of martyrdom and resurrection to which the whole continent might aspire. Its most recent destruction served as a powerful reminder of diminishing moral values, 'for all humanity a profound lesson in deep humility'.[116] But its resilience and recovery in the following decades of the twentieth century signalled hope – hope for Italian and Christian unity '[w]ithout distinction of social class, of political ideology, of party, of hatred past and potential, we must reconstruct it, stone by stone, with a deep sense of fraternal abnegation'. For as one writer observed, and many others ostensibly believed: 'in the slow rise of the Abbey will rise our redemption'.[117]

114 Ibid.
115 Ibid.
116 Comm. Rudolfo Terenzio, untitled document, Fondo "Ricostruzione di Montecassino," Private Archive of Montecassino, reprinted in Avagliano, 'Montecassino "com'era e dov'era"', pp. 153–154.
117 Ibid., p. 153.

By this measurement, the future of Europe – 'l'unità della nuova Patria'[118] – depended on Monte Cassino's uninterrupted place in the tradition of European history and Western culture. Transcending its essentialist medieval, religious, and coenobitic origins in the sixth century, the abbey had come to symbolise a universal human experience of suffering and hope. The many historical experiences comprising its 'destruction tradition' served to justify this cultural identity, whose emic construction over the past 1,400 years was transformed into a more universal, post-war legacy surrounding Europe's reconstruction and unity.

118 Ibid., p. 154.

Epilogue: Lighthouse

Abstract

Monte Cassino stands today as a rich and symbolic lesson in history. The abbey's manifold experience with destruction and recovery reveals a profound transformation of historical meaning and value, which is manifested in the twenty-first century. This epilogue reflects on the representation of Monte Cassino's history as the centre of Western culture, learning, and civilisation – a legacy that has repeatedly shaped and propelled its 'use-value'. This assigned relevance – from the early Middle Ages to the present day – takes much of its meaning from the abbey's 'destruction tradition' – the interplay between 'destruction' and 'recovery', death and resurrection, adversity and perseverance.

Keywords: World Heritage; UNESCO; culture; value; tradition

> '[T]hat constant reminder of Heaven.'[1]

Monte Cassino is a European asset. This concluding statement needs little qualification. It is an observation informed by the various arguments underwriting this book, which have charted the evolution of this triumphalist idea from the abbey's origins to the present day. Rebuilt after its most recent destruction during the Second World War, the abbey's current incarnation is on full public display. Overlooking the Liri Valley, the Land of Labour, the confluence of the Rivers Liri, Rapido, and Garigliano, the hastily rebuilt – and now languishing – town of Cassino, and various prominent military cemeteries (Polish and American), it stands as an historic monument engineered to the point of iconic veneration. It is certainly not what it once was or intended to be; although the historical (Benedictine) records like to represent a continuity of tradition, the abbey's manifold experience with

---

1   Pope Benedict XVI, 'Homily'.

destruction and recovery reveals a profound transformation of historical meaning and value.

Monte Cassino is an impressive 'workshop'[2] and product of human imagination, memory, and industry. Its historical and religious significance has metamorphosised over fourteen centuries into an international product for cultural consumption and appreciation. Universal recognition of its exalted cultural, historical, and religious status has made it a popular tourist destination. The abbey's website boasts that 'thousands of pilgrims and visitors from all around the world come to this threshold' every day of the year. They walk through the cloisters, visit the Basilica which claims to house the tombs of Saints Benedict and Scholastica, then journey below to its crypt and view the rich mosaics. 'But it is in the museum', it is noted,

> where finally visitors can see the magnificent paintings, the wonderful manuscripts and ancient books. They can go through the history of the Abbey from the very beginning till today and grasp why Montecassino Abbey is known as the Lighthouse of Western Civilization.[3]

The abbey stands today as a rich, symbolic lesson in history. While other medieval monasteries might claim a similar fate during their existence, none compares to Monte Cassino's singular and unique experience across fourteen centuries: its destruction by human actors and natural forces repeatedly inspired a process of material, cultural, and spiritual recovery that remains unrivalled in the historical record. As a monument atop a sacred mountain, a home to the remains of Saint Benedict and his sister, Monte Cassino has become regarded as the 'lighthouse'[4] of a deep Christian past and ancestry. The representation of its history as the centre of Western culture, learning, and civilisation has repeatedly shaped and propelled its 'use-value' in precisely this historical context. This assigned relevance – from the early Middle Ages to the present day – takes much of its meaning from the abbey's 'destruction tradition' – the interplay between 'destruction' and 'recovery', death and resurrection, adversity and perseverance.

This historical concept is integral to understanding Monte Cassino's true character and identity. It describes and explains the abbey's

---

2   See Pohl, *Werkstätte der Erinnerung*.
3   Cited on the abbey's website: 'Visit Montecassino'.
4   This expression was perhaps first used on 25 November 1953, in Cardinal Schuster's letter to Abbot Rea about the importance of Monte Cassino for monastic observance, for the contemplative life, for prayer (*Ildefonso Schuster – Ildefonso Rea*, no. 182, p. 253.)

self-representation and enduring legacy, carefully cultivated over time. Its framework and interplay reveal the abbey's 'distinct orders of experience'[5] and its accompanying historical discourse – that is, its usable past. Notwithstanding the damage wrought against the abbey between the sixth and twentieth centuries, it always survived. This was not a matter of mere chance, but a concerted effort by a host of internal and external players to reanimate its spirit through more than just material reconstruction.

As this book has demonstrated, the abbey's true identity is manifested through this dominant historiographical tradition. That identity has been constructed and carefully fostered over time: a linear, continuous, and triumphalist sense of the past made possible through the incorporation of catastrophic events into the abbey's main and cohesive narrative. As a rhetorical exercise in counterfactual history, we might justifiably ask whether Monte Cassino would even exist today without these defining historical experiences and their ensuing historical arc.

One thing is certain: the Cassinese narrative – that dominant historical tradition examined throughout this book – has been conceived *in relation to* these events. Just how this religious community of celibate, primarily European monks contributed to a universal framework of human experience is a complex question. But as this book has shown, the abbey's conceptualisation of its own suffering and resurrection – Monte Cassino's shared reality – gave witness to precisely this outcome and historical representation.

Without a doubt, these experiences have only increased the abbey's cultural value and international esteem. For many, Monte Cassino and the spiritual lessons of its patron saint continue to offer incorruptible wisdom for the modern world. On Benedict's feast day in 2010, for example, Cardinal Tarcisio Bertone (Segretario di stato del santo padre) addressed the abbey's role in the formation of European identity. In this ongoing search, which continues '[e]ven today', he noted, the abbey and its founder provide 'a new and lasting unity' and the power 'to arouse an ethical and spiritual renewal that draws on the continent's Christian roots'. Searching for 'true progress', Cardinal Bertone encouraged his readers to 'listen today to the lesson of Saint Benedict, as a beacon for our journey'. For this saint

> remains a teacher whose school we can learn the art of living true humanism. How, at the end of the ancient age, Saint Benedict and his monks knew how to become builders and guardians of civilization, so in this age of ours, marked by a rapid cultural evolution, it is urgent to become aware

---

5   White, 'Fictions of Factual Representation', p. 122.

of the new needs and to reaffirm, at the same time, the deep adherence to perennial values.[6]

The abbey embodied these 'perennial values' through its preserved heritage: the most visible remains of its past, painstakingly reconstructed after every episode of destruction. This book has shown exactly how the abbey harnessed these experiences into a defining tradition, affirming and valorising its historical significance both inside and outside the cloister walls. In pursuing the *idea* of Monte Cassino over 1,400 years, we have seen the abbey's evolution into a national and international symbol of peace, hope, faith, goodwill, and prosperity. Assigned the role as purveyor of Western culture and civilisation, the abbey's current incarnation perpetuates its place in the 'golden chain' as a monument of unrivalled historical and religious importance.

The measure of that importance is currently being formulated and assessed in a more official capacity. In March 2016, the Permanent Delegation of Italy to UNESCO submitted an application for World Heritage status. The 'Monte Cassino complex' forms part of this ongoing bid to preserve and celebrate the 'cultural landscapes of the Benedictine settlements in medieval Italy'.[7] By way of an introductory statement, the delegation outlined the totality of eight monastic settlements which 'represent a cultural phenomenon born in the Italian peninsula and spread out through the medieval Europe'. The nomination 'focuses on medieval monastic experience in Europe and the decisive role of Benedict of Norcia and his Rule'. For it was this regulation for monastic living and behaviour that 'radiated from Italy throughout the Latin West and gave birth to a monasticism that deeply affected Europe's intellectual and political formation, the development of the continent's cultural heritage, landscape and artistic tradition'. The *Rule* 'had an effective impact on the landscape and on the rural populations throughout the Middle Ages, spurring forms of civilization and life conditions'. Its impact on European culture and world history more broadly is measured by the development of medieval (Romanesque) art and architecture, knowledge, manuscript production and the transmission of 'classical cultural heritage'.

The roots of this wholesale tradition begin and end with Monte Cassino. They do not exist, and cannot be understood historically, without a greater appreciation of its 'destruction tradition' between the sixth and twentieth

6 'Omelia del Card'.
7 See description and appended file on UNESCO's Word Heritage Convention, 'The cultural landscape of the Benedictine settlements in medieval Italy'.

centuries. The founding abbey was praised not only as a representative (living) example of uniform Benedictine adherence, but also as 'a key place for the formation and transmission of culture in Europe'. As a singular example, Monte Cassino represented a 'remarkable continuity of traditions', one that has 'perpetuated for centuries as a possible model of humanity and sustainable development'. Likewise, 'the conservation of the landscape and the preservation of the monuments in their material aspects and in their relationship with the natural environment is the result of a centuries-old spiritual tradition and sentiment'. Like all its counterparts in this heritage application, Monte Cassino speaks to a monumental and natural landscape characterised by medieval artistic, intellectual, linguistic, and architectural achievements. They are of 'outstanding universal value', it was argued, because they form part of the cultural landscape of Italy and beyond.

A set of criteria was presented as evidence for such grand claims. The monastic experience is a transcendental universal phenomenon, one which provides 'outstanding models of intellectual and social life, characterized by the balance between individual and community, the respect for diversity and the harmony between man and nature'. The material evidence of this relationship should be preserved, as its radiation from Italy and beyond

> had a deep effect on the intellectual and cultural development, shaping the medieval Mediterranean civilizations and contributing, since the Carolingian period, to the intellectual, political and economic development of modern Europe and to the formation of the Romanesque art and architecture.

'Fitting harmoniously into the natural environment,' Monte Cassino and the other religious complexes

> offer a model of coexistence, sustainable development and conservation of the environment, providing a valuable message for the contemporary society and for the future generations, who can draw the essential values for their human and intellectual formation.

They were also 'important cultural centers, in which the universal heritage of knowledge was recovered, preserved and spread through exchanges and acquisitions as the primary investments for the construction of the future'.

UNESCO has established a set of international rules to protect such value. Its Operational Guidelines for the Implementation of the World Heritage

Convention (WHC) add context to the international significance of their intervention in the above-mentioned case. Paragraph 49 explains:

> Outstanding universal value means cultural and/or natural significance which is so exceptional as to transcend national boundaries and to be of common importance for present and future generations of all humanity. As such, the permanent protection of this heritage is of the highest important to the international community as a whole.[8]

According to the delegation responsible for the application, Monte Cassino more than exceeds these standards.

That the abbey was destroyed and rebuilt throughout its existence does not diminish the overall claims of its contribution to – and essential place in – the foundations of European heritage. For reasons carefully detailed, explained, interpreted, and advanced in this book, these experiences made its claims to that past even stronger – historical witness to its birth and maturation.

The spirit of Saint Benedict was integral to this chain of religious memory. But the abbey's concrete presence also summons an irrevocable past. That past has been salvaged from extinction on several occasions over the last fourteen centuries, fostering rather than diminishing its connection with the present. It is hard to discern any 'conflict of the Present and the Past', as Longfellow wrote after his visit in the second half of the nineteenth century; what remains is a semblance of harmony and eternal symbolism in this historical relationship – a sense of the past, whose 'records and memories of past ages' reverberate 'by an echo'[9] within the abbey's walls and far beyond.

The Benedictine community of Monte Cassino is best-known because of its self-portrayal: a culture and tradition defined by the balance of destruction and recovery. The abbey's experience and triumph over adversity reveals a perpetual tale of perseverance and endurance. As this book has shown, this legacy owes a great deal to its medieval origins in central Italy. But the community's suffering and victimisation over fourteen centuries speak to a more universal human experience, one whose coherence, meaning, and value has been memorialised by these significant historical events. It is their representation, in turn, which defines the abbey's true character and identity – an enduring legacy recorded, interpreted, and shaped over more than 1,400 years.

8 UNESCO, 'Outstanding Universal Value', in 'Operational Guidelines', para. 49, p. 19.
9 Iannetta, *Henry W. Longfellow*, p. 77.

References

Manuscript Sources

Archivio Segreto Vaticano
Registra Avenionensia (Reg. Aven.) 125

Biblioteca Apostolica Vaticana
Vat. lat. 1202
Vat. lat. 1203
Vat. lat. 4939

Biblioteca dell'Abazia Montecassino
Cod. Cas. 3
Cod. Cas. 47
Cod. Cas. 175
Cod. Cas. 361

Rome, Biblioteca Casanatense 641 (B IC 18)

Printed Primary Sources (Medieval and Early Modern)

Acta Sanctorum. Accessed 26 November 2020. http://acta.chadwyck.co.uk.
Adevrald of Fleury, *Historia translationis s. Benedicti*, ed. by Jean-Paul Migne, PL 124: 901–909.
Alfanus of Salerno, *I carmi di Alfano I arcivescovo di Salerno*, ed. by Anselmo Lentini and Faustino Avagliano. Miscellanea Cassinese 38 (Monte Cassino: Pubblicazioni Cassinesi, 1974).
Amatus of Montecassino, *The History of the Normans*, trans. by Prescott N. Dunbar and Graham A. Loud (Woodbridge: The Boydell Press, 2004).
Annales Bertiniani, ed. by Georg Pertz, MGH SS rer. Germ. 5 (Hanover: Hahn, 1883).
Annales Casinenses, ed. by Georg Pertz, MGH SS 19 (Hanover: Hahn, 1866), pp. 303–320.
Annales Casinenses ex annalibus montis Casini antiquis et continuatis excerpti inde ab a. 1000 (999) usque ad a. 1098, ed. by Wilhelm Smidt, MGH SS 30, 2 (Leipzig: Hiersemann, 1934), pp. 1385–1429.
Annales Einhardi, ed. by Georg Pertz, MGH SS 1 (Hanover: Hahn, 1826), pp. 135–218.
Annales Fuldenses, ed. by Georg Pertz, MGH SS rer. Germ. 7 (Hanover: Hahn, 1891).
Annales Laureshamenses, ed. by Georg Pertz, MGH SS 1 (Hanover: Hahn, 1826), pp. 22–39.
Anonymorum monachorum Casinensium breve chronicon, in Gattola, *Ad historiam*, II, pp. 827–839.
Anonymous, *Abt Aligern von Montecassino*, ed. by Karl Strecker, MGH Poetarum Latinorum medii aevi 5, 1.2 (Leipzig: Hiersemann, 1937), pp. 344–345.
Augustine of Hippo, *De civitate Dei*, 2 vols, ed. by B. Dombart and A. Kalb, Corpus Christianorum Series Latina 47–48 (Turnhout: Brepols, 1955).
Baluze, Étienne, *Vitae papae Avenionensium: hoc est historia pontificum Romanorum qui in Gallia sederunt ab anno Christi MCCCV usque ad annum MCCCXCIV*, ed. by Guillaume Mollat

(Paris: Letouzey et Ané, 1914). Accessed 26 November 2020. http://baluze.univ-avignon.fr/read_index.html#.

Baronius, Cesare, *Annales ecclesiastici*, 38 vols (Lucca: Typis Leonardi Venturini, 1738).

Bede, *Ecclesiastical History of the English People*, ed. and trans. by Bertram Colgrave and R.A.B. Mynors (Oxford: Clarendon Press, 1969).

Chronica monasterii Casinensis, ed. by Helmut Hartmann, MGH SS 34 (Hanover: Hahn, 1980).

Chronica sancti Benedicti Casinensis, ed. by Georg Waitz, MGH SS rer. Lang. 1 (Hanover: Hahn, 1878), pp. 467–489. Trans. into Italian by Luigi Andrea Berto (Florence: Sismel – Edizione del Galluzzo, 2006).

Chronicon Brixiense, ed. by Georg Pertz, MGH SS 3 (Hanover: Hahn, 1839).

Chronicon Salernitanum: A Critical Edition with Studies on Literary and Historical Sources, and on Languages, ed. by Ulla Westerbergh (Stockholm: Almquist & Wiksell, 1956).

Chronicon Vulturnense del monaco Giovanni, 4 vols, ed. by Vincenzo Federici (Rome: Tipografia del Senato, 1925–1937).

Cicero, *Philippics*, trans. by D.R. Shackleton Bailey, rev. by J.T. Ramsey and Gesine Manuwald (Cambridge, MA: Harvard University Press, 2009).

Crónicas del Gran Capitán, ed. by Rodriguez Antonio Villa (Madrid: Bailly-Bailliére, 1908).

Cronicon siculum incerti authoris ab anno 340 ad annum 1396 in forma diary ex inedito Codice Ottoboniano Vaticano, ed. by Guiseppe De Blasiis (Naples: F. Gianini & fil., 1887).

Codicum Casinensium manuscriptorum catalogus. 3 vols, ed. by Mauro Inguanez (Montecassino: Pubblicazioni Cassinesi, 1915–1941).

Concilium in Austrasia habitum q.d. Germanicum, ed. by Albertus Werminghoff, MGH Conc. 2, 1 (Hanover and Leipzig: Hahn, 1906), pp. 1–4.

Dante, *The Divine Comedy*, trans. by John Ciardi (New York: New American Library, 1954).

De Imola, Benvenuto, *Comentum super Dantis Aldigherij Comoediam*, ed. by W. Warren Vernon (Florence: Typis G. Barbera, 1887).

Desiderius, *Dialogi de miraculis sancti Benedicti*, ed. by Gerhard Schwartz and Adolf Hofmeister, MGH SS 30, 2 (Leipzig: Hiersemann, 1934), pp. 1111–1151.

Die Urkunden Otto des III., ed. Paul Fridolin Kehr, MGH Diplomatum regum et imperatorum Germaniae, II (Hanover: Hansche, 1893), no. 333, p. 761.

Eigil, 'Vita Sturmi abbatis Fuldensis', in *Die Vita Sturmi des Eigil von Fulda. Literarkritische-historische Untersuchung und Edition*, ed. by Pius Engelbert (Marburg: N.G. Elwert, 1968).

Erchempert, *Historia Langobardorum Beneventanorum*, ed. by Georg Pertz and Georg Waitz, MGH SS rer. Germ. 1 (Hanover: Hahn, 1878), pp. 231–264.

Ex Adrevaldi Floriacensis miraculis s. Benedicti, ed. by O. Holder-Egger, MGH SS 15, 1 (Hanover: Hahn, 1887), pp. 474–497.

Gattola, Erasmo, *Ad historiam abbatiae Cassinensis accessiones*, 2 vols (Venice: Coleti, 1734).

Gattola, Erasmo, *Historia abbatiae Cassinensis*, 2 vols (Venice: Coleti, 1734).

Hunuberc of Heidenheim, 'The Hodoeporican of St Willibald', in *The Anglo-Saxon Missionaries in Germany, Being the Lives of SS. Willibrord, Boniface, Leoba and Lebuin Together with the Hodoepericon of St. Willibald and a Selection from the Correspondence of St. Boniface*, trans. by C.H. Talbot (London: Sheed and Ward, 1954), pp. 153–177.

Jaffé, Philipp, *Regesta pontificum Romanorum*, 2nd edition by S. Löwenfeld (JL = A.D. 882-1198), F. Kaltenbrunner (JK – A.D. ?-590), and P. Ewald (JE = A.D. 590–882), 2 vols (Leipzig: Veit, 1885-1888).

Le Liber Pontificalis, ed. by Louis Duchesne and Cyrille Vogel, 3 vols (Paris: E. de Boccard, 1884).

Les Miracles de Saint Benoît écrits par Adrevald Aimoin, André, Raoul, Tortaire et Hugues de Sainte Marie moines de Fleury, ed. by Eugène de Certain (Paris: Renouard, 1858).

Mabillon, Jean, *Vetera Analecta*. 4 vols (Lucca: Billaine, 1723).

Mabillon, Jean, and Michel Germain, *Museum Italicum seu collectio veterum scriptorum ex bibliothecis italicis*, 2 vols (Lucca: E. Martin, J. Boudot & S. Martin, 1687).

Maffeus, Raphael, *Commentariorum Urbanorum Octo et Tringinta Libri* (1506). Accessed 26 November 2020. https://reader.digitale-sammlungen.de/en/fs1/object/display/bsb10140068_00435.html.

Montecassino nel Quattrocento. Studi e documenti sull'abbazia Cassinese e la 'Terra S. Benedicti' nell crisi del passaggio all'età moderna, ed. by Mariano Dell'Omo, Miscellanea Cassinese 66 (Montecassino: Pubblicazioni Cassinesi, 1992).

Monumenta Germaniae Historica (Hanover and Leipzig: Hahn; Berlin: Weidmann, 1826-).

Muratori, Ludovico Antonio, *Epistolario*, ed. by Matteo Càmpori, 14 vols (Modena: Soc. Tip. Modenese, 1901).

Muratori, Ludovico Antonio, *Epitome Chronicorum Casinensium*, vol. 2, 1 (Milan: Stamperia della Società Palatina, 1723).

Patrologiae cursus completus, series Latina, ed. Jean-Paul Migne, 221 vols (Paris: Garnieri Fratres, 1844-1864).

Paul the Deacon, *Continuatio Casinensis*, ed. by Georg Pertz and Georg Waitz, MGH SS rer. Lang. 1 (Hanover: Hahn, 1878), pp. 198–200.

Paul the Deacon, *Historia Langobardorum Beneventanorum*, ed. by Georg Pertz and Georg Waitz, MGH SS rer. Lang. 1 (Hanover: Hahn, 1878).

Paul the Deacon, *Homiliae*, ed. by Jean-Paul Migne, PL 95:1565–1583.

Peter Damian, *Opusculum 36*, ed. by Jean-Paul Migne, PL 145:595–622.

Peter the Deacon, *De viris illustribus Casinensisibus opusculum*, ed. by Jean-Paul Migne, PL 173:1003–1062.

Peter the Deacon, *Ortus et vita iustorum cenobii Casinensis*, trans. by R.H. Rodgers (Berkeley: University of California Press, 1972).

Petrarch, Francesco, *Letters on Familiar Matters. Rerum Familiarum Libri*, trans. by Aldo S. Bernardo, 3 vols (Baltimore: Johns Hopkins University Press, 1982).

Pope Urban II, *Epistolae et Privilegia*, ed. by Jean-Paul Migne, PL 151:283–552.

Quatremère de Quincy, Antoine-Chrysostome, *Lettres à Miranda sur le déplacement des monuments de l'art de l'Italie* (Paris: Macula, 1989).

Radelgisi et Siginul divisio ducatus Beneventani, ed. by F. Bluhme, MGH Leges 4 (Hanover: Hahn, 1868), pp. 221–225.

Recueil des chartes de l'abbaye de Saint-Benoît-sur-Loire, vol. 1, ed. by Maurice Prou and Alexandre Vidier (Paris: Picard, 1907).

Regino of Prüm, *Chronicon*, ed. by. F. Kurze, SS rer. Germ. 50 (Hanover: Hahn, 1890).

Registrum Petri Diaconi (Montecassino, Archivio dell'abbazia, Reg. 3), 4 vols, Sources et documents, 4 (Rome: École Française de Rome, 2015).

Rudolf of Fulda, *Vita Leobae abbatissae Biscofesheimensis auct*, vol. 1, ed. by Georg Waitz, MGH SS 15, 1 (Hanover: Hahn, 1887), pp. 118–131.

Versus domni Bertharii abbatis de miraculis almi patris Benedicti, ed. by Ludwig Traube, MGH Poetae Latini aevi Carolini 3 (Berlin: Weidmann, 1896), pp. 394–398.

Vita s. Berarii, episcopi Cenomanensis et confessoris, in *Acta Sanctorum*, cols 157–163 (BHL 1177).

Vita Willibaldi episcopi Eichstetensis, vol. 1, ed. by O. Holder-Egger, MGH SS 15 (Hanover: Hahn, 1887), pp. 86–106.

Vita Wynnebaldi abbatis Heidenheimensis, ed. by O. Holder-Egger, MGH SS 15, 1 (Hanover: Hahn, 1887), pp. 106–117.

Vogüé, Adalbert de, *Grégoire le Grand: Dialogues*, 3 vols (Paris: Ed. du Cerf, 1978).

Vogüé, Adalbert de, *La règle de saint Benoit* (Paris: Ed. du Cerf, 1971).

Online and Printed Sources (Modern)

'XI-XII Centuries: Post Desiderius' "Golden Age"'. Accessed 1 February 2021. https://www.abbaziamontecassino.org/index.php/en/legacy/the-golden-age/25-xi-xii-centuries-post-desiderius-golden-age

'1943: The Removal of Treasures'. Accessed 1 February 2021. https://www.abbaziamontecassino.org/index.php/en/legacy/the-battle-of-montecassino/32-treasures-removal-montecassino-abbey-wwii

'1948 History of the United Nations War Crimes Commission and the Development of the Laws of War'. Accessed 26 November 2020. http://www.unwcc.org/wp-content/uploads/2017/04/UNWCC-history.pdf.

'Allocuzione del Segretario di Stato, Agostino Casaroli, durante la Santa Messa celebrata nella Abbazia di Montecassino', 21 March 1980. Accessed 26 November 2020. http://www.vatican.va/roman_curia//secretariat_state/card-casaroli/1980/documents/rc_seg-st_19800321_monte-cassino_it.html.

Böhmler, Rudolf, *Monte Cassino: A German View*, trans. by R.H. Stevens (Barnsley: Pen & Sword Military, 2015).

'Cable from General Marshall to General Eisenhower Regarding Protection of Artistic and Historic Monuments in Italy' (14 October 1943). Accessed 26 November 2020. https://www.eisenhowerlibrary.gov/research/online-documents/monuments-men-and-allied-effort-save-european-cultural-heritage.

Churchill, Winston, *The Second World War*, 6 vols (London: Houghton Mifflin Harcourt, 1948).

Clark, Mark W., *Calculated Risk* (New York: Harper, 1950).

'Convention (II) with Respect to the Laws and Customs of War on Land and Its Annex: Regulations Concerning the Laws and Customs of War on Land. The Hague, 29 July 1899'. Accessed 26 November 2020. https://ihl-databases.icrc.org/applic/ihl/ihl.nsf/Article.xsp?action=openDocument&documentId=C50B4EE486305FF5C12563CD00515E60.

'Convention (IV) Respecting the Laws and Customs of War on Land and Its Annex: Regulations Concerning the Laws and Customs of War on Land. The Hague, 18 October 1907'. Accessed 26 November 2020. https://ihl-databases.icrc.org/applic/ihl/ihl.nsf/Article.xsp?action=openDocument&documentId=3C43C56CFC87D4E3C12563CD005167AA.

'Costituzione dei Comitati', *Succisa Virescit* 1 (1946), 4–6.

Craven, Keppel, *Excursions in the Abruzzi and Northern Provinces of Naples*, 2 vols (London: R. Bentley, 1838).

Dickens, Charles, *American Notes and Pictures from Italy* (London: Oxford University Press, 1957).

Documenti Vaticani per la storia di Montecassino. Pontificato di Urbano V, ed. by Tommaso Leccisotti, Miscellanea Cassinese 28 (Montecassino: Pubblicazioni Cassinesi, 1952).

Einaudi, Luigi, 'Visita di S.E. il Presidente della Repubblica Italiana', *Succisa Virescit* 5 (1950), 31–32.

Eisenhower, Dwight D., 'Historic Monuments' (29 December 1943). Accessed 26 November 2020. https://text-message.blogs.archives.gov/2014/02/10/general-dwight-d-eisenhower-and-the-protection-of-cultural-property/.

Eisenhower, Dwight D., 'Notes for Use at Luncheon Given at Metropolitan Museum of Art' (2 April 1946). Accessed 26 November 2020. https://www.eisenhowerlibrary.gov/research/online-documents/monuments-men-and-allied-effort-save-european-cultural-heritage.

Eisenhower, Dwight D., 'Preservation of Historical Monuments' (26 May 1944). Accessed 26 November 2020. https://www.eisenhowerlibrary.gov/sites/default/files/research/online-documents/monuments-men/033-006.pdf.

Eustace, Rev. John Chetwode, *A Classical Tour through Italy* (London: T. Tegg, 1841).

Fuller, Major-General J.F.C., *The Second World War, 1939–45: A Strategical and Tactical History* (London: Eyre and Spottiswoode, 1948).
Gander, Leonard Marsland, *After These Many Quests*. London: Macdonald, 1949.
Gander, Leonard Marsland, 'Return to the Battlefields of Italy', *The English Review Magazine* 4, no. 1 (1950), 36–41.
Gladstone, W.E., *An Examination of the Official Reply of the Neapolitan Government* (London: J. Murray, 1852).
Gladstone, William E., *Gleanings of Past Years, 1843–1878*, 8 vols (London: Murray, 1879).
Gladstone, William E., 'Italy in 1888–89', *The Nineteenth Century: A Monthly Review* 25, no. 147 (1889), 763–780.
Gladstone, William E., *Two Letters to the Earl of Aberdeen: On the State Prosecutions of the Neapolitan Government* (London: Charles Dolman, 1851).
Grégoire, Abbé, *Oeuvres de l'Abbé Grégoire. Grégoire député à la Convention nationale*, vol. II (Paris: EDHIS, 1977).
Hall, Donald, *Eagle Argent: An Italian Journey* (London: Methuen, 1956).
Hansard: The Official Report of All Parliamentary Debates. Accessed 26 November 2020. https://api.parliament.uk/historic-hansard/index.html.
Il Bombardamento di Montecassino: diario di guerra di E. Grossetti – M. Matronola con altre testamonianze e documenti, ed. by Faustino Avagliano, Miscellanea Cassinese 41 (Montecassino: Pubblicazioni Cassinesi, 1980).
Ildefonso Schuster – Ildefonso Rea: il carteggio (1929–1954). Tra ideale monastico e grande storia, ed. by Mariano Dell'Omo (Milan: Jaca Book, 2018).
Il sepolcro di s. Benedetto, ed. by Tommaso Leccisotti et al., Miscellanea Cassinese 27, 45 (Montecassino: Pubblicazioni Cassinesi, 1951 and 1982).
Juin, Général A., 'Pèlerinage au Mont Cassin', *Mercure de France* 1004 (1947), 577–586.
'Julius Schlegel Dies; Former German Officer Saved Cassino Art Treasures', *The New York Times*, 9 August 1958, p. 13.
Kesselring, Albert, *The Memoirs of Field-Marshal Kesselring* (Stroud, Gloucestershire: The History Press, 2007).
La distruzione di Montecassino. Documenti e testimonianze (Montecassino: Tipografica Arpinate, 1950).
'La ricognizione dei sacri corpi di s. Benedetto e s. Scolastica', *Succisa Virescit* 5 (1950), 3–9.
Le Saint Siège et les Victimes de la Guerre, Janvier 1944–Juillet 1945, ed. by Pierre Blet, R.A. Graham, A. Martini, and B. Schneider, Actes et Documents du Saint Siège relatifs à la Seconde Guerre Mondiale 10 (Vatican City: Libreria Editrice Vaticana, 1980).
'Laws of War on Land. Oxford, 9 September 1880, The'. Accessed 26 November 2020. https://ihl-databases.icrc.org/applic/ihl/ihl.nsf/Article.xsp?action=openDocument&documentId=949B1F3E326772DFC12563CD0051594E.
Lieber, Francis, *Instructions for the Government of Armies of the United States in the Field* (Washington, DC: Government Printing Office, 1898).
Linklater, Eric, *The Campaign in Italy* (London: His Majesty's Stationery Office, 1951).
Longfellow, Henry Wadsworth, *Christus: A Mystery* (Boston: J.R. Osgood, 1872).
Longfellow, Henry Wadsworth, 'Terra di Lavoro', *Atlantic Monthly* 35 (1875), 161–162. Reprinted in *The Masque of Pandora and Other Poems* (Boston: James R. Osgood and Company, 1876).
Mariotti, Filippo, *La Legislazione delle belle arti* (Rome: Unione Cooperative, 1892).
Marquess Camden, 'Proceedings at Meetings of the Royal Archaeological Institute', *The Archaeological Journal* 23 (1866), 6–78, 149–156, 231–236, 299–333.
'Memorandum from General Dwight D. Eisenhower Regarding Preservation of Historical Monuments in Europe' (26 May 1944). Accessed 26 November 2020. https://www.eisenhowerlibrary.

gov/research/online-documents/monuments-men-and-allied-effort-save-european-cultural-heritage.

Morley, John, *Life of Gladstone*, 3 vols (New York: Macmillan, 1903).

'Mr Gladstone on Italy', *The Spectator* 62 (4 May 1889), 599–600.

Notes on the Repair of Ancient Buildings Issued by the Society for the Protection of Ancient Buildings (London: The Committee: Sold by B.T. Batsford, 1903).

'Notiziario di Montecassino', *Succisa Virescit* 5 (1950), 30–35.

'Omelia del Card. Tarcisio Bertone, Segratario di Sato del santo Padre' (21 March 2010). Accessed 26 November 2020. http://www.vatican.va/roman_curia/secretariat_state/card-bertone/2010/documents/rc_seg-st_20100321_montecassino_it.html.

Pacis Nuntius: Paolo VI a Montecassino. 24 ottobre 1964 (Montecassino, 1965).

'Pellegrini alle sacre ossa di s. Benedetto e s. Scolastica', *Succisa Virescit* 5 (1950), 26–29.

Petrella, E., 'Lettere inedite del Mabillon, del Germain, del Montfaucon, dell'Estiennot, del Ruinart e del Fontanini', *Rivista storica benedettina* 7 (1912), 229–293.

Pope Benedict XVI, 'Celebration of Vespers with the Benedictine Abbots and the Community of Benedictine Monks and Nuns Gathered in the Archabbey of Monte Cassino (May 24, 2009)'. Accessed 26 November 2020. http://w2.vatican.va/content/benedict-xvi/en/homilies/2009/documents/hf_ben-xvi_hom_20090524_vespri-montecassino.html.

Pope Benedict XVI, 'Homily of His Holiness Benedict XVI', May 24, 2009. Accessed 26 November 2020. https://w2.vatican.va/content/benedict-xvi/en/homilies/2009/documents/hf_ben-xvi_hom_20090524_cassino.html.

Pope John Paul II, 'Address of His Holiness John Paul II at the Cemetery of Monte Cassino' (18 May 1979). Accessed 26 November 2020. https://w2.vatican.va/content/john-paul-ii/en/speeches/1979/may/documents/hf_jp-ii_spe_19790517_montecassino-cimitero.html.

Pope John Paul II, 'Address of His Holiness John Paul II to the Monks of the Abbey of Monte Cassino' (May 18, 1979). Accessed 26 November 2020. https://w2.vatican.va/content/john-paul-ii/en/speeches/1979/may/documents/hf_jp-ii_spe_19790517_montecassino-abbazia.html.

Pope John Paul II, 'Discorso di Giovanni Paolo II al Clero, ai Religiosi e ai Laici' (20 September 1980). Accessed 26 November 2020. https://w2.vatican.va/content/john-paul-ii/it/speeches/1980/september/documents/hf_jp-ii_spe_19800920_clero-laici-cassino.html.

Pope Paul VI, 'Consecrazione delle chiesa dell'archicenobio di Montecassino' (24 October 1964). Accessed 26 November 2020. https://w2.vatican.va/content/paul-vi/it/homilies/1964/documents/hf_p-vi_hom_19641024_montecassino.html.

Pope Paul VI, *Pacis Nuntius* (24 October 1964). Accessed 26 November 2020. http://w2.vatican.va/content/paul-vi/it/apost_letters/documents/hf_p-vi_apl_19641024_pacis-nuntius.html.

Pope Pius XII, *Fulgens Radiatur: Encyclical of Pope Pius XII on St. Benedict* (1947). Accessed 26 November 2020. http://w2.vatican.va/content/pius-xii/en/encyclicals/documents/hf_p-xii_enc_21031947_fulgens-radiatur.html.

Pope Pius XII, 'Pope Pius XII to President Roosevelt', in *Foreign Relations of the United States Diplomatic Papers, 1943* (Washington, DC: US Government Printing Office, 1943), vol. 2, pp. 916–917.

'Project of an International Declaration Concerning the Laws and Customs of War. Brussels, 27 August 1874'. Accessed 26 November 2020. https://ihl-databases.icrc.org/ihl/INTRO/135.

Rea, Ildefonso, 'Pro Montecassino', *Succisa Virescit* 1 (1946), 2–4.

'Records of the American Commission for the Protection and Salvage of Artistic and Historic Monuments in War Areas [Roberts Commission] (RG 239)'. Accessed 26 November 2020. https://www.archives.gov/research/foreign-policy/related-records/rg-239.

'Relazione dei periti nominati con decreto di S. Ecc. Ildefonso Rea Abate Ordinario di Montecassino per la ricognizione dei resti mortali dei Santi Benedetto e Scolastica', *Succisa Virescit* 5 (1950), 10–15.

'Relazione della commissione per lo studio del piano di massimo dei lavori di ricostruzione dell'abbazia di Montecassino', in Michela Cigola, *L'Abbazia Benedettina di Montecassino. La storia attraverso le testimonianze grafiche di rilievo e di progetto* (Cassino: F. Ciolfi, 2005), pp. 163–172.

Schuster, Cardinal Ildefonso, 'Una testimonianza', *Succisa Virescit* 5 (December 1950), 22–23.

'Segni di nuova vita', *Succisa Virescit* 5 (1950), 1–2.

Senger und Etterlin, General Frido von, 'Monte Cassino', *The New English Review Magazine* 2, no. 4 (1947), 250–252.

Senger und Etterlin, General Frido von, *Neither Fear nor Hope: The Wartime Career of General Frido von Senger und Etterlin, Defender of Cassino*, trans. by George Malcolm (London: Macdonald, 1960).

'Suppression and the early 20th century'. Accessed 1 February 2021. https://www.abbaziamontecassino.org/index.php/en/legacy/modern-era/161-suppression-and-the-early-20th-century.

'Tre anni di ricostruzione, 1947–1950', *Succisa Virescit* 5 (1950), 16-19.

'Treaty on the Protection of Artistic and Scientific Institutions and Historic Monuments' (15 April 1935). Accessed 26 November 2020. https://ihl-databases.icrc.org/ihl/INTRO/325?OpenDocument.

UNESCO, 'Convention for the Protection of Cultural Property in the Event of Armed Conflict with Regulations of the Convention 1954'. Accessed 26 November 2020. http://portal.unesco.org/en/ev.php-URL_ID=13637&URL_DO=DO_TOPIC&URL_SECTION=201.html.

UNESCO, 'The Cultural Landscape of the Benedictine Settlements in Medieval Italy' (18 March 2016.) Accessed 26 November 2020. https://whc.unesco.org/en/tentativelists/6107/.

UNESCO, 'Operational Guidelines for the Implementation of the World Heritage Convention'. UNESCO World Heritage Centre, 2017. Accessed 26 November 2020. https://whc.unesco.org/en/guidelines/.

UNESCO, *Protection of Mankind's Cultural Heritage: Sites and Monuments* (Paris, 1970).

United Nations General Assembly, 'Reconstruction of the Countries Members of the United Nations Devastated by War', A/RES/28, 2 February 1946. Accessed 26 November 2020. http://www.worldlii.org/int/other/UNGA/1946/.

'Visit Montecassino'. Accessed 1 February 2021. https://www.abbaziamontecassino.org/index.php/en/visit-montecassino.

Newspapers

Clark, Charles Upson, 'History Repeats', *The New York Times*, 12 February 1944, p. 12.

D.L., 'Protagonista nella sventura: L'Abate Diamare', *L'Osservatore Romano*, no. 38, 15 February 1974, pp. 6–7.

D'Onorio, B. 'L'Abate Rea e la ricostruzione', *L'Osservatore Romano*, no. 38, 15 February 1974, p. 6.

'Il terzo anniversario della distruzione di Montecassino', *L'Osservatore Romano*, no. 39, 16 February 1947, p. 2.

'I monumenti e la guerra', *L'Osservatore Romano*, no. 40, 18 February 1944, p. 1.

'Italien hat Julius Schlegel nicht vergessen', *Die Welt*, 16 March 1998. Accessed 26 November 2020. https://www.welt.de/print-welt/article596847/Italien-hat-Julius-Schlegel-nicht-vergessen.html.

Kamm, H. '40 Years Later, the Message of Monte Cassino: Pax', *The New York Times*, 27 February 1984, p. 2.

'La pace generatrice di rinascita e di ricostruzione – La Chiesa e il mondo hanno bisogno della vita monastica – Funzione insostituibile dell'uomo recuperato', *L'Osservatore Romano*, no. 248, 25 October 1964, p. 1.

'La tragica ora di Montecassino', *L'Osservatore Romano*, no. 40, 18 February 1944, p. 1.

Leccisotti, T. 'A Montecassino sono state rinvenute le ossa di San Benedetto e di Santa Scholastica', *L'Osservatore Romano*, no. 184, 7–8 August 1950, p. 2.

Lentini, A. 'Montecassino tra rovina e risurrezione', *L'Osservatore Romano*, no. 38, 15 February 1974, p. 6.

Guitton, J. 'Ricordo di una illustre visita', *L'Osservatore Romano*, no. 38, 15 February 1974, p. 6.

Matronola, M. 'Pensieri di pace', *L'Osservatore Romano*, no. 38, 15 February 1974, p. 6.

McCormick, Anne O'Hare, 'The Symbolic Battle for Monte Cassino', *The New York Times*, 2 February 1944, p. 18.

'Monks Thankful for Aid: Vicar of Montecassino Abbey Writes to Relief Head Here', *The New York Times*, 3 February 1946, p. 7.

Pantoni, A. 'Nella luce dell'odierna riconsacrazione: la basilica di Montecassino attraverso i secoli', *L'Osservatore Romano*, no. 247, 24 October 1964, p. 6.

Pantoni, A. 'Rinvenuti tra le macerie i documenti del passato', *L'Osservatore Romano*, no. 38, 15 February 1974, pp. 6–7.

'Per restituire l'uomo a se stesso', *L'Osservatore Romano*, no. 248, 25 October 1964, p. 3.

'Pope Bitter, Berlin Declares', *The New York Times*, 18 February 1944, p. 3.

'"Qua la pace troviamo, qua la pace rechiamo": "beata pacis visio"', *L'Osservatore Romano*, no. 248, 25 October 1964, p. 3.

'Sain Benedetto da Norcia patrono dell'Europa: Il Breve Pontificio che sancisce la proclamazione solenne', *L'Osservatore Romano*, no. 248, 25 October 1964, p. 2.

Scarpitti, Giovanni, 'Nuove pagine sulle vicende o sulle glorie di Montecassino', *L'Osservatore Romano*, 16 December 1946, p. 2.

Sulzberger, C.L. 'Clark Order Prohibits 5th Army from Attacking Church Property: Courtesy to Vatican Handicaps Advance as Enemy Is Said to Use Religious Sites for Artillery Observation', *The New York Times*, 29 January 1944, p. 5.

Secondary Sources

Adacher, Sabina, Faustino Avagliano, and Gugliemo Orofino, *L'età dell'abate Desiderio, I. Manoscritti Cassinesi del secolo XI*, Miscellanea Cassinese 59 (Montecassino: Pubblicazioni Cassinesi, 1989).

Avagliano, Faustino, 'Il culto di san Bertario a Montecassino', in *Montecassino. Dalla prima alla seconda distruzione. Momenti e aspetti di storia cassinese (Secc. VI–IX)*, Miscellanea Cassinese 55 (Montecassino: Pubblicazioni Cassinesi, 1987), pp. 401–428.

Avagliano, Faustino, 'Montecassino "com'era e dov'era" (1944–1964): l'abate Rea huius loci restitutor', in *Il Lazio meridionale dal 1944 agli anni Settanta. Politica, economia e società nelle fonti storiche e nelle testimonianze dei protagonisti (Cassino, 11–13 dicembre 2002)* (Milan: Franco Angeli, 2006), pp. 136–157.

Avagliano, Faustino, 'Montecassino nella descrizione di Don Angelo Pantoni del 1945', *Napoli nobilissima: Rivista di arti, filologia e storia* 6 (2005), 107–132.

Avagliano, Faustino, 'Montecassino nel primo Ottocento', in *Il monachesimo in Italia tra Vaticano I e Vaticano II*, Italia Benedetinna 15 (Cesena: Badia di Santa Maria del Monte, 1995), pp. 529–560.

Avagliano, Faustino, 'Monumenti del culto a San Pietro a Montecassino', *Benedictina* 14 (1967), 57–76.
Avagliano, Faustino, and Oronzo Pecere. *L'età dell'abate Desiderio*, 3, 1. *Storia arte e cultura* (Montecassino: Pubblicazioni Cassinesi, 1992).
Bartolini, Domenico, *Di s. Zaccaria papa e degli anni del suo pontificato: commentarii storico-critici* (Regensburg: Federico Pustet, 1879).
Beau, Antoine, *Le Culte de les reliques de saint Benoît et de sainte Scholastique* (Paris: Picard, 1980).
Beau, Antoine, 'Rapport anatomique', *Studia monastica* 21 (1979), 37–108.
Berland, J.M., 'Présence du corps de saint Benoît à Fleury-sur-Loire du Haut Moyen Âge à nos jours', *Studia monastica* 21 (1979), 265–302.
Berto, Luigi Andrea, 'Erchempert, a Reluctant Fustigator of His People: History and Ethnic Pride in Southern Italy at the End of the Ninth Century', *Mediterranean Studies* 20, no. 2 (2012), 147–175.
Berto, Luigi Andrea, 'Oblivion, Memory, and Irony in Medieval Montecassino: Narrative Strategies of the "Chronicles of St. Benedict of Cassino"', *Viator* 38, no. 1 (2007), 45–62.
Bertolini, Paolo, 'I Langobardi di Benevento e Monte Casino la prima Ricostruzione', in *Montecassino. Dalla prima alla seconda distruzione momenti e aspetti di storia Cassinese (secc. VI-IX)*, Miscellanea Cassinese 55 (Montecassino: Pubblicazioni Cassinesi, 1987), pp. 55–100.
Betts, Paul, and Corey Ross, 'Modern Historical Preservation – Towards a Global Perspective', *Past & Present* 226 (2015), 7–26.
Bloch, Herbert, 'The Bombardment of Monte Cassino (February 14–16, 1944): A New Appraisal', *Benedictina* 20 (1973), 383–424.
Bloch, Herbert, *Monte Cassino in the Middle Ages*. 3 vols (Cambridge, MA: Harvard University Press, 1988).
Bloch, Herbert, 'Monte Cassino's Teachers and Library in the High Middle Ages', in *Settimane di studio nel Centro italiano di studi sull'alto medioevo* 19 (1971) (Spoleto, 1972), pp. 563–613.
Blumenson, Martin, 'The Bombing of Monte Cassino'. *American Heritage*, vol. 19, issue 5 (August 1968). Accessed 26 November 2020. https://www.americanheritage.com/bombing-monte-cassino#1.
Blumenson, Martin, *Salerno to Cassino*. The Mediterranean Theater of Operations, vol. 3 (Washington, DC: United States Army, 1969).
Bonini, Cesare, *Petronace, restauratore ed abate di Montecassino* (Brescia, 1915).
Boynton, S. *Shaping Monastic Identity: Liturgy and History at the Imperial Abbey of Farfa, 1000–1125* (Ithaca, NY: Cornell University Press, 2006).
Bracciolini, Gian Francesco Poggio, *Two Renaissance Book Hunters*, trans. by Phyllis W. Goodhart Gordan (New York: Columbia University Press, 1974).
Brechter, Suso, 'Die Frühgeschichte von Montecassino nach der Chronik Leos von Ostia im Codex lat. monacensis 4623', in *Liber Floridus* (= *Feschrift Paul Lehmann*) (St Ottilien: Eos Verlag der Erzabtei, 1950), pp. 271–286.
Brechter, Suso, 'Monte Cassinos erste Zerstörung. Kritischer Versuch einer zeitlichen Fixierung', *Studien und Mitteilung zur Geschichte des Benediktiner-Ordens* 56 (1938), 109–150.
Bremner, G.A., 'E.A. Freeman and G.G. Scott: An Episode in the Influence of Ideas', in *Making History: Edward Augustus Freeman and Victorian Cultural Politics*, ed. by G.A. Bremner and Jonathan Conlin, Proceedings of the British Academy 202 (Oxford: Oxford University Press, 2015), pp. 177–196.
Brown, G. Baldwin, *The Care of Ancient Monuments; an Account of the Legislative and Other Measures Adopted in European Countries for Protecting Ancient Monuments and Objects and Scenes of Natural Beauty, and for Preserving the Aspect of Historical Cities* (Cambridge: Cambridge University Press, 1905).

Brown, Peter, *The Rise of Western Christendom: Triumph and Diversity, A.D. 200–1000*. 2nd ed. (Oxford: Blackwell Publishing, 2003).

Burckhardt, Jacob, *Civilization of the Renaissance in Italy*, trans. by S.G.C. Middlemore (Kitchener, ON: Batoche, 2001).

Butler, E.C., 'The Monte Cassino Text of St. Benedict's Rule', *The Journal of Theological Studies* 3 (1902), 458–468.

Butler, Perry, *Gladstone: Church, State, and Tractarianism: A Study of His Religious Ideas and Attitudes, 1809–1859* (Oxford: Clarendon Press, 1982).

Caddick-Adams, Peter, *Monte Cassino: Ten Armies in Hell* (London: Arrow Books, 2013).

Carman, John, 'Legacies of War in Creating a Common European Identity', *International Journal of Heritage Studies* 9 (2003), 135–150.

Carr, David, 'The Reality of History', in *Meaning and Representation in History*, ed. by Jörn Rüsen (New York: Berghahn Books, 2006), pp. 123–136.

Casini, Lorenzo, 'International Regulation of Historic Buildings and Nationalism: The Role of UNESCO', *Nations and Nationalism* 24, no. 1 (2017), 131–147.

Caspar, Erich, 'Echte und gefälschte Karolingerurkunden für Monte Cassino', *Neues Archiv der Gesellschaft für ältere deutsche Geschichtskunde* 33 (1908), 55–73.

Caspar, Erich, *Petrus Diaconus und die Monte Cassineser Fälschungen: ein Beitrag zur Geschichte des italienischen Geisteslebens im Mittelalter* (Berlin: J. Springer, 1909).

Cavalli, Alessandro, 'Memory and Identity: How Memory Is Reconstructed after Catastrophic Events', in *Meanings and Representations in History*, ed. by Jörn Rüsen (New York: Berghahn Books, 2006), pp. 169–182.

Cavallo, Guglielmo, *L'età dell'abate Desiderio, II. La decorazione libraria*, Miscellanea Cassinese 60 (Montecassino: Pubblicazioni Cassinesi, 1989).

Chadwick, Owen, 'Young Gladstone and Italy', *The Journal of Ecclesiastical History* 30 (1979), 243–259.

Chamard, Dom François, *Les reliques de saint Benoît* (Paris: Ligugé, 1882).

Chapman, John, 'A propos des martyrologues', *Revue bénédictine* 20 (1903), 285–313.

Chapman, John, 'La restauration du Mont-Cassin par l'abbé Petronax', *Revue bénédictine* 21 (1904), 74–80.

Chklaver, Georges, 'Projet d'une Convention pour la Protection des Institutions et Monuments consacrés aux Arts et aux Sciences', *Revue de droit international* 6 (1930), 589–592.

Choay, Françoise, *The Invention of the Historic Monument*, trans. by Lauren M. O'Connell (Cambridge: Cambridge University Press, 2001).

Cigola, Michela, *L'Abbazia Benedettina di Montecassino. La storia attraverso le testimonianze grafiche di rilievo e di progetto* (Cassino: F. Ciolfi, 2005).

Cigola, Michela, 'L'Abbazia di Montecassino. Disegni di rilievo e di progetto per la conoscenza e la memoria', *Disegnare Idee Immagini* 14 (1997), 43–52.

Citarella, Armand O., 'The Political Chaos in Southern Italy and the Arab Destruction of Monte Cassino in 883', in *Montecassino. Dalla prima alla seconda distruzione momenti e aspetti di storia Cassinese (secc. VI–IX)*, Miscellanea Cassinese 55 (Montecassino: Pubblicazioni Cassinesi, 1987), pp. 163–180.

Citarella, Armand O., and Henry M. Willard, *The Ninth-Century Treasure of Monte Cassino in the Context of Political and Economic Developments in South Italy*. Miscellanea Cassinese 50 (Montecassino: Pubblicazioni Cassinesi, 1983).

Clark, Francis, 'The Authorship of the Gregorian Dialogues: A Challenge to the Traditional View', *Studia Patristica* 18 (1990), 120–132.

Clark, Francis, *The 'Gregorian' Dialogues and the Origins of Benedictine Monasticism* (Leiden: Brill, 2003).

Clark, Francis, *The Pseudo-Gregorian Dialogues*. 2 vols (Leiden: Brill, 1987).
Clement, John G., *The Necessity for the Destruction of the Abbey of Monte Cassino* (Fort Leavenworth, 2002).
Coccolo, Francesca, 'Law No. 1089 of 1 June 1939', in *Cultural Heritage: Scenarios 2015–17*, ed. by Simona Pinton and Lauso Zagato (Venice: Edizioni Ca' Foscari, 2017), pp. 195–210.
Colombo, Alessandro, 'The Laws of Suppression in Italy: Characteristics and Effects', in *Religious Institutes in Western Europe in the 19th and 20th Centuries*, ed. by Jan De Maeyer, Sofie Leplae, and Joachim Schmiedl (Leuven: Leuven University Press, 2004). pp. 263–276.
Conlin, Jonathan, 'Development or Destruction? E.A. Freeman and the Debate on Church Restoration, 1839–51', *Oxoniensia* 57 (2012), 137–152.
Coulter, Cornelia C., 'Boccacio and the Cassinese Manuscripts of the Laurentian Library', *Classical Philology* 43 (1948), 217–230.
Cowdrey, H.E.J., *The Age of Abbot Desiderius: Montecassino, the Papacy, and the Normans in the Eleventh and Early Twelfth Centuries* (Oxford: Clarendon Press, 1983).
Cowdrey, H.E.J., 'Desiderio abate di Montecassino', in *L'età dell'abate Desiderio*, 3, 1. *Storia arte e cultura*, ed. by Faustino Avagliano and Oronzo Pecere (Montecassino: Pubblicazioni Cassinesi, 1992), pp. 17–32.
D'Amelio, Giuliana, *Stato e Chiesa: La legislazione ecclesiastica fino al 1867* (Milan: Giuffrè, 1961).
Dantier, Alphonse, *Les monastères Benedictins d'Italie: Souvenirs d'un voyage littéraire au dela des Alpes*, 2 vols (Paris: Didier, 1867).
Davril, Anselmus, 'Concusion générale', *Studia monastica* 21 (1979), 423–428.
Davril, Anselmus, 'Historique des travaux sur les reliques de saint Benoît et de sainte Scholastique en France', *Studia monastica* 21 (1979), 7–16.
Davril, Anselmus, 'La tradition cassinienne', *Studia monastica* 21 (1979), 377–408.
Dell'Omo, Mariano, '1944–1964, la ricostruzione di Montecassino "com'era e dov'era". Da specchio di rovine e di polvere a simbolo di unità spirituale dell'Europa', in *La ricostruzione dell'Abbazia di Montecassino* (Rome: Gangemi Editore, 2014), pp. 11–17.
Dell'Omo, Mariano, 'A proposito dell'esilio romano dei monaci cassinesi dopo la distruzione longobardia di Montecassino', in *Montecassino. Dalla prima alla seconda distruzione momenti e aspetti di storia Cassinese (secc. VI–IX)*, Miscellanea Cassinese 55 (Montecassino: Pubblicazioni Cassinesi, 1987), pp. 494–512.
Dell'Omo, Mariano, 'Cronaca delle celebrazioni cassinesi nel XV centenario della nascita di s. Benedetto', *Monastica* II (1984), 359–378.
Dell'Omo, Mariano, *Montecassino Medievale: Genesi di un simbolo, storia di una realtà. Saggi sull-identità cassinese tra persone, istituzione, consuetudini e cultura*. Biblioteca della Miscellanea Cassinese 15 (Montecassino: Pubblicazioni Cassinesi, 2008).
Dell'Omo, Mariano, *Montecassino. Un'abbazia Nella Storia* (Montecassino: Pubblicazioni Cassinesi, 1999).
Dell'Omo, Mariano, 'Per la storia dei monaci-vescovi nell'Italia normanna del secolo XI: ricerche biografiche su Guitmondo di La Croix-Saint-Leufroy vescovo di Aversa', *Benedictina* 40 (1993), 9–34.
Dell'Omo, Mariano, 'Tommaso Leccisotti e Montecassino: un grande storico al servizio di un grande archivio (Dalle drammatiche vicende degli ultimi mesi del 1943 ai grandi lavori eruditi del secondo '900)', *Benedictina* 62 (2015), 39–58.
Deshusses, Jean, and Jacques Hourlier, 'Saint Benoît dans les livres liturgiques', *Studia monastica* 21 (1979), 143–204.
De Witte, Dom Charles-Martial, 'Notes sur la découverte des ossements de Saint Benoît et de Sainte Scolastique au Mont Cassin en 1484', *Benedictina* 10 (1956), 259–266.

Dickens, Jack, 'William Gladstone: Providence and the People, 1838–1865', *The Chicago Journal of History* 8 (2017), 49–68.

Diem, Albrecht, 'The Carolingians and the Regula Benedicti', in *Religious Franks: Religion and Power in the Frankish Kingdoms: Studies in Honour of Mayke de Jong*, ed. by Dorine van Espelo, Bram van den Hoven van Genderen, Rob Meens, Janneke Raaijmakers, Irene van Renswoude, and Carine Van Rhijn (Manchester: Manchester University Press, 2016), pp. 243–261.

D'Onorio, Bernardo, Giovanni Spinelli, and Vincenzo Pirozzi, *L'Abbazia di Montecassino: storia, religione, arte* (Milan: Silvana, 1986).

Dormeier, Heinrich, *Montecassino und die Laien im 11. und 12. Jahrhundert*, MGH Schriften 27 (Stuttgart: Anton Hiersemann, 1979).

Dümmler, Ernst, 'Lateinische Gedichte des neunten bis elften Jahrhunderts', *Neues Archiv der Gesellschaft für ältere deutsche Geschichtskunde* 10 (1885), 331–357.

Dunn, Marilyn, *The Emergence of Monasticism: From the Desert Fathers to the Early Middle Ages* (Oxford: Blackwell Publishing, 2000).

Durkheim, Émile, *Elementary Forms of Religious Life*, trans. by Carol Cosman (Oxford: Oxford University Press, 2001).

Eck, Diana, 'Mountains', in *Encyclopedia of Religion*, ed. by Lindsay Jones (Macmillan Reference USA, 2005), 9:6212–6215.

Engelbert, Pius, 'Regeltext und Romverehrung zur Frage der Verbreitung der Regula Benedicti im Frühmittelalter', in *Montecassino. Dalla prima all second distruzione momenti e aspetti di storia cassinese (secc. VI–IX)*, Miscellanea Cassinese 55 (Montecassino: Pubblicazioni Cassinesi, 1987), pp. 133–162.

Ettinger, A., 'La Corrispondenza dei Benedettini Maurini con Montecassino', *Rivista storica benedettina* 8 (1913), 29–48.

Fabiani, Luigi, *La Terra di S. Benedetto: Studio storico-giuridico sull'Abbazia di Montecassino dall'VIII al XIII secolo*, 3 vols, Miscellanea Cassinese 33–34, 42 (Monte Cassino: Pubblicazioni Cassinesi, 1968).

Fagnoni, Anna Maria, 'I Dialogi di Desiderio nella Chronica monasterii Casinensis', *Studi Medievali* 34 (1993), 65–94.

Falco, Giorgio, 'Lineamenti di storia cassinese nei secoli VIII e IX', *Casinensia* II (1929), 457–548.

Ferrari, Guy, *Early Roman Monasteries. Notes for the History of the Monasteries and Convents at Rome from the V through the X Century* (Vatican City: Pontificio Istituto di Archeologia Cristiana, 1957).

Ferry, John Rowe, 'Erchempert's *History of the Lombards of Benevento*: A Translation and Study of Its Place in the Chronicle Tradition', PhD dissertation, Rice University, 1995.

France, John, 'The Occasion of the Coming of the Normans to Southern Italy', *Journal of Medieval History* 17 (1991), 185–205.

Frank, Hieronymus, 'Die älteren Zeugnisse für das Fest de hl. Benedikt am 21. März', in *Vir Dei Benedictus. Eine Festgabe zum 1400. Todestag des heiligen Benedikt*, ed. by Raphael Moliter (Münster: Aschendorff, 1947), pp. 333–339.

Fratadocchi, Tommaso Breccia, *La ricostruzione dell'abbazia di Montecassino* (Rome: Gangemi Editore, 2014).

Fried, Johannes, *Der Schleier der Erinnerung: Grundzüge einer historischen Memorik* (Munich: C.H. Beck, 2004).

Furet, François, *In the Workshop of History*, trans. by Jonathan Mandelbaum (Chicago: University of Chicago Press, 1984).

Galdi, Amalia, 'S. Benedetto tra Montecassino e Fleury (VII-XII secolo)', *Mélanges de l'École française de Rome – Moyen Âge* 126 (2014), 557–574.

Galli, Déodat, *Saint Benoît en France* (Fleury-sur-Loire: Éditions de Fleury, 1950).

Galli, Paolo Antonio Constantino, and José Alfredo Naso, 'Unmasking the 1349 Earthquake Source (Southern Italy): Paleoseismological and Archaeoseismological Indications from the Aquae Iuliae Fault', *Journal of Structural Geology* 31 (2009), 128–149.

Geary, Patrick, *Furta Sacra: Thefts of Relics in the Central Middle Ages* (Princeton: Princeton University Press, 1990).

Geary, Patrick, *Phantoms of Remembrance: Memory and Oblivion at the End of the First Millennium* (Princeton: Princeton University Press, 1994).

Giovannoni, Gustavo, *L'Abbazia di Montecassino* (Florence: Electa Editrice, 1947).

Giovannoni, Gustavo, 'Rilievi ed opere architettoniche del Cinquecento a Montecassino', in *Casinensia* II (Montecassino-Sora, 1929), pp. 305–335.

Goffart, Walter, 'Le Mans, St. Scholastica, and the Literary Tradition of the Translation of St. Benedict', *Revue bénédictine* 77 (1967), 107–141.

Grégoire, Réginald, 'Montecassino ospitava alcuni eremeti nel 717?', *Benedictina* 25 (1978), 413–416.

Grégoire, Réginald, *Storia e agriografia a Montecassino*, Biblioteca della Miscellanea Cassinese 12 (Montecassino: Pubblicazioni Cassinesi, 2007).

Guiraud, J.-F., *Économie et société autour du Mont-Cassin au XIIIe siècle*, Miscellanea Cassinese 81 (Montecassino: Pubblicazioni Cassinesi, 1999).

Hallinger, Kassius, 'Benedikt von Monte Cassino. Sein Augstieg zur Geschichte, zu Kult und Verehrung', *Regulae Benedicti Studia* 10–11 (1981–1982), 77–89.

Hallinger, Kassius, 'Papst Gregor der Grosse und der heiilger Benedikt', in *Commentationes in Regulam S. Benedicti*, ed. by Basilius Steidle, Studia Anselmiana 42 (Rome: Herder, 1957), pp. 231–319.

Hartog, François, *Regimes of Historicity: Presentism and Experiences of Time*, trans. by Saskia Brown (New York: Columbia University Press, 2015).

Harvey, David C., 'Heritage Pasts and Heritage Presents: Temporality, Meaning and the Scope of Heritage Studies', *International Journal of Heritage Studies* 7, no. 4 (2001), 319–338.

Head, Thomas, *Hagiography and the Cult of Saints: The Diocese of Orléans, 800–1200* (Cambridge: Cambridge University Press, 1990).

Heath, Christopher, 'Third/Ninth-Century Violence: "Saracens" and Sawdān in Erchempert's Historia', *Al-Masaq: History-Writing and Violence in the Medieval Mediterranean* 27 (2015), pp. 24–40.

Heller-Roazen, Daniel, 'Tradition's Destruction: On the Library of Alexandria', *Obsolescence* 100 (2002), 133–153.

Hervieu-Léger, Danièle, *Religion as a Chain of Memory*, trans. by Simon Lee (Cambridge: Polity Press, 2000).

Hirsch, Ferdinand, 'Amatus von Monte Cassino und seine Geschichte der Normannen', *Forschungen zur deutschen Geschichte* 8 (1868), 203–325.

Hirsch, Ferdinand, 'Desiderius von Monte Cassino als Papst Victor III', *Forschungen zur deutschen Geschichte* 7 (1867), 1–112.

Histories of the Aftermath: The Legacies of the Second World War in Europe, ed. by Frank Biess and Robert G. Moeller (New York: Berghahn Books, 2010).

Hodges, Richard, *Light in the Dark Ages: The Rise and Fall of San Vincenzo al Volturno* (Ithaca, NY: Cornell University Press, 1997).

Hodges, Richard, 'The Sack of San Vincenzo al Volturno', *History Today* 47, no. 7 (1997), 19–26.

Hoffmann, Hartmut, 'Chronik und Urkunde in Montecassino', *Quellen und Forschungen aus italienischen Archiven und Bibliotheken* 51 (1971), 93–206.

Hoffmann, Hartmut, 'Das Chronicon Vulturnense und die Chronik von Montecassino', *Deutsches Archiv für Erforschung des Mittealters* 22 (1966), 179–196.

Hoffmann, Hartmut, 'Der Kalender Leo Marsicanus', *Deutsches Archiv für Erforschung des Mittealters* 21 (1965), 82–149.

Hoffmann, Hartmut, 'Die älteren Abtslisten von Montecassino', *Quellen und Forschungen aus italienischen Archiven und Bibliotheken* 47 (1967), 224–354.

Hoffmann, Hartmut, 'Die Anfänge der Normannen in Süditalien', *Quellen und Forschungen aus italienischen Archiven und Bibliotheken* 49 (1969), 95–144.

Hoffmann, Hartmut, 'Studien Zur Chronik von Montecassino', *Deutsches Archiv für Erforschung des Mittealters* 29 (1973), 59–162.

Hoffmann, Hartmut, 'Zur Geschichte Montecassinos im 11. und 12. Jahrhundert', in *Montecassino und die Laien im 11. und 12. Jahrhundert*, MGH Schriften 27 (Stuttgart: Anton Hiersemann, 1997), pp. 1–23.

Houben, Hubert, 'L'influsso Carolingio sul monachesimo meridionale', in *Montecassino. Dalla prima alla seconda distruzione momenti e aspetti di storia Cassinese (secc. VI–IX)*, Miscellanea Cassinese 55 (Montecassino: Pubblicazioni Cassinesi, 1987), pp. 101–132.

Houben, Hubert, 'Malfattori e benefattori, protettori e sfruttatori: i Normanni e Montecassino', in *L'età dell'abate Desiderio*, 3, 1, ed. by Faustino Avagliano and Oronzo Pecere, *Storia arte e cultura* (Montecassino: Pubblicazioni Cassinesi, 1992), pp. 123–151.

Hourlier, Jacques, 'La lettre de Zacharie', *Studia monastica* 21 (1979), 241–252.

Hourlier, Jacques, 'La translation après les sources narratives', *Studia monastica* 21 (1979), 213–239.

Hourlier, Jacques, 'La translation de sainte Scholastique au Mans', *Studia monastica* 21 (1979), 313–334.

Hourlier, Jacques, 'Le témoignage de Paul Diacre', *Studia monastica* 21 (1979), 205–212.

Howe, John, *Church Reform and Social Change in Eleventh-Century Italy: Dominic of Sora and His Patrons* (Philadelphia: University of Pennsylvania Press, 1997).

Howe, John, 'The Conversion of the Physical World: The Creation of a Christian Landscape', in *Varieties of Religious Conversion in the Middle Ages*, ed. by James Muldoon (Gainesville: University Press of Florida, 1997), pp. 63–80.

Iannetta, Sabatino, *Henry W. Longfellow and Montecassino. His Rhode Island Friendship. His Birthplace* (Boston: B. Humphries, 1940).

Iannetta, Sabatino, *Triumph of Life: Destruction and Restoration of Montecassino* (Arpino: Tipografica Arpinata, 1960).

'Il rinvenimento delle sacre ossa di S. Benedetto e S. Scolastica', *Bollettino Diocesano* 3 (1950), 73–79.

Immonen, Teemu, 'Building the Cassinese Monastic Identity: A Reconstruction of the Fresco Program of the Desiderian Basilica (1071)', PhD dissertation, University of Helsinki, 2012.

Inguanez, Mauro, 'Lettere di Gladstone all'abate Luigi Tosti sulla conciliazione', *Nuova Antalogia* 72 (1937), 162–177.

Inguanez, Mauro, *Montecassino* (Montecassino: Pubblicazioni Cassinesi, 1949).

Jallonghi, Ernesto, 'Borbonici e Francesi a Montecassino (1796–1799)', *Archivio storico per le province Napoletane* 34 (1909), 222–251.

Jallonghi, Ernesto, 'D. Ottavio Fraja Fangipane aschivista cassinese (1763–1843)', *Bulletino del'Istituto storico italiano per il Medio Evo e Archivio Muratoriano* 47 (1932), 226–245.

Jallonghi, Ernesto, 'Montecassino nel primo cinquantenario del secolo XIX (1806–56)', *Rivista storica benedttina* 7 (1912), 195–222, 415–431.

Koselleck, Reinhart, *Futures Past: On the Semantics of Historical Time*, trans. by Keith Tribe (Cambridge, MA: MIT Press, 1985).

Koselleck, Reinhart, *The Practice of Conceptual History: Timing History, Spacing Concepts*, trans. by Todd Samuel Presner et al. (Stanford: Stanford University Press, 2002).

Kreutz, Barbara, *Before the Normans: Southern Italy in the Ninth and Tenth Centuries* (Philadelphia: University of Pennsylvania Press, 1991).

Lambourne, Nicola, *War Damage in Western Europe: The Destruction of Historic Monuments during the Second World War* (Edinburgh: Edinburgh University Press, 2001).

Lankila, Tommi P., 'The Saracen Raid of Rome in 846: An Example of Maritime Ghazw', in *Travelling Through Time: Essays in Honour of Kaj Öhrnberg*, ed. by Sylvia Akar, Jaakko Hämeen-Anttila, and Inka Nokso-Koivisto (Helsinki: Finnish Oriental Society, 2013), pp. 93–120.

Laporte, Jean, 'Vues sur l'histoire de l'abbaye de Fleury aux VIIe et VIIIe siècles', *Studia monastica* 21 (1979), 109–142.

Laurent, M.-H., 'Review of Il Sepolcro di S. Benedetto (Miscellanea Cassinese, 27) Mont-Cassin, 1951', *Revue d'histoire ecclésiastique* 47 (1952), 654–660.

Leccisotti, Tommaso, 'Ancora del sepolcro di S. Benedetto', *Benedictina* 7 (1953), 295–346.

Leccisotti, Tommaso, 'Aspirazioni all'unità dei Cristiani nella corrispondenza Tosti-Gladstone', *Rivista di Storia della Chiesa in Italia* 17 (1963), 115–125.

Leccisotti, Tommaso, 'D. Luigi Tosti agli inizi della sua attività intellettuale', *Benedictina* 1 (1947), 259–317.

Leccisotti, Tommaso, 'Episodi di storia Cassinese', *Benedictina* 22 (1976), 173–187.

Leccisotti, Tommaso, 'Il contributo Benedettino all'edizione di fonti storiche del medioevo d'Europa', in *Le Fonti del Medioevo Europeo. Relazioni al Convegno di Studi delle Fonti del Medioevo Europeo in occasione del 70 della fondazione dell'Istituto Storico Italiano* (Rome: Istituto Storico Italiano, 1954), pp. 268–271.

Leccisotti, Tommaso, 'Il contributo di Montecassino all'opera Muratoriana', *Benedictina* 4 (1950), 207–240.

Leccisotti, Tommaso, 'Il racconto della dedicazione della Basilica desideriana nel codice Cassinense 47', in *Le vicende della dedicazione della Basilica di Montecassino attraverso la documentazione archeologica*, Miscellanea Cassinese 36 (Montecassino: Pubblicazioni Cassinesi, 1973), pp. 212–225.

Leccisotti, Tommaso, 'Il recente rinvenimento delle reliquie di S. Benedetto e di S. Scolastica e la loro ricognizione', in *Il sepolcro di S. Benedetto*, Miscellanea Cassinese 27 (Montecassino: Pubblicazioni Cassinesi, 1951), pp. 11–30.

Leccisotti, Tommaso, 'I monasteri fondati da s. Benedetto e il loro stato alla meta del secolo XVII', *Benedictina* 27 (1980), 63–82.

Leccisotti, Tommaso, *I Regesti dell'Archivio*, 11 vols (Rome: Ministero dell'Interno, 1964).

Leccisotti, Tommaso, 'La consacrazione della basilica cassinese nel 1727', *Benedictina* 14 (1967), 320–330.

Leccisotti, Tommaso, 'L'archivio di Montecassino dal Gattola alla soppressione del 1807', in *I Regesti dell'Archivio*, vol. 2 (Rome: Ministero dell'Interno, 1965), pp. vii–xlii.

Leccisotti, Tommaso, 'La testimonianza storica', in *Il sepolcro di S. Benedetto*, Miscellanea Cassinese 27 (Montecassino: Pubblicazioni Cassinesi, 1951), pp. 99–233.

Leccisotti, Tommaso, *Monte Cassino*, trans. by Armand O. Citarella (Montecassino: Pubblicazioni Cassinesi, 1987).

Leccisotti, Tommaso, 'Montecassino agli inizi del Cinquecento', *Benedictina* 2 (1948), 75–94.

Leccisotti, Tommaso, *Montecassino: sein Leben und seine Ausbreitung* (Basel: Thomas Morus Verlag, 1949).

Leccisotti, Tommaso, 'Sul documento che ricorda l'invenzione delle ossa di S. Benedetto e S. Scolastica, avvenuta nel 1484', *Benedictina* 9 (1955), 113–126.

Leccisotti, Tommaso, 'Una lacuna della storia di Montecassino al secolo X', *Studia Anselmiana* 18–19 (1947), 273–281.

Leclercq, Henri, 'Fleury-sur-Loire', in *Dictionnaire d'archéologie chrétienne et de liturgie*, 5.2 (Paris: Letouzey et Ané, 1922), cols 1709–1760.

Lena, Gaetana, 'Le vicende di San Germano (Cassino) e di Montecassino nel 1799', *Latium* 8 (1991), 141–174.

Lentini, Anselmo, 'Il sermone di S. Bertario su S. Scolastica', *Benedictina* 1 (1947), 197–232.

Levine, Philippa, *The Amateur and the Professional: Antiquarians, Historians and Archaeologists in Victorian England, 1838–1886* (Cambridge: Cambridge University Press, 1986).

Leyser, Conrad, *Authority and Asceticism from Augustine to Gregory the Great* (Oxford: Clarendon Press, 2000).

Leyser, Conrad, 'St Benedict and Gregory the Great: Another Dialogue', in *Sicilia e Italia Suburbicaria Tra IV e VIII Secolo: Atti Del Convegno Di Studi, Catania, 24–27 Ottobre 1989*, ed. by Salvatore Pricoco, Francesca Rizzo Nervo, and Teresa Sardella (Soveria Mannelli: Rubbettino, 1991), pp. 21–43.

Loew, Elias Avery, *The Beneventan Script: A History of the South Italian Minuscule* (Oxford: Oxford University Press, 1914).

Loud, Graham A., 'Abbot Desiderius of Montecassino and the Gregorian Papacy', *The Journal of Ecclesiastical History* 30 (1979), 305–326.

Loud, Graham A., *Church and Society in the Norman Principality of Capua, 1058–1197* (Oxford: Clarendon Press, 1985).

Loud, Graham A., 'The Liri Valley in the Middle Ages', in *Archaeological Survey in the Lower Liri Valley, Central Italy, under the Direction of Edith Mary Wightman*, ed. by J.W Hayes and I.P. Martini, British Archaeologial Reports, International Series 595 (Oxford: Tempus Reparatum, 1994), pp. 53–68 and 121–125.

Loud, Graham A., 'The Norman Counts of Caiazzo and the Abbey of Montecassino', in *Monastica I Scritti raccolti in memoria del xv centenario della nascità di S. Benedetto*, Miscellanea Cassinese 44 (Monte Cassino: Pubblicazioni Cassinesi, 1981), pp. 199–217.

Loud, Graham A., 'Southern Italy in the Tenth Century', in *The New Cambridge Medieval History*, ed. by Timothy Reuter, vol. 3 (Cambridge: Cambridge University Press, 2000), pp. 624–645.

Lowenthal, David, *The Past Is a Foreign Country – Revisited* (Cambridge: Cambridge University Press, 2016).

Markus, R.A., 'How on Earth Could Places Become Holy?: Origins of the Christian Idea of Holy Places', *Journal of Early Christian Studies* 2, no. 3 (1994), 257–271.

Marazzi, Frederico, 'Montecassino e s. Vincenzo al Volturno: ragionamenti sui criteri progettuali dei "grandi monasteri" fra VIII e IX secolo', in *Sodalitas: Studi in memoria di don Faustino Avagliano*, vol. I, ed. by Mariano Dell'Omo, Frederico Marazzi, Fabio Simonelli, and Cesare Crova (Montecassino, 2016), pp. 619–645.

Martin, Jean-Marie, 'L'*Epitome Chronicorum Casinensium*: Les Carolingiens vus du Mont-Cassin', in *Sodalitas: Studi in memoria di don Faustino Avagliano*, vol. I, ed. by Mariano Dell'Omo, Frederico Marazzi, Fabio Simonelli, and Cesare Crova (Montecassino, 2016), pp. 647–658.

McCready, William D., 'Abbot Desiderius, Alberic of Montecassino, and the Writing of the "Dialogi de miraculis Sancti Benedicti"', *The Journal of Medieval Latin* 9 (1999), 102–120.

McCready, William D., 'Dating the Dialogues of Abbot Desiderius of Montecassino', *Revue bénédictine* 108 (1998), 145–168.

McCready, William D., 'Leo of Ostia, the Montecassino Chronicle, and the Dialogues of Abbot Desiderius', *Mediaeval Studies* 62 (2000), 125–160.

McCurrach, Catherine C., 'The Veneration of St. Benedict in Medieval Rome: Parish Architecture, Monumental Imagery, and Local Devotion', PhD dissertation, University of Michigan, 2005.

Meeder, Sven, 'Monte Cassino and Carolingian Politics around 800', in *Religious Franks: Religion and Power in the Frankish Kingdoms: Studies in Honour of Mayke de Jong*, ed. by Dorine van Espelo, Bram van den Hoven van Genderen, Rob Meens, Janneke Raaijmakers, Irene van Renswoude, and Carine Van Rhijn (Manchester: Manchester University Press, 2016), pp. 279–295.

Melville, Gert, 'Montecassino', in *Erinnerungsorte des Christentums*, ed. by Christoph Markschies and Hubert Wolf (Munich: C.H. Beck, 2010), pp. 322–344.

Melville, Gert, *The World of Medieval Monasticism*, trans. by James D. Mixson (Collegeville, MN: Cistercian Publications/Liturgical Press, 2016).

Metcalfe, Alex, *The Muslims of Medieval Italy* (Edinburgh: Edinburgh University Press, 2008).

Mews, Constant, 'Gregory the Great, the Rule of Benedict and Roman Liturgy: The Evolution of a Legend', *Journal of Medieval History* 37 (2011), 125–144.

Meyvaert, Paul, *The Codex Benedictus: An Eleventh-Century Lectionary from Monte Cassino*, 2 vols (New York: Johnson Reprint Corporation, 1982).

Meyvaert, Paul, 'L'invention des reliques Cassiniennes de Saint Benoit en 1484', *Revue bénédictine* 69 (1959), 287–336.

Meyvaert, Paul, 'Peter the Deacon and the Tomb of St Benedict: A Re-Examination of the Cassinese Tradtion', *Revue bénédictine* 65 (1955), 3–70.

Meyvaert, Paul, 'Problems Concerning the "Autograph" Manuscript of Saint Benedict's Rule', *Revue bénédictine* 69 (1959), 3–21.

Michel, Elizabeth, 'Reconstructing the National Narrative: Questions of Sovereignty and the Rebuilding of Montecassino, 1944–1964', PhD dissertation, New York University, 2013.

Michel, Elizabeth, 'Seeking Consensus in the Ruins: Montecassino and Italian Reconstruction', *History in the Making* 1, no. 1 (2012), 64–79.

Miele, Chris, 'E.A. Freeman and the Culture of the Gothic Revival', in *Making History: Edward Augustus Freeman and Victorian Cultural Politics*, ed. by G.A. Bremner and Jonathan Conlin, Proceedings of the British Academy 202 (Oxford: Oxford University Press, 2015), pp. 139–156.

Minozzi, Giovanni, *Montecassino della storia Rinascimento* (Ferrari: Opera nazionale per il mezzogiorno d'Italia, 1925).

Mitchell, John, 'The Early Medieval Monastery as a Site of Commemoration and Place of Oblivion', in *Memory & Oblivion*, Proceedings of the XXIXth International Congress of the History of Art Held in Amsterdam, 1–7 September 1996 (Dordrecht: Springer, 1999), pp. 455–465.

Morin, Germain, 'La Translation de S. Benoît et La Chronique de Leno', *Revue bénédictine* 19 (1902), 337–356.

Morin, Germain, 'Les quatres plus anciens calendriers du Mont-Cassin', *Revue bénédictine* 25 (1908), 486–497.

Morin, Germain, 'Pour le Topographie ancienne du Mont Cassin', *Revue bénédictine* 25 (1908), 277–303.

Mundò, Ascarius M., 'Posthuma Sancti Benedicti sive de reliquiis, de sepulchro, de festis, de translatione', in *Il sepolcro di S. Benedetto*, vol. 2, Miscellanea Cassinese 45 (Montecassino: Pubblicazioni Cassinesi, 1982), pp. 228–269.

Murray, William, 'Letter from Cassino', *The New Yorker*, 15 May 1989, pp. 112–120.

Newton, Francis L., 'The Desiderian Scriptorium at Monte Cassino: The "Chronicle" and Some Surviving Manuscripts', *Dumbarton Oaks Papers* 30 (1976), 35–54.

Newton, Francis L., 'Leo Marsicanus and the Dedicatory Text and Drawing in Monte Cassino 99', *Scriptorium* 33, no. 2 (1979), 181–205.

Newton, Francis L., 'Monte Cassino Scribes in the Eleventh Century', *Medieval and Renaissance Studies* 7 (1975), 3–19.

Newton, Francis L., *The Scriptorium and Library at Monte Cassino, 1058–1105*, Cambridge Studies in Paleography and Codicology 7 (Cambridge: Cambridge University Press, 1999).

Nietzsche, Friedrich, *The Use and Abuse of History*, trans. by Adrian Collins (New York: Liberal Arts Press, 1957).

O'Keefe, Roger, *The Protection of Cultural Property in Armed Conflict* (Cambridge: Cambridge University Press, 2006).

O'Keefe, Roger, 'Protection of Cultural Property under International Criminal Law', *Melbourne Journal of International Law* 11 (2010), 1–54.

Olivieri, Luigi, and Domenico Catalano, 'Studio anatomo-radiologico dei resti di S. Benedetto e di S. Scolastica', in *Il sepolcro di S. Benedetto*, Miscellanea Cassinese 27 (Montecassino: Pubblicazioni Cassinesi, 1951), pp. 35–64.

Pantoni, Angelo, 'Abati construttori da Petronace a s. Bertario', in *Montecassino. Dalla prima alla seconda distruzione momenti e aspetti di storia Cassinese (secc. VI–IX)*, Miscellanea Cassinese 55 (Montecassino: Pubblicazioni Cassinesi, 1987), pp. 215–229.

Pantoni, Angelo, 'Descrizioni di Montecassino attraverso i secoli', *Benedictina* 19 (1972), 539–586.

Pantoni, Angelo, 'La basilica di Gisulfo e tracce di onomastica longobarda a Montecassino', in *Atti del I Congresso internazionale di Studi Longobardi. Spoleto, 27–30 settembre 1951* (Spoleto: Presso l'Accademia Spoletina, 1952), pp. 433–442.

Pantoni, Angelo, 'La basilica di Montecassino e quella di Salerno ai tempi di san Gregorio VII', *Benedictina* 10 (1956), 23–47.

Pantoni, Angelo, *L'Acropoli di Montecassino e il Primitivo Monastero di San Benedetto*, Miscellanea Cassinese 43 (Montecassino: Pubblicazioni Cassinesi, 1980).

Pantoni, Angelo, *Le vicende della basilica di Montecassino: attraverso la documentazione archeologica*, Miscellanea Cassinese 36 (Montecassino: Pubblicazioni Cassinesi, 1973).

Penco, Gregorio, *Storia del monachesimo in Italia dalle origini all fine del medio evo* (Milan: Jaca Book, 1983).

Phillips, Mark Salber, 'Distance and Historical Representation', *History Workshop Journal* 57 (2004), 123–141.

Picasso, Giorgio, 'La sede apostolica e la ripresa di Montecassino nei secoli VIII–IX', in *Montecassino. Dalla prima alla seconda distruzione momenti e aspetti di storia Cassinese (secc. VI–IX)*, Miscellanea Cassinese 55 (Montecassino: Pubblicazioni Cassinesi, 1987), pp. 201–213.

Picasso, Giorgio, 'Montecassino e il papato nell'età di Desiderio', in *L'età dell'abate Desiderio*, 3, 1, ed. by Faustino Avagliano and Oronzo Pecere, *Storia arte e cultura* (Montecassino: Pubblicazioni Cassinesi, 1992), pp. 59–68.

Picozzi, Nicandro, 'Gli abati commendatari di Montecassino (1454–1504)', in *Montecassino nel Quattrocento. Studi e documenti sull'abbazia Cassinese e la 'Terra S. Benedicti' nell crisi del passaggio all'età moderna*, ed. by Mariano dell'Omo, Miscellanea Cassinese 66 (Montecassino: Pubblicazioni Cassinesi, 1992), pp. 115–178.

Pieri, Piero, *La battaglia del Garigliano del 1503* (Rome: Stab. L. Proja, 1938).

Pieri, Piero, 'La guerra franco-spagnola nel Mezzogiorno (1502–1503)', *Archivio storico per le province Napoletane* 72 (1952), 21–69.

Pistilli, Emilio, *La Rocca Janula di Cassino: attraverso le ricerche di L. Paterna Baldizzi e G.F. Carettoni* (Cassino: Edizioni Cassino, 2000).

Pohl, Walter, 'History in Fragments: Montecassino's Politics of Memory', *Early Medieval Europe* 10 (2001), 343–374.

Pohl, Walter, *Werkstätte der Erinnerung. Montecassino und die Gestaltung der langobardischen Vergangenheit*, Mitteilungen des Instituts für Österreichische Geschichtsforschung (Vienna: R. Oldenbourg, 2001).

Pope Benedict XVI, *Great Christian Thinkers from the Early Church through the Middle Ages* (London: SPCK, 2011).

Poupardin, René, *Les Institutions politiques et administratives des principautés lombardes de l'Italie méridionale (IXe au XIe siècles)* (Paris: Librairie ancienne Honoré Champion, 1907).

Prinz, Friedrich, *Frühes Mönchtum im Frankenreich. Kultur und Gesellschaft in Gallien, den Rheinlanden und Bayern am Beispiel der monastischen Entwicklung (4. bis 8. Jahrhundert)* (Munich-Vienna: Oldenbourg, 1965).

Prinz, Friedrich, 'Montecassino ed Europa monastica', in *Il monaco, il libro, la biblioteca. Atti del Convegno, Cassino-Montecassino, 5–8 settembre 2000*, ed. by Oronzo Pecere (Cassino: Università degli studi di Cassino, 2003), pp. 5–32.

Quentin, Henri, 'Le Martyrologe Hiéronymien et les fêtes de saint Benoît', *Revue bénédictine* 20 (1903), 351–424.

Quintavalle, Ferrucio, *La Conciliazione fra l'Italia ed il Papato nelle lettere del P. Luigi Tosti e del sen. Gabrio Casati* (Milan: Cogliati, 1907).

Raaijmakers, Janneke, *The Making of the Monastic Community of Fulda, c. 744–c. 900* (Cambridge: Cambridge University Press, 2012).

Raimondi, Ezio, 'I padri maurini e l'opera del Muratori', *Giornale Storico della Letteratura Italiana; Torino* 128, no. 384 (1 October 1951), 429–471.

Ramseyer, Valerie, 'Questions of Monastic Identity in Medieval Southern Italy and Sicily (c. 500–1200), in *The Cambridge History of Medieval Monasticism in the Latin West*, ed. by Alison I. Beach and Isabelle Cochelin (Cambridge: Cambridge University Press, 2020), pp. 399–414.

Remensnyder, Amy G., *Remembering Kings Past: Monastic Foundation Legends in Medieval Southern France* (Ithaca, NY: Cornell University Press, 1995).

Ricoeur, Paul, *Memory, History, Forgetting*, trans. by Kathleen Blamey and David Pellauer (Chicago: University of Chicago Press, 2004).

Robinson, I.S., 'Monte Cassino in the Central Middle Ages', *The Journal of Ecclesiastical History* 42, no. 2 (1991), 259–282.

Rosa, Eligio Della, *Montecassino: The Return of the Lost Madonna and the Inside Story of the Bombing of Montecassino* (New York, 1988).

Rosenzweig, Roy, and David P. Thelen, *The Presence of the Past: Popular Uses of History in American Life* (New York: Columbia University Press, 1998).

Ruskin, John, *The Seven Lamps of Architecture*, ed. by Edward Tyas Cook and Alexander Wedderburn, vol. 8, *The Works of John Ruskin* (Cambridge: Cambridge University Press, 2011).

Russo, Francesco, 'Medieval Art Studies in the Republic of Letters: Mabillon and Monfaucon's Italian Connections between Travel and Learned Collaborations', *Journal of Art Historiography* 7 (2012), 1–24.

Samuel, Raphael, *Theatres of Memory: Past and Present in Contemporary Culture*, rev. ed. (London: Verso, 2012).

Scarafoni, Camillo Scaccia, 'Il sepolcro di S. Benedetto', *Benedictina* 6 (1952), 167–171.

Scarafoni, Camillo Scaccia, 'Note su fabbriche ed opere d'arte medioevale a Montecassino', *Bollettina d'Arte* 30 (1936), 97–121.

Schmitz, Dom Philibert, *Histoire de l'Ordre de Saint Benoit*, 4 vols (Maredsous: Ed. de Maredsous, 1942).

Schreuder, D.M., 'Gladstone and Italian Unification, 1848–70: The Making of a Liberal?', *The English Historical Review*, 85, no. 336 (1 July 1970), 475–501.

Scotti, G., *L'Abate Erasmo Gattola* (Monte Cassino, 1910).

Smidt, Wilhelm, 'Die Historia Normannorum von Amatus', *Studi Gregoriani* 3 (1948), 173–231.

Smidt, Wilhelm, 'Die vermeintliche und wirkliche Urgestalt der Chronik Leos von Montecassino', *Quellen und Forschungen aus italienischen Archiven und Bibliotheken* 28 (1937), 286–297.

Smidt, Wilhelm, 'Über den Verfasser der drei letzten Redaktionen der Chronik Leos von Monte Cassino', in *Papsttum und Kaisertum. Forschungen zur politischen Geschichte und Geisteskultur des Mittelalters. Paul Kehr zum 65. Geburtstag*, ed. by Albert Brackmann (Munich: Verlag der Münchner Drucke, 1926), pp. 263–286.

Spurr, David, *Architecture and Modern Literature* (Ann Arbor: University of Michigan Press, 2012).

Stone, Lawrence, 'The Revival of Narrative: Reflections on a New Old History', *Past & Present* 85 (1979), 3–24.

Tabacco, Giovanni, 'Montecassino e l'impero tra XI e XII secolo', in *L'età dell'abate Desiderio*, 3, 1, ed. by Faustino Avagliano and Oronzo Pecere, *Storia arte e cultura* (Montecassino: Pubblicazioni Cassinesi, 1992), pp. 35–57.

Tabacco, Giovanni, *The Struggle for Power in Medieval Italy: Structures of Political Rule*, trans. by Rosalind Brown Jensen (Cambridge: Cambridge University Press, 1989).

Thatcher, Mark, 'Introduction: The State and Historic Buildings: Preserving "the National Past"', *Nations and Nationalism* 24, no. 1 (2018), 22–42.

Thatcher, Mark, 'State Production of Cultural Nationalism: Political Leaders and Preservation Policies for Historic Buildings in France and Italy', *Nations and Nationalism* 24, no. 1 (2018), 64–87.

Tosti, Luigi, *La biblioteca dei codici manoscritti di Monte Cassino*, 2 vols (Naples: Stamperia della Regia Università, 1874).

Tosti, Luigi, *S. Benedetto al parlamento nazionale* (Naples: G. Gioja, 1861).

Tosti, Luigi, *Storia della badia di Monte Cassino*, 4 vols (Naples: Napoli Cirelli, 1843).

Toubert, Pierre, 'Pour une histoire de l'environnement économique et social du Mont-Cassin (IXe-XIIe siècles)', *Comptes rendus des séances de l'Académie des Inscriptions et Belles-Lettres* 120, no. 4 (1976), 689–702.

Vidier, Alexandre, *L'Historiographie à Saint-Benoît-sur-Loire et les Miracles de Saint Benoît* (Paris: A. et J. Picard, 1965).

Violet-le-Duc, Eugène-Emmanuel, *On Restoration*, trans. by Charles Wethered (London: Sampson Low, Marston, Low, and Searle, 1875).

Vogel, Cyrille, *Medieval Liturgy: An Introduction to the Sources*, trans. by William G. Storey and Niels Krogh Rasmussen (Washington, DC: The Pastoral Press, 1986).

Von Falkenhausen, Vera, 'Montecassino e Bisanzio dal IX al XII secolo', in *L'età dell'abate Desiderio*, 3, 1, ed. by Faustino Avagliano and Oronzo Pecere, *Storia arte e cultura* (Montecassino: Pubblicazioni Cassinesi, 1992), pp. 69–107.

Waldman, Martin Raymond, 'Pavia's Twin: Power and Identity in Early Medieval Benevento (570–899 CE)', PhD dissertation, Catholic University of America, 2017.

Weber, Robert, 'Un nouveau manuscrit du plus ancien récit de la translation des reliques de St. Benoît', *Revue bénédictine* 62 (1952), 140–142.

West, G.V.B., 'Charlemagne's Involvement in Central and Southern Italy: Power and the Limits of Authority', *Early Medieval Europe* 8, no. 3 (1999), 341–367.

White, Hayden, 'The Fictions of Factual Representation', in *The Tropics of Discourse: Essays in Cultural Criticism* (Baltimore: Johns Hopkins University Press, 1978), pp. 121–134.

White, Hayden, 'The Value of Narrativity in the Representation of Reality', *Critical Inquiry* 7 (1980), pp. 5–27.

Whitten, Sarah, 'Conflict, Community, and Legal Culture in Lombard Southern Italy, 770–1070', PhD dissertation, UCLA, 2010.

Whitten, Sarah, 'Franks, Greeks, and Saracens: Violence, Empire, and Religion in Early Medieval Southern Italy', *Early Medieval Europe* 27 (2019), 251–278.

Whitten, Sarah, '*Quasi ex uno ore*: Legal Performance, Monastic Return, and Community in Medieval Southern Italy', *Viator* 44 (2013), 49–64.

Wickham, Chris, *Early Medieval Italy: Central Power and Local Society, 400–1000* (London: Macmillan, 1981).

Wickham, Chris, 'Monastic Lands and Monastic Patrons', in *San Vincenzo al Volturno, Vol. II: The 1980–1986 Excavations*, ed. by R. Hodges and J. Mitchell (London: British School at Rome, 2001), pp. 138–152.

Wickham, Chris, 'The Terra of San Vincenzo al Volturno in the 8th to 12th Centuries: The Historical Framework', in *San Vincenzo al Volturno: The Archaeology, Art and Territory of an Early Medieval Monastery*, ed. by Richard Hodges and John Mitchell (Oxford: B.A.R., 1985), pp. 227–258.

Wickstrom, John B., 'Text and Image in the Making of a Holy Man: An Illustrated Life of Saint Maurus of Glanfeuil Ms Vat. Lat. 1202', *Studies in Iconography* 16 (1994), 53–82.

Willard, Henry M., 'A Project for the Graphic Reconstruction of the Romanesque Abbey at Monte Cassino', *Speculum* 10, no. 2 (1935), 144–146.

Winandy, Jacques, 'Un témoignage oublié sur les anciens usages Cassineniens', *Revue bénédictine* 50 (1938), 254–292.

Wollasch, Joachim, 'Benedictus abbas Romensis. Das römische Element in der frühen benediktinischen Tradition', in *Tradition als historische Kraft. Interdisziplinäre Forschungen zur Geschichte des früheren Mittelalters*, ed. by Norbert Kamp and Joachim Wollasch (Berlin: W. de Gruyter, 1982), pp. 119–137.

Wood, Ian, 'Reform and the Merovingian Church', in *Religious Franks: Religion and Power in the Frankish Kingdoms: Studies in Honour of Mayke de Jong*, ed. by Dorine van Espelo, Bram van den Hoven van Genderen, Rob Meens, Janneke Raaijmakers, Irene van Renswoude, and Carine van Rhijn (Manchester: Manchester University Press, 2016), pp. 95–111.

Wood, Ian, 'Between Rome and Jarrow: Papal Relations with Francia and England from 597 to 716', *Chiese Locale e Chiese Regionali Nell'alto Medioevo* 61 (2014), 297–320.

Wühr, Wilhelm, 'Die Wiedergeburt Montecassinos unter seinem ersten Reformabt Richer von Niederaltach (d. 1055)', *Studi Gregoriani* 3 (1948), 369–450.

Zeller, Bernhard, 'Montecassino in Teano. Klösterliche Politik und lokale Eliten im Spiegel Montecassiner Privaturkunden des 10. Jarhunderts', *Römische Historische Mitteilungen* 52 (2010), pp. 121–145.

Zumbini, Benvenuto, *W.E. Gladstone nelle sue relazioni con l'Italia* (Bari: Laterza, Giuseppe & figli, 1914).

Index

abbot's house 69, 109
Aberdeen, earl of 162–3
Acciaiuoli, Angelo I, abbot of Monte Cassino 141
Adalbert, abbot of Monte Cassino 139
Adrevald of Cluny 38–9, 40, 43–4, 45
Aerial Warfare, Hague Draft Rules of 174
Agareni *see* Muslims
Agnes, empress 61
Aigulf, monk of Monte Cassino 44
Alboin, king of Lombards 90
Aldisio, Salvatore 149
Alexander II, pope 49
Alexander, Harold 113
Alexandria 67
Alfanus, archbishop of Salerno 66–7, 70, 72, 148
Aligernus, abbot of Monte Cassino 63, 64, 70, 136, 137, 139, 196
Alighieri, Dante 59, 74, 206
Amalfi, Italy 69, 94
Amatus of Monte Cassino 47–8, 65 n.62, 103
Anastasius Bibliothecarius 45, 70
Ambrose, St 70
Anastasius 45, 70
Andrea, king of Hungary 106
Andrea I, abbot of Faenza 144
Angelarius, abbot of Monte Cassino 101, 137
Angevins 15, 105
Antiquaries, Society of 166
Apennine Mountains 13, 90, 102, 137
Apollo, altar of 38, 53, 56, 57, 63, 82, 135
  see also John the Baptist, St, chapel of
Apuleius 71, 75
Aquinas, Thomas 115
Aquino, Italy 64, 139
Archaeological Institute 118, 167
archaeology 53, 167
architecture 65, 69, 76, 79, 112, 145, 148, 171, 172, 176, 181, 184, 185, 216, 217
archivists, monastic 18, 21, 43, 52, 101, 105, 109, 116, 145–6, 192, 197, 198
Argyrus, Marianus 139
armistice, Italian (1943) 114
art collection 115
asceticism 14, 31, 32, 131
Assisi, Italy 148
astronomy 71
Atenulf, prince of Campania 137–8
Atenulfus, abbot of Monte Cassino 65
Athens, School of 58
Atti, Francesco d', abbot of Monte Cassino 141
Augustine, St 70, 201
Austria 162

Avellino, Italy 180
Avignon, France 105, 106, 143

Baldwin, abbot of Monte Cassino 139
Bari, Italy 95, 97
Bartholomew, St, chapel of 68
Becker, Maximilian Johannes 114, 118, 119
Bede, St 40, 70
Bell, George, bishop of Chichester 175, 176
Benedict of Nursia/Norcia, St 13–25, 29–54
  birth 39
  death 37–8
  foundation of Monte Cassino 15–25
  legend of 29–54
  life as a hermit 13–15
  miracles 14, 31, 39, 41, 47–8, 58, 96–7
  patron of Europe 15, 31, 54, 203–6
  relics 53, 62, 101, 118–19, 128
    disputes over 37–51
  tomb at Monte Cassino 36, 37, 43, 44, 48, 49–50, 51, 63, 73, 76, 96, 119, 124, 147, 164, 214
  translations 38–9, 42–50, 53
Benedict, St, chapel of 135
Benedict VIII, pope 42
Benedict XIII, pope 50–1, 145, 205
Benedict XVI, pope 30, 35, 62, 201
Benedictine monasticism 16, 21, 30, 32, 34, 36, 71, 73, 110, 111, 132, 134, 137, 165, 178, 186, 201, 207
Benevento, Italy 143
Benevento, duchy of 17, 67, 90, 95, 97, 100, 134, 137, 138
Benvenuto de Imola 73
Berarius, bishop of Le Mans 44
Bertharius, St, abbot of Monte Cassino 41–2, 46, 49, 63, 97, 196
  cult of 103
  martyrdom 17, 100–1, 136–7
Bertone, Tarcisio, cardinal 215
Beuron school 145
bishop, abbots' role as *see* Cassino, diocese of
Boccaccio, Giovanni 73–5
Böhmler, Rudolf 112, 121, 183
Bollandus, Jean 39
Bonaparte, Joseph, king of Naples 109, 111
Bonomi, Ivanoe 148
Boniface, St 56 n.7
books *see* library, monastic
Bourbon restoration 110
Bowyer, George 160
Bracciolini, Gian Francesco Poggio 75
Brescia, Italy 130, 132
bronze doors 17, 69, 79, 145, 180
Browning, Oscar 167

Brussels Declaration (1874)   173
Burkhardt, Jacob   172

Caffarelli, Simplificius, abbot of Monte Cassino   50
Cairo, Monte   88
calligraphy   71
Capua, Italy   17, 60, 63, 95, 97, 98, 102, 137–9
Carloman, mayor of the palace   60, 134
Carloman, king of the Franks   45–6, 136
Carolingian reform (of monastic life)   33, 36–7, 61
Casalucense, Italy   148
Casaroli, Agostino   208
Cassian, John   70
Cassinese Benedictine Congregation   107
Cassini, Gennaro   149
Cassino (town), Italy   14, 18, 63, 82, 109, 114, 146, 155, 208, 213
Cassino, diocese of   102, 110, 111, 123
Cassinum (ancient town)   55
Castelli (architects)   150
catapani   137
Cava, abbey of   114, 147
cemeteries, military   73, 205, 213
Chamard, François   39
Championnet, Jean-Antoine Étienne   108
chapter house   69
Charlemagne, emperor   41, 61, 90, 134
Chigi-Albani, Ludovico   151
Chronica sancti Benedicti Cassinensis   22, 96, 138, 195
Chronicon monasterii Casinensis   45, 48, 63, 65, 66, 68, 70, 71, 72, 100, 104, 130, 133, 135, 137, 140, 195, 196–7
chronosophy   194
Churchill, Winston   113, 120, 123
Cicero   56, 70
Cini, Bartholomeo   167
Cistercians   33
Cîteaux, France   34
civilisation, idea of   15, 18, 24, 118, 159, 160, 161–4, 166, 167, 168, 169, 171, 173, 175, 177, 180, 181, 188, 207, 209, 210, 213, 214, 216
Clarendon, earl of   166, 169
Clark, Mark W.   88, 113, 182
Clementi, Nicola   123
cloister   22, 65, 69, 73, 79, 80, 105, 107, 124, 146, 152, 153, 170, 192, 214, 216
Clovis II, king of Neustria and Burgundy   44
Cluny, France   33
commenda   106, 107, 144
consecrations   37, 131, 162, 205
  of 1071   49, 69, 72
  of 1727   51, 145
  of 1938   101
  of 1946   148
  of 1964   154–5, 199, 201, 204
Constantine, pope   45

Constantine, abbot of Monte Cassino   32
Constantini, Giovanni   149, 185
Constantinople   67, 68, 69, 79, 90
  Hagia Sophia   69, 72
Convention for the Protection of Historic Buildings and Works of Art in Times of War (1937)   174
Cordova, Consalvo di   107
Corsica   94

Danube, river   90
Deiber, lieutenant   122
Desiderius, abbot of Monte Cassino *see* Victor III, pope
'destruction tradition' of Monte Cassino   16–18, 21, 24–5, 87–125, 186, 188, 189, 191, 194, 199, 211, 214
  by earthquake (1349)   17, 81, 102–6, 140, 141, 143, 144, 145, 195
  by Lombards (c. 577)   15, 17, 32, 34, 36, 37, 44, 45, 90–4, 101, 123, 130, 131, 133, 147, 195, 196
  by Saracens (883)   15, 17, 34, 62, 64, 70, 94–102, 103, 108, 123, 136, 137, 138, 195–6
  by the Allies (1944) *see* Monte Cassino, battle of (1944)
Diamare, Gregorio, abbot of Monte Cassino   101, 114–15, 116 n.152, 118–19, 120, 121–2, 123, 148, 199
Dickens, Charles   80
dormitory   63, 69, 141
Dubois, Jean   39

Einaudi, Luigi   186
Eisenhower, Dwight D.   174–5, 178, 180–1
Engelburga, empress   97
England   33, 162, 166, 168
Erchempert   22, 70, 95, 97, 100, 136, 137, 138
Esculapius   71
Eton College   167
Eulogimenopolis *see* Cassino (town)
Europe, idea of   15, 20, 24, 31, 35, 54, 159, 160, 162–3, 166, 179, 188, 189, 191, 203–11, 215–18
Evans, Bradford   87 n.2, 123
exemptions, jurisdictional   36, 60, 97, 137, 163, 167

Faggis, Angelo de, abbot of Monte Cassino   145
Fansaga, Cosimo   145
Farfa, Italy   148
Ferdinand IV, king of Naples   108, 110
Fifth Army (United States)   114, 120
finances, monastic   64, 90, 134, 136, 137, 139
Fitzalan, viscount   177
Fleury (Saint-Benoît-sur-Loire), France   38–40, 42, 43, 44, 45, 46, 47, 50, 52–3
Florence, Italy   75, 169
Florentinus   114 n.6

INDEX

France 31, 33, 40, 42, 43, 44, 46, 47, 50, 162, 166, 172, 175, 172, 177, 179, 181, 188, 198, 204, 208, 210, 216, 217, 218
Fratadocchi, Giuseppe Breccia 150
Frederici, Giovanni Battista 109
Frederick II, emperor 103, 105
Freyburg, Bernard 113, 182
Frontinus, Julius 75
Fuller, J. F. C. 182
furta sacra (relic theft) 43

Gaeta, Italy 94, 107
Garigliano, river 17, 59, 76, 96, 100, 107, 114, 213
Garigliano, battle of (915) 100
Garigliano, battle of (1503) 107
Garioald 135
Gattola, Erasmo 76–7, 145, 197–8
Geddes, lord 179
Gelasian Sacramentary 40
Gellone, martyrology of 40
geography 76
Germain, Michel 77, 197
Germanus, St 63
Germany 33, 40, 61, 166
gifts *see* patronage
Gisulf, abbot of Monte Cassino 39, 62, 63, 66, 134
Gisulf II, duke of Benevento 64, 134–5
Gisulf, prince of Salerno 69
Gladstone, William 161–5, 166
Goebbels, Joseph 121
Göring, Hermann 117
Goths 60, 177, 178
Gravaldi, Serafino 150
Greece 67
Grégoire, Abbé 172
Gregorius (Byzantine general) 137
Gregory the Great, St 29, 45, 115, 168
  altar of 65, 67
  Dialogues on the Life and Miracles of the Italian Fathers 29–32, 34, 35, 38, 44, 53, 56, 62, 91, 92, 132, 194
Gregory of Tours 70
Gregory II, pope 130
Gregory IX, pope 103
Grimoald, king of the Lombards 90
Guglielmelli, Arcangelo 77
Guiglielmo II, abbot of Monte Cassino 141
Guiscard, Robert 116
Gustav Line 114, 171

Hague Convention II (1899) 173
Hague Convention IV (1907) 176
Hall, Donald 153, 187
Hauterive (Alta Ripa), France 33
Henry II, emperor 47, 48, 61, 140
Henry III, emperor 61
Herculaneum, Italy 180
heritage 15, 19, 20, 24, 25, 34, 37, 62, 89, 93, 114, 124, 130, 148, 150, 153, 154, 159, 161, 168, 171,

Hieronymian Martyrology 31, 40
Hilary of Poitiers, St 70
historiography 23, 30, 54, 93, 191–2, 193, 194, 195, 197, 198, 215
Holy Years 145
Honoratus, abbot of Monte Cassino 32
Honorius II, pope 104
Hope, Beresford 160
Horace 70
Hubbard, John 159
Hungary 90, 151
Hunuberc of Heidenheim 132

ICCROM 181
ICOMOS 181
infirmary, monastic 69
Inguanez, Mauro 115
'iniquitous ordinance' (1868) 111, 149
Innocent II, pope 103
Innocent VI, pope 106
internationalism 22
Ippocrates 71
Italy, reunification of *see* Risorgimento

Jacovitti, Antonio 150
Jerome, St 70
John I, abbot of Monte Cassino 137, 138, 139, 195
John II, abbot of Monte Cassino 140
John III, abbot of Monte Cassino 65
John VIII, pope 97
John IX, pope 42
John XII, pope 42
John XV, pope 42
John XXII, pope 105
John of Aragon, abbot commendatory of Monte Cassino 49
John of Ephesus 56 n.7
John Antonio I Carafa, king of Naples 50
John the Baptist, St, chapel of 38, 53, 56, 63, 67, 92, 135
John Paul II, pope 205, 207
Jonas of Bobbio 60
Jordanes 70
Juin, Alphonse 81
Julius Caesar 56
Jupiter, temple of 56
Justinian, emperor 70, 72

Kesselring, Albert 117, 122

Lamberti, Giovanni 108
landholdings 64
landscape *see* geography
Landulf I, prince of Capua 137
Landulf II, prince of Capua 64, 69
Lang, Cosmo Gordon, archbishop of Canterbury 176

Lateran I, ecumenical council 58
Latham, lord 178
Lavoro, Terra di (Land of Labour) 59, 169, 174, 213
Le Cointe, Charles 39
Le Donne, Faustino 151
Le Mans, France 38, 42, 44, 45
Leiberich, Carl Mack von 108
Leo II, pope 45
Leo VI, pope 137
Leo X, pope (Medici, Giovanni dei, abbot of Monte Cassino) 106
Leno, Italy 43
Leccisotti, Tommaso 43, 53, 71, 101, 105, 106, 108, 116, 118–19, 121, 144, 146, 149, 151, 192, 198, 199
library, monastic 69–71, 73, 74, 77, 108, 109, 112, 122, 131, 145, 153, 161, 169, 178, 180, 196, 198, 214
  evacuation of (1943) 115–18
Lieber Code (1863) 173
'lighthouse', Monte Cassino as 15, 214
Liri, river 14, 59, 64, 96, 108, 114, 139, 185, 213
liturgy 31, 33, 38, 39, 40, 41, 70, 80, 138, 147, 151, 163, 195, 204–5, 207
Liutprand, king of the Lombards 90
Lombards 15, 17, 32, 34, 36, 37, 39, 44, 60–1, 90–1, 92–5, 98, 101, 123, 130–1, 134, 137, 138, 147, 187, 195–6
Longfellow, Henry Wadsworth 74, 82, 169–70, 218
longue durée 24, 83
looting 95, 109, 117, 187
Lorsch, Annals of 42
Lothar, emperor 98
Louis II, emperor 42, 61, 63, 97, 98
Louis XII, king of France 106
Louvain Library, Belgium 174

Mabillon, Jean 43, 75, 76–7, 78, 197
MacMillan, Norman 117
Maelzer, general 116
Maffeus, Raphael 50
Maglione, cardinal 183
Maielpoto, abbot of Monte Cassino 139
Maio, abbot of Volturno 98, 136
malaria 147, 208
Malta, Sovereign Military Order of 151
Maredsous, France in39
Marinus I, pope 42
Mark Antony 56
Marseilles, France 141
Marshall, George C. 175
Marsi, count of 69
Marsicanus, Leo, abbot of Monte Cassino 22, 35, 63, 72, 93, 95, 96, 99–101, 130, 131, 133, 138, 195, 198
Martin of Tours, St, chapel of 17, 56, 63, 69, 100, 101, 135, 136
Mary, St, altar of 67
Maternus, Julius Firmicus 75

Matthieu, Maurice 108
Matronola, Martino, abbot of Monte Cassino 191
Maurists 75, 197
Medici, Giovanni dei, abbot of Monte Cassino *see* Leo X, pope
Medici, Onorato 198
Medici, Pietro di 145
Mellitus, archbishop of Canterbury 56
memory, historical 15, 17, 19, 22–5, 30, 34, 45, 46, 47, 51, 54, 62, 75, 83, 101, 130, 132, 166, 171, 177, 192, 193, 196, 203, 207, 208–9, 214, 218
Metropolitan Museum of Art, New York 181
Michael VII Dukas, emperor 72
Miller, Walter 123
Millet, Simon-Germain 39
Monte Cassino, battle of (1944) 18, 51, 77, 81, 87–8, 112–25, 145, 152, 171, 183, 188, 205
Montefiascone, Italy 144
Morley, John 162
mosaic floors 17, 67, 68, 145, 214
Mummolus, abbot of Fleury 44
Munding, Emmanuel 115
Muratori, L. A. 197
museum of Monte Cassino 17, 214
music 71, 153, 168, 207
Muslims 94, 95 *see also* Saracens

Naples, Italy 51, 52, 91, 94, 95, 97, 102, 114, 119, 180
Naples, kingdom of 18, 102, 106, 107, 108, 109, 141, 144
Narses 90
nationalism 18, 21, 22, 162
Newdegate, Charles 160
Nicholas, St, church of 65, 68
Noce, Angelo VI della, abbot of Monte Cassino 50, 51
Norcia, Italy 13
Normans 15, 17, 65, 69, 103–5, 187, 195

oak, St Benedict's 20, 21
Oderisius, abbot 47, 104
Office, Divine 34, 77, 143
Olivier, general 108
Optatus, abbot of Monte Cassino 45
Orvieto, Italy 117
Ostia, Italy 95
Ostrogoths 90
Otto I, emperor 42
Otto II, emperor 42
Otto III, emperor 42
Ottomans 60
Oxford Manual (1880) 173

Pandulf II, prince of Capua 64, 100
Pan-American Union 174
Pannonia *see* Hungary
Pantoni, Angelo 123–4, 149–50
Papal States 162

Parliament of Italy   111, 161, 166
Parliament of the United Kingdom   159, 162–4
patronage   44, 64, 134, 140, 144, 150, 151
Paul VI, pope   154–5, 199, 201, 202, 206
    Pacis Nuntius   203–5
Paul the Deacon   31, 35, 38, 39, 41, 42, 61, 70, 91, 92, 93, 130, 131, 132, 138, 194
Pavia, battle of (744)   90
peace   15, 20, 66, 96, 103, 105, 106, 107, 112, 114, 136, 139, 140, 149, 154, 155, 162, 163, 169, 190–1, 199, 201, 202, 203, 204, 206, 208–10, 216
Pelagius, cardinal   105
Pepin the Short, king of the Franks   136
Perone, Cristoforo   50
Perugia, Italy   148
Peter the Deacon   23, 32, 45, 48–9, 70, 100, 104, 130, 195, 196, 198
Petrarch   102
Petronax, abbot of Monte Cassino   17, 36, 41, 64, 92, 93, 101, 130, 131–5, 136, 194, 196
Piedimonte, Italy   88, 162
Pietro IV, abbot of Monte Cassino   144
pilgrimage   44, 49, 60, 132, 144, 145, 153, 164, 201, 214
Pius VII, pope   109
Pius XII, pope   177, 183, 202, 204, 206
    Fulgens Radiatur   59, 127–8, 149, 189, 190
Plato   58
Pliny the Elder   71
Po Valley   90
Poles   88, 147, 152, 205, 213
Pompeii, Italy   180
Posta, Angelo II della, abbot of Monte Cassino   141
Poto, abbot of Monte Cassino   135
Public Works, Italian Ministry of   112, 148, 149, 185

Quincy, Antoine Quatremère de   172

Radelchis   97
Rapido, river   59, 64, 114, 213
Ratchis, king of the Lombards   60, 134, 135
Ravenna, Italy   90–1
Rea, Ildefonso, abbot of Monte Cassino   51, 148
rebuilding of Monte Cassino (from 1944)   52, 151–6
refectory, monastic   63, 141, 143, 152, 153
Regensburg, Germany   43
Regino of Prüm   39
restorations of Monte Cassino   63, 102, 129–30
    of 718   34, 36, 64, 131–4
    of 966   139–40
    of 1365   141–4
    of 1486   50
    of 1649   79
    of 1938   101
    see also rebuilding of Monte Cassino (from 1944)

Revolutionary Army, French   18, 172
Rheims Cathedral, France   174
Richard, prince of Capua   69, 104
Richerius, abbot of Monte Cassino   65, 103–4, 196
Ricoeur, Paul   193
Risorgimento   110, 162, 165, 174
Roberts Commission   178
Rocca Janula   63, 103
Rock, Dr   168
Roerich Pact (1935)   174
Roger II, king of Sicily   103, 116
Rome, Italy   13, 15, 31, 40, 51, 59, 66, 67, 76, 91, 94, 98, 102, 109, 112, 114, 117, 119, 132, 149, 153, 168, 171, 176–7
    Cassinese monks in (c. 577–c. 718)   17, 32, 34, 92–3, 130–1
    Castel Sant'Angelo   118, 148
    Keats-Shelley House   118
    Lateran Palace   32, 92, 93, 131
    Lombard siege of   90
    San Paolo fuori le Mura   136
    Sant'Anselmo, abbey of   88, 116, 121
    Saracen attack on   95, 96, 100
    Vatican City   61, 116, 117, 118, 176
Roosevelt, Franklin   151, 175, 177, 178
Ruini, Meuccio   148
Rule of St Benedict   20, 31, 32–7, 47–8, 54, 58, 61, 62, 71, 73, 75, 101, 133, 138, 141, 143, 148, 195, 199, 207, 209, 216
    manuscript of   92–3, 131, 137
Ruskin, John   184

sacramentaries   31, 40, 70
Sacred Art, Pontifical Commission for   185
Saint-Bertin, Annals of   95, 97
Saint-Gall, Switzerland   37
Salconio, Francisco   123
Salerno, Italy   95
Samuel, viscount   178
San Germano *see* Cassino (town)
San Salvatore, priory of   62, 63, 65, 97, 99–100, 134, 136
Santa Giustina of Padua, congregation of *see* Cassinese Benedictine Congregation
Santarelli, Ippolito   101
Saracens   15, 17, 34, 62, 64, 70, 108, 123, 139, 178, 187
    attack on Monte Cassino   94–102, 103, 136, 137, 138, 195
    see also Muslims
Sardinia   94
Sawdān, emir of Bari   97, 98
Schism, Papal   105
Schlegel, Julius   114–16, 118–19, 153
Schuster, Ildefonso, cardinal-archbishop of Milan   52, 147, 148, 149, 214 n.4
Scloccheto, Girolamo II, abbot of Monte Cassino   50

scriptorium, monastic. 70–1, 75, 112, 196
Second World War *see* Monte Cassino, battle of (1944)
secularism 24
Seneca 70
Senger und Etterlin, Frido von   121, 122, 175, 182
Sergius, duke of Naples 69
Sergius, duke of Sorrento 69
Severus, St 65
Scholastica, St 15, 37, 38, 41, 42, 43, 44, 46, 49, 50, 51, 53, 63, 121, 131, 135, 147, 152, 153, 192, 214
Sicily 94, 95, 96, 110
Siconulf 97, 136
Simon, John 179
Simplicius, abbot of Monte Cassino 32
Sinai, Mount 72
Spoleto, Italy 116
Spoleto, duchy of 90, 100, 134
Squarcialupi, Ignazio 145
Stanley, George 160, 166
Stanthorpe, Philip 166
Stephen II, pope 46
Stephen V, pope 137–8
Sturmi, abbot of Fulda 61, 134
Subiaco, Italy 13, 14 n.6
Switzerland 33, 37

Tacitus 75
Teano, Italy 17, 35, 64, 101, 131, 137, 138, 196
Terence 70
Teudelapius, duke of Spoleto 91
Theobald, abbot of Monte Cassino 65, 70, 140
Theodericus, king of the Saxons 61
Tittmann, Harold H. 183
Tosti, Luigi 138, 164–5, 166, 167, 169, 198
Totila, king of the Goths 60
tradition, role of *see* 'destruction tradition' of Monte Cassino

treasury, monastic 105, 108, 135
Tupini, Umberto 149

UNESCO 181, 216, 217
United Nations 150, 151
Urban II, pope 49, 165
Urban V, pope 18, 141–4
  Monasterium Cassinense 143

Vacquerie, Picard de la, bishop of Orléans 53
Valentianus, abbot of the Cassinese community in Rome 32, 92
Valva, count of 69
Vandals 178
Varro, Marcus Terentius 56
Versailles, Treaty of (1919) 174
Via Casilina 15, 59
Victor III, pope (Abbot Desiderius) 17, 47, 48, 49, 65–72, 76, 79, 96–7, 140, 154, 196
Victor Emmanuel I, king of Italy 160
Viollet-le-Duc, Eugène-Emmanuel 184
Virgil 70
Vitalian, pope 45
Vitruvius 71
Volturno, Italy 97, 98, 131, 132, 139

Walker, Fred L. 183
war, laws of *see* Brussels Declaration; Hague Convention IV; Lieber Code; Oxford Manual
Washington Conference on Limitation of Armaments (1922)
Washington Pact *see* Roerich Pact
Willibald, bishop of Eichstatt 60, 132–3, 195
Willibrord, St 40
Wilson, Henry Maitland 87
Woden 168
World Heritage Status 216

Zacharias, pope 34, 45, 131, 195